Andy
Warhol
was a
Hoarder

Andy Warhol was a Hoarder

Inside the Minds of History's Great Personalities

Claudia Kalb

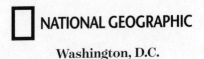

NATIONAL GEOGRAPHIC

Washington, D.C.

Published by National Geographic Partners, LLC
1145 17th Street NW, Washington, DC 20036

Library of Congress Cataloging-in-Publication Data

Kalb, Claudia.
   Andy Warhol was a hoarder : inside the minds of history's great personalities / Claudia Kalb. -- 1st Edition.
      pages cm
   Includes bibliographical references.
   ISBN 978-1-4262-1466-0 (hardback)
   1. Fame--Psychological aspects. 2. Celebrities--Psychology--Biography. I. Title.
   BJ1470.5.K35 2016
   616.890092'2--dc23
                              2015024370

Since 1888, the National Geographic Society has funded more than 12,000 research, exploration, and preservation projects around the world. National Geographic Partners distributes a portion of the funds it receives from your purchase to National Geographic Society to support programs including the conservation of animals and their habitats.

National Geographic Partners, LLC
1145 17th Street NW
Washington, DC 20036-4688 USA

Become a member of National Geographic and activate your benefits today at natgeo.com/jointoday.

For information about special discounts for bulk purchases, please contact National Geographic Books Special Sales: ngspecsales@ngs.org

For rights or permissions inquiries, please contact National Geographic Books Subsidiary Rights: ngbookrights@ngs.org

Interior Design: Katie Olsen
Cover and Interior Illustrations: Allison Bruns

Printed in the U.S.A.
16/QGF-CML/2

For my parents, Phyllis and Bernard Kalb
And for Steve, Molly, and Noah
With love and gratitude

Contents

~

Introduction

WHY DID ANDY WARHOL FILL hundreds of boxes with old postcards, medical bills, and pizza crust? What made Marilyn Monroe overdose on sedatives? Why did Charles Darwin suffer from stomachaches, and Howard Hughes insist on turning doorknobs with Kleenex? These are some of the questions that launched this book: a journey into the wonder and anguish of the mind as told through the lives of 12 celebrated figures who reshaped the world. Albert Einstein's theory of relativity transformed our understanding of time and space. Abraham Lincoln's Emancipation Proclamation freed slaves. George Gershwin's "Summertime" intoxicated the soul. Almost all of these characters were enormously accomplished in science, business, politics, or the arts—but every one of them also exhibited behaviors associated with a mental health condition like autism, depression, anxiety, addiction, and obsessive-compulsive disorder.

In many ways, historical figures are no saner or zanier than the rest of us. While their public lives have been fodder for books, movies, and splashy headlines, their psyches reveal characteristics that many of us will recognize in our spouses, children, friends— even ourselves. We all craft public personas and tussle with internal dramas. Rich or poor, musician or accountant, boomer or millennial, most of us have *something* going on—a compulsion to line up pencils, a knack for blowing up friendships, an ego that jeopardizes a promotion, a powerlessness over potato chips. I, for one, have been known to triple-check the stove before leaving the house, hang on to old magazines and catalogs, and bawl over sappy commercials. But where is the line between "normal" behavior and a psychological problem? When is shyness a personality trait, and when is it social anxiety disorder? What makes yanking on your hair trichotillomania rather than just a bad habit? At what point do you treat sadness with Prozac?

Our understanding of mental health has evolved dramatically from the days when our ancestors drilled holes in one another's brains to excise supernatural possession by demons. Over the centuries, people with psychological ailments have endured a rash of treatments, from leeches to electroshock therapy. Freud, with his theories of unconscious repression, launched the "talking cure" in the first half of the 20th century; then came the cascade of psychotropic drugs, from the tranquilizer Miltown in the 1950s to Prozac in the 1980s. Today, the brain and the mind are viewed as inextricably linked, and scientists are pushing to pinpoint the biological blueprints of mental health conditions. Intriguing findings are emerging: Activity in a specific area of the brain can predict if a patient with depression will do better with an antidepressant or talk therapy; people with schizophrenia have less brain tissue in the earliest stages of the illness; low levels of oxytocin, a hormone linked to social behavior, have been linked to higher levels of anxiety.

With each new discovery, however, comes the daunting reality that there is so much more to learn. The human brain is infinitely complex and unpredictable—a breathtaking mass of tissue comprising some 100 billion neurons and immeasurable capacity. That one organ can power our most basic needs (breathing, eating, walking), foster our intellect, *and* preside over random thoughts and amorphous feelings is as impossible to fathom as the breadth of the universe. Doctors know far more about the mechanisms underlying heart disease or diabetes than they do about mental disorders, and diagnostic tools are more precise for most physical ailments. X-rays pick up bone breaks; thermometers measure fever; blood tests detect infection. The brain is different. While you can image it for tumors and blood clots, you cannot scan it for bipolar or borderline personality disorders. And even if you could, would you be able to "see" these conditions with any clarity? Symptoms crisscross and overlap. Boundaries blur. Depression and anxiety often coexist with each other and with other conditions, including addiction, autism, and eating disorders. The notion that mental disorders are distinct entities has begun to change. Researchers recently discovered, for example, that a group of the same genetic variations is associated with five seemingly different conditions: autism, attention deficit hyperactivity disorder (ADHD), bipolar disorder, depression, and schizophrenia.

A mental health assessment is subjective, based largely on what a patient's symptoms look like and what he or she tells the doctor. For now, the best that clinicians can do is to compare this against descriptive information and a checklist of symptoms contained in the American Psychiatric Association's 947-page reference book called the *Diagnostic and Statistical Manual of Mental Disorders*, or *DSM*. Although it serves a vital purpose in guiding mental health professionals toward diagnoses and treatment, the diagnostic manual has long been controversial. Critics charge that the diagnostic criteria lack validation and are overly inclusive. Since it debuted in 1952, the number of distinct mental disorders has increased from 80 to 157 in the fifth and most recent edition of the *DSM* (known as the *DSM-5*), published in 2013. With each new condition comes the possibility that an otherwise healthy person with run-of-the-mill quirks will be given a diagnosis and a medication he or she doesn't need. Is your headache a symptom of caffeine withdrawal, one of the new diagnostic categories, or just punishment for too many lattes? If you gorge on french fries, do you have a binge eating disorder? Or is it the old eyes-bigger-than-your-stomach problem?

Despite these valid concerns, the *DSM* is the standard reference guide relied on by most mental health professionals today, and I used it as a framework to understand the symptoms and behaviors of the figures I've profiled here. To unveil the details of their experiences and their struggles, I mined published medical reports, biographies, autobiographies, and, when available, letters and diaries. For historical and contemporary views about mental health generally, and about the specific conditions I profiled, I consulted numerous books and journal articles and interviewed professionals with a range of expertise, including neuroscientists, psychiatrists, psychoanalysts, clinical psychologists, and academic researchers. My goal in presenting these portraits was not to assign labels but to contextualize mental health characteristics using both historical and contemporary psychiatry, and to explore the mysteries of the brain and human behavior.

What drives creative genius, intellectual brilliance, and ingenious leadership? And what lies beneath?

Several of the figures in these pages had confirmed mental illnesses, which they wrote about and talked about publicly. Princess Diana described her trials with the eating disorder bulimia nervosa in secret taped interviews that were later published and in a television interview with the BBC. On a trip abroad early in her marriage to Prince Charles, Diana recalled, "I spent my whole time with my head down the loo." First Lady Betty Ford recounted her addiction to prescription drugs and alcohol in her autobiographies and dedicated her life after the White House to helping others recover at her renowned Betty Ford Center in Rancho Mirage, California. She was adamant about reducing stigma by being honest. "Getting sober," she wrote, "is tough, tough work."

A number of these profiles were inspired by long-standing debates about what the person's ailment was, or if it even existed. Abraham Lincoln's melancholy has been scrutinized for decades: Was he just a sad man? Or did he have a pattern of clinical depression? Lincoln's story elicits a compelling and much debated question: Is there an upside to mental illness? There is fascinating research brewing here, especially in the area of mood disorders and their link to creativity. In Lincoln's case, some experts argue that he could not have been depressed and steered the country through such turbulent times; others say that his despair made him a better leader. Across the Atlantic, Lincoln's contemporary Charles Darwin suffered for years on end as he was compiling his theory of evolution. His chronic and debilitating symptoms, which he documented in meticulous health diaries, have inspired dozens of medical studies and a slew of diagnoses, from panic disorder to irritable bowel syndrome. I make a case for anxiety based on historical data and diagnoses put forward by mental health professionals, but it is in no way conclusive. The man who unraveled one of the greatest riddles in the universe left us a mystery that may never be solved: What made him so sick—his body, his mind, or both?

Nowhere is the debate over "normal" and "abnormal" more fraught than in the childhood disorders of attention deficit hyperactivity disorder and autism spectrum disorder, both of which have increased in prevalence significantly over the last two decades. Two of the figures profiled in these pages exhibited early childhood behaviors that would have made them candidates for diagnostic assessments had they lived in the 21st century. Albert Einstein was socially awkward and had a habit of focusing intensively on solitary subjects. Several experts have suggested that he exhibited symptoms of high-functioning autism, a condition that until recently might have been diagnosed as Asperger's disorder. George Gershwin, one of Einstein's younger contemporaries, was restless, unruly, and hyperactive as a boy, leading one psychiatrist to propose that today he would have almost certainly been hauled off to a child psychologist and tested for ADHD. Both Einstein's and Gershwin's stories are relevant to a critical question debated today: When is a diagnosis warranted in children, and what kind of impact will it have? Would Gershwin have written *Rhapsody in Blue* on Ritalin?

A number of the figures here received valuable psychological counseling, including Princess Diana and Betty Ford. But others had ineffective therapy or none at all. Marilyn Monroe exhibited symptoms consistent with borderline personality disorder, a condition deemed wholly untreatable during the era in which she sought help. Today, innovative behavioral therapies can be enormously beneficial, allowing patients to lead productive lives. Could Monroe have been saved? There's no evidence that Howard Hughes, who spent weeks holed up in a sealed screening room, ever received treatment for what was almost certainly obsessive-compulsive disorder. It is possible that medication or counseling could have helped rid him of his overwhelming preoccupation with germs. People with narcissistic personality disorder rarely seek treatment, because they're often oblivious to their behavior. It's their spouses and children who end up on the couch. Frank Lloyd Wright's narcissism was legendary, and it blemished relationships, both personal and professional. His remedy was not to find help but to surround himself with admirers.

Introduction

Several of the conditions profiled here appear for the first time in the latest *DSM*. Hoarding, previously viewed as a subtype or symptom of obsessive-compulsive disorder, has earned stand-alone status. The term is used loosely by many of us who squirrel away old books or new shoes. But when does "hoard," the descriptive verb, become hoarding disorder? And what's the difference between a "collector" and a "hoarder," anyway? Andy Warhol provides more than one clue. In addition to his stockpile of boxes, he left a town house jammed with everything from Fiestaware to Tiffany lamps. Gambling disorder, played out convincingly by Fyodor Dostoevsky both in life and in his novels, also makes its debut in the most recent *DSM*, breaking new ground as the first behavioral addiction alongside alcohol, cannabis, inhalant, and other substance use disorders. Stay tuned: Internet gaming disorder could be next. Finally, there's gender dysphoria, which has emerged as a new conceptualization of what used to be known as gender identity disorder. Christine Jorgensen, the first American widely known to seek sex-reassignment surgery in the 1950s, and a celebrity in her day, opens the door to an exploration of why transgender might be considered a psychiatric condition at all.

Investigating the ills of historical figures is controversial terrain. Mental health professionals are trained not to proffer diagnoses for patients they have never met. Given the inherent complexities of interpreting the mind, it is wise to be cautious. At the same time, leading medical journals routinely publish articles about what might have ailed celebrity "patients" based on historical records and accounts, and these reports often launch interesting discussions and debates, which can help raise the public consciousness about mental health. One study about King George III's hair found that it was tainted with arsenic, which might have contributed to his madness. Numerous journals have printed reports about what ailed Mozart, including bipolar disorder and Tourette syndrome. Every year, the University of Maryland School of Medicine hosts a conference in which they present a case study of a historical figure. Since the program launched in 1995, experts have proposed diagnoses for everyone from Christopher Columbus (arthritis caused by an infection) and Edgar Allan Poe (rabies) to Florence Nightingale (bipolar disorder with psychotic features) and General George Custer (histrionic personality disorder). In some cases, a figure from the past may reveal even more about himself than a patient in the office. When asked in a magazine interview how well he knew Darwin, Dr. Ralph Colp, Jr., who spent decades studying the scientist's illness, answered: "Probably much better than I know some of my living friends and patients."

Mental illness can be debilitating and deadly. Throughout the course of my research, I made discoveries that deepened my admiration for these 12 figures and the troubles and triumphs they experienced. Before researching Marilyn Monroe, I had a simplistic view of her as Hollywood goddess; I came away feeling enormous sympathy for a woman whose tragic childhood left her empty and searching for a sense of self. Princess Diana also underscored the deep divide between public image and internal pain. One of the most photographed women in the world, she inspired fashion trends and raised compassion for humanitarian causes—but beneath the ball gowns and the smiles, she was exceedingly insecure. Christine Jorgensen, about whom I knew little, impressed me with her determination to break social mores and bravely fulfill her deeply felt identity as a woman. Frank Lloyd Wright and his colossal ego wowed me. I wouldn't have wanted to work for him, but I would have loved to have met him. Darwin surprised me the most. I had no idea that the great naturalist was exhausted, dizzy, and retching while writing *On the Origin of Species*. I still can't grasp how he managed to get it done.

Introduction

Ultimately, this book is about crossways and connections—between the mind and the brain, between public images and internal struggles, between the way people are wired and the way they behave, between famous people and the rest of us. It turns out that the lives of some of these historical figures intersected in very tangible ways. Darwin and Lincoln were born on the same day, February 12, 1809. Einstein loved reading Dostoevsky; in a letter written in 1920, he called *The Brothers Karamazov* "the most wonderful thing I've ever laid my hands on." Frank Lloyd Wright had dinner with Einstein and designed a house for Marilyn Monroe and her third husband, Arthur Miller. Monroe's hero was Lincoln. Howard Hughes and George Gershwin traveled in Hollywood circles, and both dated Ginger Rogers. Andy Warhol printed silk screens of Einstein, Monroe, and Princess Diana. But what they shared, above all, was being human. My hope is that telling these stories will highlight the psychological challenges we all face—no matter how big or small—and maybe even eradicate some of the cultural stigma that can go along with them. By learning more about these fascinating icons, we may discover a greater appreciation for the depths of human experience and behavior—and gain a greater understanding of ourselves.

Marilyn Monroe

"**MR. PRESIDENT, MARILYN MONROE.**" With those words, the epic scene began. It was May 19, 1962, at Madison Square Garden. Despite warnings from advisers and her own anxiety about performing, Marilyn Monroe had agreed to serenade President John F. Kennedy at a grand fund-raiser and celebration of his 45th birthday. Actor Peter Lawford, the president's brother-in-law, stood at the podium and extended his arm to welcome the actress. Spotlights lit the dark stage. A drumroll sounded. The actress, however, was nowhere to be seen. Lawford went at it again. "A woman about whom it truly may be said she needs no introduction. Let me just say, here she is . . ." Again, the extended arm. The spotlights. The drumroll. Again, nothing.

Finally, as Lawford launched into yet another attempt, Monroe emerged, shimmying across the stage in a fur coat and flesh-colored gown so tight it was reportedly sewn together on her body. As she cozied up to the podium, Lawford made his final introduction: "Mr. President, the *late* Marilyn Monroe."

Monroe put her hands over her eyes to shield herself from the glare of the spotlight, which electrified her platinum hair and the 2,500 rhinestones decorating her dress. It was a moment rich with anticipation and bawdy curiosity. Some 15,000 people sat expectantly in the audience, including Ella Fitzgerald, Jack Benny, Robert Kennedy, and, of course, the president. Monroe caressed the microphone, exhaled deeply, then crooned her tribute: "Happy birthday to you, happy birthday to you, happy birthday, Mr. Pres-i-dent, happy birthday to you." She sang in a breathy voice imbued with her trademark mix of innocence and sensuality. "Thanks, Mr. President, for all the things you've done, the battles that you've won," she went on, to the familiar tune of "Thanks for the Memory," "the way you deal with U.S. Steel and our problems by the ton, we thank you so much." With that, she threw her hands up in the air and jumped up, awkwardly, in her heels. "Everybody, happy birthday!"

Monroe's appearance didn't last long, but it left an indelible mark on American culture. It was perceived by some as a public airing of Monroe's alleged sexual relationship with JFK. One newspaper columnist wrote that the actress's performance was like "making love to the President in direct view of 40 million Americans." (The first lady had declined to attend.) The event stoked Monroe's two provocative images as sex symbol and ditzy blonde. The first she seemed to encourage; the second she came to hate. Kennedy thanked the actress, saying, "I can now retire from politics after having had 'Happy Birthday' sung to me in such a sweet, wholesome way." The crowd roared.

Lawford's use of the word "late" was meant to be a ribbing of Monroe's notorious and exasperating tardiness in her personal and professional life. In retrospect, it haunts like the grim reaper. Three months after her tribute to the president, she would indeed be the late Marilyn Monroe. "Our angel, the sweet angel of sex," as Norman Mailer famously referred to her, would be dead at the age of 36.

MARILYN MONROE IS AND ALWAYS has been everywhere. Instantly recognizable, ever tantalizing. Just weeks after she was interred in a crypt at the Westwood Village Memorial Park Cemetery in Los Angeles, Andy Warhol debuted his famous silk screen diptych of Monroe's face—50 images, half in color, half in black-and-white. Performers from Madonna to Scarlett Johansson have transformed themselves into Marilyn Monroe look-alikes, with her seductive smile and platinum hair. In 2015, the cosmetic company Max Factor announced a new ad campaign featuring the actress as their "global glamour ambassador." No matter that she's long gone—her allure is eternal.

Underneath it all, however, Marilyn Monroe was a profoundly troubled and complicated woman who yearned for love and stability. Dozens of biographers have told her story, complete with sordid details that may or may not be true. All varieties of literary heavyweights have weighed in, including Mailer, Diana Trilling, Joyce Carol Oates, and Gloria Steinem. But nobody has completely figured her out. Monroe was a paragon of contradiction. She loved children and desperately wanted to be a mother, but conflicting accounts say she may have had several abortions. She was the embodiment of life, beauty, and sensuality, and yet self-destructive and suicidal. Great disparities exist in how she perceived herself and how she has been viewed by others. Was she a manipulator who abused her privileges of stardom? Or was she used by a greedy Hollywood industry that exploited her for money? A good actress, or a woman hired just for her looks? Flighty or shrewd? A willing victim of sexual stereotyping, or a feminist before her time? Depends on whom you ask.

What is clear is that Monroe suffered severe mental distress. Her symptoms included a feeling of emptiness, a split or confused identity, extreme emotional volatility, unstable relationships, and an impulsivity that drove her to drug addiction and suicide—all textbook characteristics of a condition called borderline personality disorder. "Borderline," in this context, does not mean "marginal" or "almost." The word dates back to the Freudian era, when a New York psychoanalyst used it to refer to patients whose symptoms lay on the border between two camps of psychological impairment: neurosis (depression and anxiety) and psychosis (schizophrenia and delusional disorder). Borderline patients were found to be very despondent at times, a key symptom of depression. Like people with schizophrenia, they often had unrealistic ideas and tended to be paranoid. And they exhibited features of antisocial personality, with their impulsive behavior and their unwillingness to cooperate. "They seemed to be a little bit this and a little bit that, and it wasn't clear that there was any center," says Dr. John Gunderson, a professor of psychiatry at Harvard Medical School and a pioneer in the field. "They didn't fit into any other diagnostic category."

To this day, borderline personality disorder is poorly understood by the public and even by mental health professionals, who often confuse it with depression and bipolar disorder. For patients, feelings of frustration, desolation, anger, and emptiness become all-consuming as they search, often in vain, for relief. Marilyn Monroe spent her short life seeking a cure. She never had the chance to find it.

FROM DAY ONE OF MARILYN MONROE'S LIFE, nothing was as it seemed. Her mother, whose given name was Gladys Pearl Monroe, gave birth to her daughter on June 1, 1926, in the charity ward of Los Angeles County Hospital. She named the baby Norma Jeane, though the "e" at the end would be inconsistent throughout her life. Gladys had a son and a daughter with her first husband, John Newton Baker, a man she had married when she was just 15. At the hospital, Gladys claimed that the children were dead, even though they were living with their father in Kentucky. She listed her second husband, from whom she was apparently separated, as the baby's father, but misspelled his name as Edward Mortenson instead of Edward Mortensen. Later, she alleged that Stanley Gifford, a man she worked with as a film cutter at Consolidated Film Industries in Hollywood, was the baby's real father. She subsequently changed her daughter's name from Norma Jeane Mortenson to Norma Jeane Baker, which would later be replaced by Marilyn Monroe when the actress began her career in Hollywood. It was a labyrinth of confusion that marked the beginning of Monroe's lifelong quest to figure out who she was—and who, if anybody, she belonged to.

People with borderline personality disorder often experience significant traumas early in life—separation from a parent, death of a parent, or neglect from caregivers. Gladys was a troubled mother, unable to provide for her newborn. She had little money and suffered from severe mood swings and possibly postpartum depression. When Norma Jeane was just a few weeks old, her mother paid a strict churchgoing couple five dollars a week to become foster parents, a contract that would last for about seven years.

Gladys visited on weekends, but she remained an enigma to her daughter. The actress later recalled that when she called her foster mother "Mama," the woman told her, "I'm not your mother, the one who comes here with the red hair, she's your mother." But the red-haired mother didn't act like one. She didn't kiss her child or hold her in her arms. Even when Norma Jeane went to her mother's home, she felt uncomfortable and out of place. "I used to be frightened when I visited her and spent most of my time in the closet of her bedroom hiding among her clothes," Monroe recalled in her autobiography, *My Story*. "She seldom spoke to me except to say, 'Don't make so much noise, Norma.' " Later, Monroe would say, "I was a mistake. My mother didn't want to have me."

Gladys was clearly incapable of providing the comfort, love, and stability her daughter needed. Young Norma Jeane coped by crafting an imaginary relationship with the man she believed to be her father. At her mother's house, she saw a photograph of a handsome man with a thin mustache wearing a slouch hat. Her mother said it was her father; Norma Jeane thought he looked like Clark Gable. Monroe would never know her father's true identity, but nothing could stop her from envisioning him in her life. She imagined him waiting for her after school and kissing her forehead after she had her tonsils out. "The night I met his picture I dreamed of it when I fell asleep," she recalled. "And I dreamed of it a thousand times afterward. That was my first happy time, finding my father's picture."

Grace McKee, a fellow Hollywood film-cutter and friend of Gladys's, would become something of a surrogate mother to Norma Jeane. With McKee's help, Gladys took her daughter back from foster care when she was about seven years old, and they moved into a house near the Hollywood Bowl with a British couple, who helped pay the rent. For a while, there was some semblance of a normal life, with McKee providing the affection Norma Jeane so desperately needed. She remembered Aunt Grace, as she called her, saying, "Don't worry, Norma Jeane. You're going to be a beautiful girl when you grow up. I can feel it in my bones," while the two stood in line for bread at Holmes Bakery in Los Angeles. "Her words made me so happy that the stale bread tasted like cream puffs."

But this interlude was short-lived. One morning during breakfast, when Norma Jeane was about eight, a clamor erupted from the stairway near the kitchen. "It was the most frightening noise I'd ever heard. Bangs and thuds kept on as if they would never stop," Monroe later recalled. The bangs and thuds turned out to be her mother having a nervous breakdown, alternating between screams and laughter. She was whisked off to the Norwalk State Hospital, where she was diagnosed with paranoid schizophrenia. The place held family history; Gladys's mother had died there years earlier after being diagnosed with what is now known as bipolar disorder.

Researchers have found that disrupted family life and sexual abuse may be linked to the development of borderline personality disorder. Not long after Gladys's institutionalization, McKee took Norma Jeane to the Los Angeles Orphans Home Society, a residential shelter where she lived for a number of months before rotating through several more foster homes. Monroe later recalled wearing tattered clothes and being treated like Cinderella, forced to bathe in a dirty tub full of water. And she said she was sexually abused, possibly by a boarder in one of her foster homes.

Biographers question many of the recollections Monroe shared in interviews and in her autobiography, which was written in collaboration with the Academy Award–winning playwright Ben Hecht and published in 1974, 12 years after her death. This does not surprise experts, who say patients often dramatize their childhood experiences. "While many people who develop the disorder have had dysfunctional and neglectful families, it's also true that adult borderline patients sometimes color their backgrounds in that direction," says Gunderson. "In order to understand the early childhood of people with borderline personality disorder, you have to understand that sometimes, these were difficult kids."

Whatever the truth, what matters is the end result. For Monroe, it was deep loneliness and feelings of abandonment. "As I grew older, I knew I was different from other children because there were no kisses or promises in my life. I often felt lonely and wanted to die," she wrote. This profound emptiness is classic in borderline patients, who frequently report fearing abandonment, feeling hollow, and being uncertain of who they are. When asked, "How would you describe yourself?" they aren't sure how to respond, says Andrada Neacsiu, a clinical psychologist specializing in borderline personality disorder at Duke University Medical Center. When the question is, "Do you feel empty?" they don't hesitate. Their response: "Of course I do."

Monroe seems to have dealt with this void by dreaming about who she could become. Eager to attract the attention she had been deprived of as a child, she envisioned being "so beautiful that people would turn to look at me when I passed." Puberty made it happen. One day, 13-year-old Norma Jeane ambled across a beach in her bathing suit, and the boys started whooping. That moment, she later recalled, "I was full of a strange feeling, as if I were two people. One of them was Norma Jeane from the orphanage who belonged to nobody. The other was someone whose name I didn't know. But I knew where she belonged. She belonged to the ocean and the sky and the whole world."

One of the hallmark features of borderline personality disorder is what psychiatrists call "identity disturbance." The *DSM* defines this as a "markedly and persistently unstable self-image or sense of self." Monroe struggled with this duality throughout her life: the child, Norma Jeane; the woman, Marilyn Monroe. She often felt the presence of her younger self peering out from the grown woman. In a poignant and telling sentence in her autobiography, she revealed that "this sad, bitter child who grew up too fast is hardly ever out of my heart. With success all around me, I can still feel her frightened eyes looking out of mine. She keeps saying, 'I never lived, I was never loved,' and often I get confused and think it's I who am saying it."

Without a stable inner being—Arthur Miller, Monroe's third husband, would later describe her life as "detached and center-less"—people with borderline personality disorder are exceedingly sensitive to how they are perceived, and often find self-worth by pleasing others. "They're a little chameleon-like, adapting themselves to different people," says Dr. Joel Paris, a psychiatrist and borderline expert at McGill University. This was the thrust of Marilyn Monroe's life. As a child, she was forced to adjust to new family surroundings; on screen, she took on multiple identities; in the public spotlight, she played the seductress everyone wanted to see. It was her career that gave Monroe the only semblance of solid footing. "My work is the only ground I've ever had to stand on," she said in an interview not long before she died. "To put it bluntly, I seem to be a whole superstructure with no foundation."

All of this played out in Monroe's relationships, which were markedly intense and unstable. People with borderline personality disorder demand constant attention and reassurance, wearing out the people they turn to for support. "Many people who develop this disorder feel essentially alone and unlovable," says Gunderson. "A lot of their relationships are compensating for that." None of Monroe's three marriages lasted. She wed her first husband, a merchant marine named James Dougherty, in 1942 when she was 16, and divorced him four years later. Her second marriage, to baseball player Joe DiMaggio in 1954, was over in nine months. Among other issues, DiMaggio was infuriated by Monroe's public displays of sexuality. This came to a boiling point during the filming of a famous scene in the movie *The Seven Year Itch*. Standing over a subway grate, Monroe smiled teasingly as her skirt billowed upward and swirled around her, an alluring image that would morph into an iconic photograph. Onlookers cheered and clapped. Later, there were reports of yelling at the St. Regis Hotel and of DiMaggio roughing up Monroe. "I've had it!" he shouted. Monroe accused DiMaggio of "mental cruelty."

Monroe's third marriage, to Arthur Miller in 1956, seemed unlikely from the start: the intellectual playwright, the bombshell actress. Miller, who was still married to his first wife when he met Monroe, was intoxicated by her allure. She admired Miller's intellect and saw him, to some degree, as her savior. He accepted the role. But over the course of their five-year marriage, Monroe's insecurities and neediness wore on him. She probed the world for the slightest sign of hostility, Miller wrote in his memoir, *Timebends*, and constantly sought reassurance. Miller was unable to bear her emotional volatility, especially her ire. "Anger, relentless and unending, at last refused to give way to any ameliorating word," he wrote. "In my trying to gentle her torment, she thought her cause was being trivialized." Miller acknowledged that he had expected "the happy girl that all men loved" but discovered "someone diametrically opposite, a troubled woman whose desperation was deepening no matter where she turned for a way out."

Monroe's intellect became a divisive issue. She had quit high school to marry Dougherty, her first husband, and struggled with her lack of knowledge about the world throughout her life. She tried to remedy it, signing up for art classes that introduced her to Michelangelo, Raphael, and Tintoretto, and collecting books by Milton, Dostoevsky, Hemingway, and Kerouac. She cultivated a friendship with poet and historian Carl Sandburg and delved into his six-volume biography of Abraham Lincoln. She talked about admiring Eleanor Roosevelt and Greta Garbo. She even sent a telegram to playwright and novelist Somerset Maugham, wishing him a happy birthday.

But soon after marrying Miller, Monroe found an entry in his diary expressing his disappointment in her and suggesting that he was sometimes embarrassed by her in front of his intellectual friends. Monroe was said to be devastated and felt betrayed. Those feelings ran deep. Monroe's pattern in relationships was to experience exaltation initially and then defeat, because nobody could live up to her needs. People with borderline personality disorder, says Gunderson, "switch rapidly from idealizing somebody who's going to take care of them to viewing that same person as devalued—a failure who never cared about anybody." By the time filming started for Miller's 1961 movie *The Misfits*, which starred Monroe as a young divorcée, "it was no longer possible to deny to myself that if there was a key to Marilyn's despair, I did not possess it," Miller wrote. "With all her radiance, she was surrounded by a darkness that perplexed me."

ALTHOUGH BORDERLINE PERSONALITY DISORDER is estimated to affect as many people as schizophrenia and bipolar disorder, it is far less recognized and often misunderstood. The very nature of personality disorders (there are ten total, including narcissistic, antisocial, and avoidant) is that they are deeply ingrained and long-lasting, which distinguishes them from other major mental health conditions. Symptoms of depression, for example, surge at one time and ease at another; the characteristics of personality disorders, by contrast, persist over time. The key features of these disorders—impulsivity, an inability to sustain close relationships, and anger—are paired with an overriding inflexibility. As a result, people who have personality disorders don't do well adapting to new situations or, for that matter, changing their behavior.

Borderline personality disorder is strongly "heritable," meaning it is likely to be passed down from one family member to another. One study found that a person's risk of developing the condition is three to four times higher if a parent or sibling has it, too. Monroe came from an unstable bloodline, and she connected her torment to her genetic roots. In her autobiography, Monroe pointed to "family ghosts" who struggled with mental health issues—in addition to her mother and grandmother, her grandfather died in a mental hospital, and an uncle killed himself. "I wish I knew why I am so anguished," she once wrote in a letter. "I think maybe I'm crazy like all the other members of my family were."

The biological underpinnings of borderline personality disorder are enormously complex and barely understood. Scientists have found that cortisol, the stress hormone, and oxytocin, which plays a role in social bonding and intimacy, both appear to be dysregulated in borderline patients. Brain scans may reveal additional features, including an overactive amygdala (the control center for modulating emotions) and an underactive prefrontal cortex (an area responsible for putting the brakes on impulsivity).

In almost every case, borderline patients suffer tremendous emotional pain and are prone to the worst possible outcome: suicide. More than half of all emergency room patients admitted for suicidal behaviors have borderline personality disorder, according to one report; 10 percent of patients will succeed at killing themselves. Because of their frequent ER visits, borderline patients are known in medical circles as "frequent-fliers," and their illness has long been considered toxic and untreatable. Many patients do not, however, intend to die, and this may well have been true of Monroe, who made numerous attempts at suicide. Their actions are impulsive, rather than decisive, says Gunderson. The thinking is "If somebody saves me, then life is worth living, and if nobody is there, I'll be dead."

Proper treatment can save patients, and this is where a radical transformation has taken place over the last 50 years. Monroe did seek psychological counseling, and she was seen by leading practitioners of the day, including Dr. Ralph Greenson, a prominent Beverly Hills psychiatrist; Dr. Marianne Kris, in New York; and even Anna Freud, Sigmund Freud's youngest child. All were trained in psychoanalysis, the established treatment approach in the early to middle part of the 20th century. A classical psychoanalytic approach is grounded in listening, rather than active dialogue. Therapists often begin by asking patients, "What's on your mind?" and then wait quietly for a response. A patient's thoughts, dreams, and reactions are used to help interpret how experiences of the past might be influencing behaviors of the present. Psychoanalysis is still used in some circles today to treat a number of mental health conditions, and some people seek it out simply to better understand themselves—how their lives were shaped by early experiences, how they perceive the world, how they interact. Talking allows patients to uncover old wounds, pick at the scabs, and help their damaged cores heal.

But patients with borderline personality disorder are primed for battle mode, and when the therapist is more passive, fears and insecurities can become aggravated. Although no one is privy to the dialogue Monroe had with Greenson, her longest-running therapist, it is likely that she spent a great deal of time reliving her childhood—her absent mother, the loneliness, the isolation, and perhaps, the abuse she says she suffered. Inez Melson, Monroe's live-in business manager, once wrote a letter to Greenson saying that she was concerned that Monroe was spending "too much time thinking about her problems" and "languishing in her misery." Arthur Miller questioned Monroe's treatment in his memoir as well: "Psychoanalysis was too much like talking *about* something rather than doing it, which was the only thing she had ever believed in anyway—her life had all been put up or shut up." If only Monroe could "step out of herself and see her own worth," he wrote.

Greenson seemed to struggle with how best to handle his patient and, at some point, he decided to radically alter his traditional therapy. Because of her losses in early childhood, he tried to help create the family she never had. He invited Monroe into his home—a no-no in the therapeutic world, where the patient-therapist boundary is sacrosanct. Greenson became Monroe's surrogate father, making himself available at all times of day and night. Monroe became completely dependent on him, often extending her sessions by several hours and eating dinner with Greenson and his family, even washing the dishes. Throughout her treatment, Monroe continued to receive copious prescriptions for drugs, not just from Greenson but from other doctors as well. For years, she drowned herself in sleeping pills and sedatives—the very drugs she would overdose on the night she died—to help quell the emotional pain. "You have to say that her treatment failed her," says McGill's Joel Paris.

Greenson has been roundly criticized for the dynamics he set up with Monroe—not just because he corrupted the sacred relationship between patient and therapist but because his methods may have made her condition worse. Still, the reality is that he had to rely on the skills and tools available to him at the time. Today, therapists use radically different treatment approaches that are rooted in the conviction that patients must be active participants in their own recoveries. One of these, dialectical behavior therapy, was pioneered by the borderline expert Marsha Linehan of the University of Washington, who realized it was crucial to develop a therapy for patients at high risk for suicide with difficult-to-treat disorders. She would know: After a patient inquired if she was "one of us," Linehan went public with her experience with mental illness in 2011 and spoke out about her severe distress and the suicide attempts that came with it. Institutionalized, often in seclusion, at a Hartford clinic at the age of 17 in 1961, Linehan burned her wrists with cigarettes, cut her arms and legs, and banged her head against the wall. Linehan now suspects that the symptoms she exhibited in the hospital and for some time afterward were similar to borderline personality disorder. But she was given a diagnosis of schizophrenia—one she finds highly unlikely—and was prescribed drugs, psychoanalysis, and electroshock treatments. None of it helped. "I was in hell," Linehan told the *New York Times*. "And I made a vow: when I get out, I'm going to come back and get others out of here."

The approach Linehan devised starts with having patients acknowledge their traumatic pasts. Rather than dwell on their emotional injuries, however, they learn skills to help them move on. Rooted in problem solving, the method focuses on establishing a balance between acceptance and change. Through a series of exercises, patients are taught how to regulate their emotions and control their impulsivity. Learning how to reduce self-destructive behaviors linked to the disorder, like abusing drugs and alcohol and cutting arms and wrists, is critical. Patients are also encouraged to try soothing activities to calm their powerful and erratic emotions, like taking a deep breath, going for a walk, or calling a friend for a chat.

Andy Warhol Was a Hoarder

Unlike the psychoanalysts of Monroe's day, therapists who practice dialectical behavior therapy and other related approaches take a hands-on approach to their patients. They talk to them, they give them direction, they don't allow them to stew. "It's become much less about either living through the past, à la Freud, or trying to replace the missing mother," says Paris. Instead, "you have to go forward." Patients often find much needed relief and affirmation when they discover that their clinicians are willing to not only validate their suffering but also believe in their ability to get better. In general, people tiptoe around borderline patients, says Neacsiu, so when clinicians treat them as equals, "they find it incredibly rewarding."

There are no specific medications used to treat borderline personality disorder. Many patients, misdiagnosed with bipolar disorder, depression, or schizophrenia, receive antidepressants or antipsychotics. Sometimes, these medicines can improve symptoms that overlap from one condition to the next, such as mood swings. But they are temporary fixes that cannot touch the complexity of what really needs to be done: reorganizing the way one understands and manages one's life. Only the patient can do that. The ultimate goal, says Neacsiu, is to "replace pills with skills." With the breakthrough in active therapy, borderline personality disorder has morphed from one of the most untreatable of mental illnesses to one with a high potential for a positive outcome. "There's a lot of good news here," says Paris.

Marilyn Monroe was, of course, not your typical patient. She was one of the most watched, sexualized, parodied, and idolized celebrities in history. She was the embodiment of beauty despite the pain and despair she felt inside. Is it possible that, with today's treatment, she might have learned to accept her tormented past and moved forward, living a decent, if not, satisfied life? "Absolutely," says Gunderson.

Arthur Miller wrote that Monroe lived "as though she were a mere passenger in her life." Had she been taught to seize the wheel, Marilyn Monroe might have had a very different destiny.

⌒

ON JUNE 1, 1962, MARILYN MONROE celebrated her 36th birthday on the set of the romantic comedy *Something's Got to Give*. Photos show her smiling behind the dance of glittering cake candles. One week later, she was fired. Monroe, who played the lead role (a housewife who discovers that she has been declared legally dead after being lost at sea), had consistently arrived late for rehearsals or hadn't shown up at all, claiming that she was sick with fever, headaches, and sinus problems. Her unexcused trip from Hollywood to Madison Square Garden in the middle of filming to serenade President Kennedy caused even more delays and roiled the executives at Twentieth Century–Fox.

Over the next couple of months, Monroe sat for photo shoots and interviews, including her last, with *Life* magazine's Richard Meryman. In his story, published on August 3, Monroe shared her indignation with the way studio execs treat their stars, her desire to give her fans her very best performance, and the capriciousness of fame. "You know," she told Meryman, "most people really don't know me." Over the course of several days of interviews, Meryman wrote in a follow-up account, Monroe veered from tired to lively to late. One day, he waited for hours as she had her hair done, made phone calls, and busied herself with errands around the house in her bare feet and curlers. During their numerous conversations, Monroe's jumbled feelings cascaded tellingly as she talked. "Her inflections came as surprising twists and every emotion was in full bravura, acted out with exuberant gestures,"

Meryman wrote. "Across her face flashed anger, wistfulness, bravado, tenderness, ruefulness, high humor and deep sadness."

On the early morning of August 5, Monroe was found naked and dead in her bedroom in Los Angeles with a telephone in one hand. Empty pill bottles were scattered nearby; sedatives were identified in her blood. The coroner ruled her death a probable suicide, but conspiracy theories—including that the Kennedys did her in—have never stopped swirling. Even in death, Monroe never got the chance to rest.

Over the course of her 16-year career, Monroe acted in 29 movies, including *Some Like It Hot*, for which she won a Golden Globe Award. The stage was where she lived; off it, she struggled to survive. Beauty and fame came big to Marilyn Monroe, but simple contentment did not. "I was never used to being happy," she said in her interview with Meryman, "so that wasn't something I ever took for granted."

Howard Hughes

MARTIN SCORSESE'S FILM *The Aviator* opens with a young Howard Hughes standing naked in front of a crackling fire as he waits to be bathed by his mother, Allene. Scorsese's filming of the scene is deliberately slow and methodical, punctuating the weightiness of every image, every word, every nuance. We see one of Allene's hands reach forward, shot close up in dramatic light. We see her carefully remove soap from a soap dish and plunge her hands into a tub filled with water. We see her begin to gently bathe her young son.

It is somewhere around 1913, a time when contagious illnesses are sickening patients without modern medicine to cure them. "Q-U-A-R-A-N-T-I-N-E," Allene Hughes says softly to Howard.

"Quarantine," the boy responds. "Q-U-A-R-A-N-T-I-N-E. Quarantine." "You know the cholera?" his mother asks. "Yes, Mother," Howard says. "You've seen the signs on the houses where the coloreds live?" she asks. "Yes, Mother," he says, his face softly shadowed. "You know the typhus?" she asks, her eyes searching the contours of her son's face. "I do, Mother," he says. "You know what they can do to you?" she asks, cupping her hands around his cheeks. "Yes, Mother." Allene Hughes pauses, then shakes her head slowly back and forth. "You are not safe," she says.

The scene is dramatic, perhaps overly so, but those four words perfectly define Howard Hughes's existence on the big screen and in life. The ambitious billionaire thrived on risky dalliances in romance, business, and his beloved airplanes—barely surviving after he crashed a military reconnaissance jet he had designed into a Beverly Hills neighborhood not far from the Los Angeles Country Club golf course. But it was the turbulence inside Hughes's mind that would ultimately ruin his life.

Throughout Scorsese's Oscar-winning film, in which Hughes is portrayed by Leonardo DiCaprio, snippets of Hughes's phobias, fixations, and nonsensical urges appear, recede, then resurface, ever more magnified. There's the moment when Katharine Hepburn, played by Cate Blanchett, asks Hughes what he has wrapped around the steering wheel of his airplane. "Cellophane," he says matter-of-factly. "If you had any idea of the crap people carry around on their hands." There's the sink scene, where Hughes scrubs his hands so hard they bleed, and the incident in the public bathroom, where he can't bring himself to pick up a paper towel and pass it to a man on crutches who asks for help. "I, uh, I really can't do that," Hughes says, looking pained. There's the nonsensical repetition of phrases, as he mutters "show me all the blueprints, show me all the blueprints, show me all the blueprints," more than 30 times in an increasingly rapid clip.

And then, in the most horrifying scene of all, there's a middle-aged Howard Hughes, holed up in a screening room, unshaven and gaunt, a prisoner of his own internal chaos. At various times, he sits naked in a white leather chair; he paces around the room, bathed in a blinking red light; he obsesses about how to complete the most minute tasks. "That milk is bad," he says out loud to himself. "I shouldn't pick up the bottle of milk with my right hand, and I shouldn't take the top off with my left hand, put it in my pocket, my left pocket." Later, he urinates into an empty glass bottle and places it next to dozens of others lined up neatly in a row. Standing naked in front of them, he flashes back to his childhood and spells out the word his mother drilled into his head: "Q-U-A-R-A-N-T-I-N-E."

A man of enormous achievement—a filmmaker, an engineer, a test pilot, a billionaire—Hughes was a master at controlling the people and circumstances around him, but he could not rein in the tortured meanderings of his mind. We now know that Hughes's bizarre behaviors were features of obsessive-compulsive disorder, or OCD, a debilitating condition that affects more than two million American adults, one-third of whom develop symptoms as children. Dr. Jeffrey Schwartz, a research psychiatrist and OCD expert at UCLA's School of Medicine, carefully studied Hughes's condition and served as DiCaprio's personal coach to enhance the actor's understanding of the disorder. "There's nothing mild about OCD. It's a serious disease," says Schwartz. And Hughes had it bad. "He was a walking encyclopedia of severe OCD symptoms."

❧

HOWARD ROBARD HUGHES, JR., WAS BORN on Christmas Eve of 1905 in Houston, Texas. Hughes's father, born in Missouri and raised in Iowa, was a bit of a rambunctious child who later dropped out of Harvard and then law school at the University of Iowa. But he had a keen intelligence, and great curiosity about mechanics and engineering. After dabbling in law and mining, Hughes Sr. was lured to east Texas by the promise of gushing oil fields. It was there that he met his wife, Allene Gano, the debutante daughter of a Dallas judge, and settled down to make his fortune.

Young Howard inherited attributes from both his parents. Like his father, he was fascinated by mechanical design and spent much of his childhood tinkering with gadgets, once concocting a make-shift radio out of parts from the family doorbell. When his mother said no to a motorcycle, he and his father built a motorized bicycle instead, which Howard rode proudly through the neighborhood streets. It was such a celebrated achievement that a photographer from the local paper showed up to take a picture.

Allene Hughes, tall and dark, doted on her only child, with whom she shared a quiet demeanor. Young Howard—shy, intro-verted, and socially awkward—had few friends, but he and his mother were exceedingly close. Allene worried about her son incessantly, rarely letting him out of her sight and creating what some remember as a wall of loneliness and alienation. Even after finally consenting to send Howard to summer camp in the Pocono Mountains of Pennsylvania, she found it impossible to fully let go and sent notes to the staff imploring them to look after her son and help him through his homesickness, according to Donald L. Barlett and James B. Steele's biography *Howard Hughes: His Life and Madness*. The camp director wrote back, telling her that How-ard was "an interesting little chap, full of fun and well liked" and showed no signs of missing his family. But nothing quelled her unease. The next summer, in 1917, she wrote another letter asking Howard's counselor to monitor her son's emotional and physical well-being. He continued to suffer from "supersensitiveness," as she called it, and a tendency to get his feelings hurt. She even worried about pain in the soles of his feet. While acknowledging that her concerns might be excessive, Hughes's mother wrote that she could not help herself: "I am trying hard to overcome too much anxiety over my one chick, but don't seem to make much headway."

It is not clear when or why Allene Hughes developed such angst about her child, and such an intense fear of germs and disease. It may have been fueled by the epidemics she grew up with. Although the turn of the 20th century in the United States was a time of great expansion and ingenuity—oil fields burgeoning; steel production booming; highways, railroads, and telephones connecting people nationwide—nobody had figured out how to stop people from contracting infectious diseases and dying. Germ theory—the realization that contagious illnesses were caused by microorganisms invading the body—had prompted improvements in sanitation, tempering epidemics of typhoid, cholera, and tuberculosis, which had killed tens of thousands of Americans in the 1800s. But with few vaccines available, and antibiotics decades from discovery in the early 1900s, the risk of deadly disease hovered like thunder on the horizon. This was the era, after all, of Mary Mallon, the Irish cook who was accused of sickening dozens of people with typhoid fever, at least three of whom died. "Typhoid Mary," as she was known, admitted to rarely washing her hands. She was quarantined for the first time in 1907, just two years after Allene Hughes gave birth to her baby boy, and again in 1915, when Howard was nine years old.

Hughes's mother likely felt overwhelmed by the responsibility of keeping her child safe in such a seemingly dangerous world. The enemy was everywhere and yet invisible, lurking in a cough or a handshake. Polio was on the loose, too, striking healthy people in towns and cities across the country during the summer months. Tens of thousands were affected—some paralyzed, others killed. Public health campaigns attempted to raise awareness, but no doubt instilled fear in people already primed with worry. One polio pamphlet underscored the importance of washing and decontaminating: "Keep your children clean. Bathe them frequently. See that they keep their hands particularly clean. Be sure that each child has [his] own clean handkerchief. Keep your house unusually clean. Don't allow a fly in it."

Hughes suffered numerous bouts of routine childhood illnesses, but his mother, especially, fixated on every symptom, no matter how minor. In 1919, he gave his parents a terrible scare when he was suddenly unable to walk. Fearing that Howard had been stricken with polio, Hughes Sr. flew an expert from New York's Rockefeller Institute for Medical Research to the family's home in Texas to try to cure his 13-year-old son. The doctor, however, could find no evidence of the dreaded virus—and despite being confined to a wheelchair for several months, young Howard fully recovered. To this day, it's unclear what went wrong, leading some to wonder if the boy was feigning his illness. Whatever caused his symptoms, the episode only reinforced Allene Hughes's excessive worries about her son's health—a pattern of fear that would reverberate throughout Howard Hughes's life.

DESPITE HIS QUIET CONDUCT AND social unease, Howard Hughes was filled with ambition, grit, even rebelliousness. These qualities emerged after both his parents died suddenly, when he was still a teenager. In 1922, his mother entered the hospital for what was considered minor uterine surgery. She was supposed to return home that same day, but never regained consciousness after undergoing anesthesia. She died at the age of 39. Just two years later, Howard Sr., outwardly spry and healthy at 54, slumped to the floor in the middle of a business meeting, the victim of a lethal heart attack.

The loss of his mother and father affected Hughes profoundly. Already primed with fears about illness, he was now fated to worry that he, too, might meet an early demise. Raymond Fowler, a psychologist who was commissioned to write a psychological autopsy after Howard Hughes's death in 1976, spent years reviewing Hughes's personal records and interviewing people who knew him. In his account, Fowler described Hughes becoming depressed and preoccupied by his health after his parents' deaths. The "loss of the only two people with whom he had a close relationship," Fowler wrote, "deepened his fears of death and increased his vulnerability to later disorders."

Hughes was, however, able to harness whatever emotional fortitude he had and set out to claim his independence when he was just 18 years old. Barely an adult, he rebuffed attempts by his grandparents and Rupert Hughes, his father's brother, to provide him a guardian, turning instead to the inheritance he received from his father's estate. The money was mostly bankrolled in shares of the Hughes Tool Company, the successful business Howard Hughes Sr. had founded to manufacture a revolutionary oil well drilling bit that could grind through hard rock. Young Howard had no interest in running the business's day-to-day affairs but was happy to reap its financial benefits. Not long after his father died, Hughes dropped out of Rice University and married Ella Rice (her great uncle had founded the original Rice Institute). A Houston socialite two years his senior, she wed Howard in the early summer of 1925.

Within just a few months, the young couple had packed up their belongings and moved to Hollywood, where Hughes set his sights on the competitive world of moviemaking. Though inexperienced in cinema, he had mingled with Hollywood producers and actors at the home of his uncle Rupert, who had become a successful scriptwriter. And Hughes had two other advantages: family money and bullish determination. In just a few years, he would make his first big box-office hit, *Two Arabian Knights*, a comedy featuring the zany adventures of a pair of American soldiers on the lam from a World War I POW camp.

Hughes's achievements in Hollywood surpassed the expectations of skeptics, who initially viewed him as nothing more than an amateur with wads of money. In 1929, the inaugural year of the Academy Awards, *Two Arabian Knights* won an Oscar for directing, and a second film Hughes produced, *The Racket*, was nominated for outstanding picture. His successes propelled Hughes to celebrity status. But he also overworked himself, spending endless hours on sets or in editing rooms, and straining his marriage.

Around this time, in his early 20s, Hughes's disconcerting behaviors began to emerge. Obsessive-compulsive disorder often strikes in adolescence or early adulthood, when life is in flux. For Hughes, one of the condition's earliest manifestations was fear of germs, a phobia he shared with his mother. He "gargled often and avoided people with colds," Fowler wrote in his analysis. "One time, when he found out that an actress with whom he had been having an affair had been exposed to venereal disease, he stuffed all of his clothes in canvas bags and ordered them burned."

Anxiety and stress are triggers for OCD, and Hughes was bedeviled by both, especially during filming and production of his epic World War I movie, *Hell's Angels*. Shooting began in October 1927, just after *Two Arabian Knights* debuted, and continued almost incessantly for more than three years as Hughes fixated on every detail, editing and reediting film at all hours. Hughes's demands went beyond those of even the most difficult Hollywood taskmasters. OCD is characterized by perfectionism and an overwhelming need to control one's environment—qualities that defined the way Hughes operated. He insisted on using authentic fighter planes rather than replicas, requiring a ground crew of more than 100 mechanics. He demanded that scenes be filmed repeatedly to get a portrayal he deemed powerful and realistic. At one point, he wanted a more imposing backdrop for a sequence that involved dozens of warring aircraft diving through the sky. The clear blue vistas of Southern California were too flat—he needed puffy white stuff—but nature refused to cooperate, so Hughes moved his filming operation north to Oakland, where he found the clouds he was looking for.

The film racked up costs of almost $4 million (about $54 million in today's dollars), an extravagance that shocked even Hollywood, and wore out the people who worked for him. His wife, fed up with his relentless schedule, packed up and moved back to Texas in the midst of filming. (They were divorced in 1929.) But Hughes carried on, with tireless intensity. He was unbendable, even when his vision was reckless. Advised to abandon his plan to have one of the planes spin down to earth, Hughes ordered it done anyway, killing one of his mechanics in a fiery crash.

Despite these tribulations, *Hell's Angels* made Hughes a big man in Hollywood and fueled his passion for aviation as both hobby and business. Two years before Hughes was born, the Wright brothers had succeeded in flying the first powered plane for 59 seconds; by the time he was five, they were manufacturing airplanes and training pilots. Flying saturated Hughes's childhood, and he wanted in on all of it as he grew up—the new machines, the soaring heights, the adventure. An accomplished pilot, Hughes liked to take his small planes out at night off the California coastline before returning to the busy lights of Los Angeles in the dark. Being high in the air offered him solitude and a kind of mastery over his surroundings that was unattainable anywhere else. In his account, Fowler suggested that flying may have alleviated Hughes's anxiety: "For Hughes, the landings were a reassuringly familiar activity that helped him avoid social stresses while allowing him to control at least some part of his environment."

Flying was an escape from what Hughes liked least about the world below: the clamor of celebrities and the never ending film extravaganzas and soirees. He was a "different man in the air," Barlett and Steele note in their biography. "No longer the shy, tense, highly nervous man people saw on the ground, aloft he was at ease behind a dizzying array of toggle switches and gauges, integrated with the sound of the engine, the feel of the controls, the magnificent view of the earth."

Hughes loved airplanes, and he was determined to make them better and faster—fast enough, even, to set new flying records. In 1932, he formed the Hughes Aircraft Company, a division he created out of his father's tool company, and soon after built the Hughes H-1, a racing jet. Taking the controls himself, Hughes took the plane up over a flat expanse of land in Southern California and gunned it to 352 miles an hour, setting a new speed record before running out of gas and crash-landing in a beet field. In 1938, he set his sights even higher, aiming to beat his competitors at circling the globe. In his twin-engine passenger plane, Hughes and his crew made it from New York to Paris in just 16.5 hours, slashing Lindbergh's transatlantic record by half. The entire trip, full circle, took 91 hours, setting a new world record. As he approached New York City, "twenty-five thousand cheering, hysterical people were there to greet him," according to Barlett and Steele. A ticker-tape parade followed the next day, with more than one million fans lining the sidewalks to see Hughes, the aviator, in person.

None of these achievements, however, could undo the growing turmoil in Hughes's mind, which would snowball when he became tangled up in a fiasco over an infamous flying boat. In 1942, during World War II, Hughes received a government contract to build the largest aircraft ever designed to transport military supplies and personnel. The H-4 Hercules, as he named it, was to be constructed out of wood with a wingspan bigger than a football field and a weight of about 200 tons. It was an intoxicating proposition for Hughes, but it was also impossibly ambitious. The government didn't help when it proposed a formidable challenge: Build it in ten months.

Given the scope of the project, Hughes sensed that it would be unworkable from the start, but he agreed to it anyway, amping up his stress. "The more he thought about potential problems, the more he worried and the less he slept," write Barlett and Steele in their biography. Within the first year, Hughes had missed numerous deadlines and burned through much of the $9.8 million the government allocated for the project. But he was obsessed with getting it done. Told that the contract was being canceled in the winter of 1944, he flew to Washington and worked tirelessly to convince the higher-ups to grant him a temporary reprieve. But the "Spruce Goose," as critics derisively called it, was doomed. By the time Hughes finished building it, the war was over.

The Hercules project left Hughes strung out and exhausted. By then, his preoccupation with germs and the precautions he took to avoid them had "gone beyond what most people regard as normal," according to Fowler. And a new symptom had emerged: Hughes began repeating instructions to the people who worked for him, either in person or in copious memoranda he dictated. In a memo about communication, he wrote, "a good letter should be immediately understandable . . . a good letter should be immediately understandable . . . a good letter should be immediately understandable" and "think your material over in order to determine its limits . . . think your material over in order to determine its limits . . . think your material over in order to determine its limits."

Repetition is a core feature of OCD. It often plays out in the fixations people develop, but it can surface in speech as well, as it did with Hughes. There are a variety of reasons for both manifestations. In some cases, it's a struggle with perfectionism; an action or word has to be repeated over and over again until it feels just right. In other instances, it's an effort to neutralize bad thoughts ("I've offended God") or fears about terrible things that might happen ("My brother is going to crash his car"). The hallmark of OCD, which is believed to affect up to 3 percent of the population, is the pairing of recurrent obsessions, which are intrusive thoughts, feelings, and images ("I forgot to turn off the stove" or "Germs are everywhere"), and compulsions, which are purposeful attempts to protect, escape, or reduce discomfort (checking and rechecking the stove or repeatedly washing one's hands).

Checking and washing are the most common and well-known manifestations of OCD, but symptoms can vary widely. Some people feel the need to organize books, papers, or clothing in a particular order; others are obsessed with counting or odd routines, like touching a doorpost a specific number of times before entering a room. In one of its most challenging forms, OCD can grip people with fears about causing grave harm to other people, like sexually abusing a child or even killing a spouse. Without knowing for sure that something bad is *not* going to happen, people with OCD devise irrational methods to keep everything under control. "One common theme that connects them all is intolerance of uncertainty," says Jason Elias, an OCD specialist at the Obsessive Compulsive Disorder Institute at McLean Hospital in Belmont, Massachusetts.

Plenty of people have borrowed the term "OCD" to make fun of the way they feel compelled to alphabetize their spices or wash their tennis shoes. And many of us *do* exhibit OCD-like characteristics every now and then—running back to the front door to make sure it's locked or stepping over cracks in the sidewalk. But more often than not, these behaviors are quirky and short-lived; they don't cause us ongoing distress, significantly impede our lives, or drive our family members *too* crazy. A severe case of clinical obsessive-compulsive disorder, on the other hand, can be as debilitating as the worst case of depression. The constant pattern of repetition may help reduce uncertainty by creating the appearance of warding off trouble and keeping people safe—but it is enormously stressful and a terrible burden to bear. Some people with OCD commit suicide to escape the constant barrage of messages and impulses. "It's horrible," says Elias. "It's torture from the inside."

THE CHARACTERISTICS OF OBSESSIVE-COMPULSIVE disorder have been around for as long as humans have been scanning the horizon for danger. Some evolutionary psychologists believe the condition may be an extreme overreaction to the early warning systems that protected us against deadly threats and disease and were vital to survival. A prehistoric human who kept an obsessive lookout for a saber-toothed cat might have noticed the animal coming sooner and escaped faster than his cool-as-a-cucumber cave mates. We're not the only ones who exhibit compulsive behaviors: Birds overpick at their feathers, pigs chew excessively on chains, cats pace and gnaw on fabric, and dogs lick at their paws and flanks so vigorously they develop ulcers and infections. It's impossible to know if animals actually obsess—but, like humans, their behaviors sometimes develop after stressful experiences, such as injury or loss of a companion.

Numerous historical figures are believed to have struggled with the condition, dating back to Martin Luther, the German monk who led the Protestant Reformation movement in the early 1500s. He is thought to have suffered from a particular form of OCD called scrupulosity, in which obsessions revolve around purity, committing sins, and going to hell. Luther was said to have been so consumed by such transgressions that he held lengthy confessions with his priest, in which he repeated his worries for hours at a time. By the late 19th century, modern conceptions of obsessive-compulsive disorder began to evolve. It was around this time that Nikola Tesla, the Serbian inventor, exhibited some of his famous symptoms: He counted his steps, insisted on having 18 napkins on the dinner table, and became obsessed with germs and the number three.

OCD is often confused with obsessive-compulsive personality disorder, a separate, and distinctly different, diagnosis. People with obsessive-compulsive personality disorder are preoccupied with orderliness and precision and are often rigidly stubborn and inflexible when it comes to rules and morals. They tend to think that they're right and that everyone else should be as persnickety as they are. They are not, however, plagued by the obsessions and compulsions of OCD. Above all, they lack one hallmark characteristic: insight. People with true OCD are painfully aware of how debilitating their thoughts and behaviors are but cannot figure out how to stop them. They are locked in a never ending duel with their brains.

Hughes's brand of OCD ran the gamut from germ phobias to rituals about how his clothes needed to be hung and the order in which his food had to be served. Petrified of germs, he required his assistants to wash their hands and put on white cotton gloves before presenting documents. Newspapers had to be delivered in stacks of three, allowing Hughes to grasp the middle, and presumably cleanest, copy.

As his symptoms intensified, Hughes fluctuated between functional and paranoid. He suffered his first severe psychological breakdown in 1944 in the midst of the Spruce Goose fiasco and another in 1958, when he holed himself up in a private film screening room, watched movies around the clock, and then slept for more than 24 hours straight. Hughes's obsessions revolved around precision and routine. His menu consisted of just a few items served repeatedly: whole milk, Hershey's bars with almonds, pecan nuts, and Poland bottled water. Everything had to be delivered in a brown paper bag rolled back at the outer edges and held at a 45-degree angle from his aide's body. Hughes then used Kleenex to reach into the bag and pull out the goods. None of this served him well. "He deteriorated physically and lost so much weight that his employees thought he would die," Fowler wrote.

During his seclusions, which also took place in a private bungalow at the Beverly Hills Hotel, Hughes issued an edict that "nobody ever goes into any room, closet, cabinet, drawer, bathroom or any other area used to store any of the things which are for me—either food, equipment, magazines, paper supplies, Kleenex—no matter what. It is equally important to me that nobody ever opens any door or opening to any room, cabinet or closet or anything used to store any of my things, even for one-thousandth of an inch, for one-thousandth of a second. I don't want the possibility of dust or insects or anything of that nature entering."

Andy Warhol Was a Hoarder

Even the smallest tasks required painstaking instructions. Take the three-page directive on opening a can of fruit. One step required that his assistants wash the can with soap first and then scrub it "from a point two inches below the top of the can." The label was to be soaked and removed and the can cleaned with a sterile brush "over and over until all particles of dust, pieces of paper label, and, in general, all sources of contamination have been removed." Serving the fruit mandated a new set of rules, requiring the server to always keep his head and upper body at least one foot away from the can and to present it with "absolutely no talking, coughing, clearing of the throat, or any movement whatsoever of the lips."

Windows and doors were sealed with masking tape. Kleenex became Hughes's defense against the world—he used it incessantly and demanded others do the same. In a memorandum about how to remove his hearing aid cord from the bathroom cabinet (Hughes suffered a moderate case of hearing loss for most of his life), his instructions required that six to eight Kleenexes be used to grasp the doorknob and turn on the water, six to eight more to open the cabinet, and fifteen to twenty additional to turn the faucet off. And then there was this: "The door to the cabinet is to be opened using a minimum of fifteen Kleenexes. (Great care is to be exercised in opening and closing the doors. They are not to be slammed or swung hastily so as to raise any dust, and yet exceeding care is to be exercised against letting insects in.) Nothing inside the cabinet is to be touched—the inside of the doors, the top of the cabinet, the sides—no other objects inside the cabinet are to be touched in any way with the exception of the envelope to be removed."

Hughes created his own "private mental institution—his very own asylum," according to Barlett and Steele, where aides accommodated every one of his demands, no matter how preposterous. Each one of Hughes's directives was compiled in a manual for staff members to follow. When Hughes said he liked a grilled cheese sandwich that came from a certain eatery on Sunset Boulevard, the "Grilled Cheese Sandwiches" report was created with instructions on how to prepare it exactly the same way every time. "The waitress and cook were requested to be certain that any knife or cutting board, anything touching the sandwiches, be free from the odor of onion," the report read. "To make a grilled cheese sandwich, the grill cook followed this procedure: two pieces of heavily buttered bread were placed separately on the grill, buttered sides down and a slice of cheese was placed on each. Then, after sufficient grilling, the two slices were joined to form one sandwich."

During this time, Hughes was married to the actress Jean Peters, his second wife, who quickly found herself living under the strange rituals dictated by her husband. The two watched movies together, but Hughes required that they live separately. His wife had her own bungalow at the Beverly Hills Hotel, and was instructed to call "Operations," the staff who manned Hughes's phone calls, when she wanted to reach him. In one of his directives, Hughes made it clear to his underlings that if his wife were to become sick, she needed his permission to seek treatment. "Under no circumstances should she be allowed to go see a doctor either at an office, a hospital or any place else, until HRH has talked to her first," he ordered. Somehow, the marriage lasted 13 years until the two were finally divorced in 1971.

Studies have found that obsessive-compulsive disorder runs in families, and it is very possible that Hughes inherited a genetic vulnerability to the condition. His mother's intense phobias about germs and illness likely had some impact, whether handed down through DNA or modeled through behavior. "Allene Hughes exerted an overpowering influence on his development," write Barlett and Steele. "If she was not worried about his digestion, feet, teeth, bowels, color, cheeks, weight, or proximity to others with contagious diseases, she was anxious about what she called his 'supersensitiveness,' nervousness, and inability to make friends with other boys. If Howard had no inherent anxieties in those directions as a small boy, he certainly had them by the time he reached adolescence. His mother helped instill in him lifelong phobias about his physical and mental state."

Genes are rarely the sole cause of illness, and scientists are on a quest to pinpoint other risk factors as well. Intriguing research has found that some children who suffer from strep infections may go on to develop sudden cases of OCD, possibly because their immune systems overreact to the bacteria and attack the brain. In Hughes's case, another factor may have played a role: plane crashes. Traumatic injuries to the brain have been known to trigger psychiatric disorders, especially depression, and there have been case reports of brain injuries leading to OCD. Hughes's passion for flying was boundless, and he took enormous risks during test flights, which resulted in several serious crashes. His first injury took place in 1928 during the filming of *Hell's Angels*, when he insisted on performing a risky maneuver and hit his head in a crash. In 1943, his plane went down into a lake in Nevada. The worst, by far, was his test flight of the military reconnaissance aircraft in 1946. Because of an oil leak, the plane pitched and lost altitude, crashing in Beverly Hills. Hughes broke ribs and a collarbone, crushed his chest, and suffered third-degree burns. He barely survived. An autopsy report allegedly later revealed that he had cracked his skull at least three times.

Researchers have uncovered some compelling clues about the biological underpinnings of obsessive-compulsive disorder. Neurological studies of people with OCD have found increased activity in several parts of the brain, including areas that are responsible for detecting errors and making decisions. The message that says "lock the door" keeps going and going until what is normally a vital mental warning system becomes a constant and debilitating intrusion. In people with OCD, this particular region of the brain "doesn't give up," says McLean Hospital's Elias.

As with other mental health conditions, OCD exists on a continuum, with some people suffering more recurring thoughts and ritualistic behaviors than others. Symptoms often overlap with other conditions. Researchers have discovered a close biological link between OCD and Tourette syndrome, which is characterized by rapid and repetitive movements called tics. Many people with OCD struggle with attention deficit hyperactivity disorder, depression, and anxiety. Serotonin, one of the neurotransmitters implicated in mood disorders, may also play a role in OCD, so treatment often includes antidepressants and anti-anxiety medications.

Behavioral therapy has evolved significantly over the last few decades. Early on, therapists were afraid to confront patients with their worst phobias, concerned that they might upset them more than help them. But today, exposure and response prevention therapy, or ERP—rooted in facing one's fears—is used frequently. Patients are guided to undertake the very actions that worry them most: They must leave the house without checking the door or halt their counting routines, no matter how strongly they believe something bad will happen as a result. The therapy can be exceedingly challenging, especially early on when patients become agitated, fearing they have lost control. But about two-thirds of patients who stick with ERP respond well and learn to tamp down the obsessions and compulsions. "Eventually, the tasks they are assigned can be completed comfortably even in the presence of uncertainty or anxiety," says Elias. "This restores their confidence and quality of life."

Andy Warhol Was a Hoarder

Dr. Jeffrey Schwartz, the UCLA researcher, believes in an alternative approach that harnesses the significant insight that OCD patients often exhibit, which he uses to retrain their minds. Schwartz's techniques are based in mindfulness, a practice that focuses on living in the present and viewing one's thoughts and feelings with less judgment and reactivity. During treatment, Schwartz encourages patients to talk back to their OCD. Instead of allowing distorted notions to dictate their actions, patients learn to identify their obsessions as a symptom they can control. Rather than give in, the person might say, "That's just a false message, and I don't have to listen to it." In a series of exercises, patients are trained to understand that their intrusive thoughts are happening because their brains are "stuck in gear," as Schwartz describes it. They learn to ignore their obsessions, shift away from destructive behaviors, and refocus on more productive and energizing activities. In time, with significant practice, their reactions can become much bolder and more confident: "Go ahead, make my day. Just *try* to make me wash my hands one more time." Schwartz believes that people have the power to rewire their brains. In experiments he conducted in the 1990s, Schwartz performed PET scans on the brains of his patients and found that the overactivity in their brains declined after mindfulness treatment.

Hughes never had the benefit of any kind of therapy. "Obsessive-compulsive reaction," as it was previously called, was known to exist in Hughes's day, but there is no evidence that he was ever diagnosed or received appropriate care for his debilitating illness. In the late 1960s, researchers began testing an early antidepressant called clomipramine in patients with symptoms of OCD; it was later approved as a beneficial medication. But Hughes's timing was off by about ten years, says Schwartz. Instead, he became addicted to painkillers, which were first prescribed to him after his 1946 plane crash. For decades, he used codeine on a regular basis, often at dangerously high doses. "In his later years when he had little left except his vast wealth," wrote Fowler, the psychologist, "he clung to his drugs because, as he said, they were his only pleasure."

Hughes might have benefited from a mindfulness approach to OCD early on, Schwartz posits. He had an engineer's mind, and the capacity to think about problems and organize solutions. Above all, he had a strong will. "He was an ideal therapeutic candidate," says Schwartz. But Hughes's OCD spiraled out of control until the chaos started to look like order—perhaps because there was no urgency to make it stop. Most people suffering from OCD struggle to keep their symptoms in check so they can support themselves or their families. They don't have a choice; they must function so that they can bring home a paycheck. Schwartz speculates that because of Hughes's powerful position—he never endured financial hardship and always had people obeying his controlling edicts—he had little motivation to fend off his urges. "Not only did he not resist them, he indulged them," Schwartz says. "That is a prescription for getting disastrous OCD."

⌒

THROUGHOUT HIS LIFE, Howard Hughes suffered tremendous pain, both physical and emotional. Scores of people worked with him, and he had numerous relationships with Hollywood stars, from Katharine Hepburn to Ava Gardner and Ginger Rogers. He married and divorced twice. But nobody, in the end, could save him.

In his final days, Hughes holed himself up at the Acapulco Princess Hotel in Mexico in a state of delirium and dehydration, hooked on codeine. After suffering a seizure that rendered him unconscious, Hughes was put on a stretcher and carried out to a small jet bound for Houston, the city of his birth. He never made it. During the course of the flight, on April 5, 1976, Hughes's heart stopped. He was 70 years old and weighed just 93 pounds. Two days later, he was buried next to his mother and father in Houston's Glenwood Cemetery.

In an interview after *The Aviator* debuted, Leonardo DiCaprio talked about his reaction to first seeing the film script and wondering how such a brilliant and successful man could also be so troubled. Hughes had "all the resources in the world, but was somehow unable to find any sense of peace or happiness," DiCaprio said. He could soar to great heights, but he could not, in the end, leave his troubles behind.

Andy Warhol

THE ANDY WARHOL MUSEUM, housed in an old warehouse building with an ornate terra-cotta facade, sits across the Allegheny River from Pittsburgh's downtown business center. Step inside and you are transported back to the rousing art world of the 1960s and '70s, encapsulated in Warhol's innovative and rebellious work: the Campbell's Soup silk screens, the Brillo box installation, the "Silver Clouds" balloons, the silk screens of skulls and celebrities, the haunting self-portraits with spiky hair, and the artist's infamous "oxidation" works—created in a medium described by Christie's auction house as "copper metallic pigment and urine on canvas."

But one rainy September afternoon in 2013, it was what was *not* on display that enticed a band of Warhol enthusiasts to splash through puddles on Sandusky Street and grab a seat in the museum's theater. There, museum catalogers were about to unveil the contents of one of the artist's famed Time Capsules, a sprawling collection of Warhol memorabilia housed in 569 cardboard boxes, 40 filing cabinets, and one large trunk. Other capsules, which museum staff members had been diligently documenting and archiving, contained empty toothbrush boxes, silverware swiped from the Concorde, photographs, restaurant bills, Campbell's Soup cans, worn underwear—and even a mummified human foot. As the theater lights dimmed, anticipation surged. "I heard there was a slice of Caroline Kennedy's 16th birthday cake in one of the boxes!" one man whispered.

On stage, a somewhat worn cardboard box dated "1967–1969" sat ceremoniously under a spotlight, like a black hat on a magician's table. "Aren't you guys excited?" a museum cataloger asked as she pulled back the cardboard flaps, her hands covered in blue protective gloves. Over the course of an hour, she and a colleague dug into the box in front of their rapt audience, pulling out a seemingly random assortment of items: a prescription for 250 milligrams of tetracycline; a Christmas card; a query from *Playboy* asking Warhol what he'd do first if he were elected president; *Newsweek* and *Time* magazines; a letter from a wannabe actor who hankered to be in one of Warhol's films; a news clipping about Valerie Solanas, the actress who pleaded guilty to shooting Warhol in 1968; a past-due $3,000 bill from Dr. Giuseppe Rossi, the surgeon who saved Warhol's life; and a handful of carbon copies of old checks so brittle they were practically falling apart. "These are not the kinds of things that you're meant to keep forever," the cataloger said.

And yet Warhol did just that. He could not help himself. With his silver wig, skinny jeans, and provocative work, the artist's public persona exuded image, drama, sexuality, and edginess. He was a paragon of counterculture, the face of pop art and its brash embrace of consumerism. But behind the cameras and canvases, Warhol had another, less celebrated preoccupation: He was an accumulator of epic proportions. The man loved to shop, and he did it whenever and wherever he could—five-and-dime stores, antique stores, high-end galleries. "He was a voracious consumer of just about everything," says Matt Wrbican, the Warhol Museum's chief archivist. In addition to the 610 Time Capsules, which he packed with some 300,000 items, the artist crammed his Manhattan home with so much stuff—pearl necklaces, Miss Piggy memorabilia, Bakelite bracelets, Lichtenstein drawings—that "you had to climb over things" to get around, one visitor told *New York* magazine after his death.

Hoarding has existed for at least as long as Dante's 14th-century epic poem: *The Divine Comedy* condemned hoarders to the fourth circle of hell, where they would spend eternity at war with their nemeses, the wasters. Today, many of us use the word nonchalantly to describe a bad habit that junks up our living rooms with magazines and our closets with shoes. Warhol's cache was in a league all its own. With his vast array of goods, he was one of the most important collectors of the 20th century, but he also displayed classic characteristics of hoarding.

What makes Warhol's story so captivating is that he luxuriated in such divergent worlds—the upscale and the mundane—and left behind a monumental mix of both. For most of us, it's difficult to fathom accumulating Picassos and American Empire furniture. But junk mail, old checks, and outdated catalogs? We can identify with that. It's a little bit of all of us.

Andy Warhol Was a Hoarder

IT IS HARD TO IMAGINE ANDY WARHOL living anywhere other than the artsy mecca of New York City. But his childhood began and ended on the gritty streets of working-class Pittsburgh. Andrew Warhola (he later dropped the "a") was born on August 6, 1928, to Ondrej and Julia Warhola, Czechoslovakian immigrants and churchgoing Catholics. The youngest of three boys, Andy stood out as a shy, effeminate, and artistic child. He was also sickly. At the age of eight, he suffered the first of several bouts of Sydenham's chorea, a neurological disease caused by infection. The illness triggers involuntary muscle movements and can discolor the skin. Warhol developed blotches on his face and was self-conscious about his appearance throughout his life. Often unwell and socially isolated, he found comfort in comic books, celebrity magazines, and drawing—a talent he may have inherited from his mother, who made handicrafts out of tin cans and crepe paper when she wasn't earning much needed cash cleaning homes.

Life for the Warhola family was often a struggle—his father, a construction worker, traveled frequently; the Depression weighed heavily—but young Warhol found joy in the faraway world of stardom and the arts. Passionate about movies, he created a photo scrapbook of Hollywood stars, including Henry Fonda, Mae West, and his beloved Shirley Temple. As a teenager, he took free classes at the Carnegie Museum of Art on Saturday afternoons and later enrolled in the Carnegie Institute of Technology, paid for by savings left by his father, who, after spending much of his life traveling to coal mines, died after drinking contaminated water when Warhol was just 13. At art school, Warhol developed an ink-blotting technique that would become one of his signature styles early on. But he also provoked his instructors with unconventional approaches, once cutting a painting into four parts and presenting them as separate projects, according to art critic David Bourdon in his biography, *Warhol*. A memorable incident occurred in early 1949, when the young artist submitted a painting of a man with his finger up one nostril to the annual exhibition of the Associated Artists of Pittsburgh. The piece, titled *The Broad Gave Me My Face, But I Can Pick My Own Nose*, was rejected.

In the summer of 1949, after graduating with a degree in pictorial design, Warhol moved to New York City to seek work as a commercial artist. Within just a few months, he had published a series of drawings to accompany an article in *Glamour* magazine, and was quickly sought after for his energetic and playful illustrations. A diligent artist and persistent networker, Warhol developed an active and diverse freelance business in the 1950s, drawing pictures for the major fashion magazines, designing sprightly Christmas cards for Tiffany & Co., illustrating album covers for Vladimir Horowitz, Arturo Toscanini, and Count Basie, and winning awards for his jaunty depictions of footwear featured in advertisements by the I. Miller shoe company. He even made a published artist out of his mother, who lived with him in Manhattan for almost 20 years before her death in 1972. Julia Warhola's elegant handwriting accompanied many of her son's early illustrations, and he published a series of her feline drawings in a small book titled *Holy Cats by Andy Warhol's Mother*.

By 1960, Warhol's success in commercial art allowed him the freedom to experiment with new ideas. By then, Robert Rauschenberg and Jasper Johns were remaking abstract expressionism and covering canvases with familiar imagery—newspapers, photos, the American flag. Warhol shifted his focus from whimsical illustrations to groundbreaking pop images of consumer goods: Coca-Cola bottles, Brillo pads, Del Monte peach tins, and his iconic Campbell's Soup cans. Using silk screen on canvas, the artist found a new niche with his eclectic representations of Jackie Kennedy,

Andy Warhol Was a Hoarder

Elizabeth Taylor, Elvis Presley, baseball, car crashes—even the electric chair. Suddenly, the skinny, socially challenged kid from the Iron City was whipping up controversy and achieving what he sought most of all: fame.

He was also cultivating a passion for stuff. A lot of it. Looking back, it's interesting to note that Warhol had a thing for multiplicity in almost every area of his life—more was always better than less. His silk screens are clearly defined by their repetitions: 100 Marilyn Monroes, 210 Coca-Cola bottles, 14 orange images of a mangled vehicle. Art critics have probed the esoteric meaning of this—the commodification of celebrity, the dulling down of horror—but in a most simplistic way, Warhol's serial images flaunted the artist's preoccupation with abundance. He sought numbers in people, too. Lonely as a child, he amassed flocks of "associates," showing up at social events with many of them in tow. "He became notorious for taking his entourage everywhere, most annoyingly to private gatherings," wrote Bourdon, who was a friend and part of Warhol's inner circle. "If a hostess thought she had invited Andy by himself, she was likely to be aghast when he walked in followed by several companions." As Warhol admitted, "It was like one whole party walking into another one whenever we arrived."

It was Warhol's accumulation of physical items, however, that shocked his closest companions and triggered spirited debates about the motivation behind his "possession obsession," as the Warhol Museum aptly dubbed one of its exhibits. By his own admission, the artist had trouble getting rid of anything: "My conscience won't let me throw anything out, even when I don't want it for myself," he wrote in his 1975 book *The Philosophy of Andy Warhol (From A to B and Back Again)*. Nothing exemplified this better than his 610 Time Capsules, which Warhol began filling in 1974. The boxes were initially intended to store items during a relocation of his studio, known as the Factory. But for years after the move, Warhol continued to use them as a place to stash everyday items that he swept off his desk: lunch receipts, tickets stubs, doctors' bills, letters, postage stamps. "At the Factory, he often drove his colleagues crazy by saving virtually everything, from the canceled stamps on incoming mail to the exhausted batteries in his tape recorder," according to Bourdon. The boxes were an easy out, because Warhol never had to get rid of anything. It all went in—even junk he picked out of the trash—and was shipped off to storage. Later, Warhol wrote: "I want to throw things right out the window as they're handed to me, but instead I say thank you and drop them into the box-of-the-month."

A persistent inability to part with belongings is one of the defining characteristics of hoarding disorder, a mental health condition that appears as a distinct diagnosis for the first time in the most recent edition of the *DSM*. Soon after he moved in to an apartment on the Upper East Side of Manhattan in the 1950s, Warhol began filling it with furniture, artwork, books, and decorative objects, including a stuffed peacock he discovered in a taxidermy shop. "Clutter was an indispensable element of Warhol's habitats, and his parlor-floor apartment came to resemble a scavenger's pleasure palace," wrote Bourdon. Collecting, which harkened back to Warhol's childhood fascination with celebrity photos, soon became a passion for accoutrements high and low, whether it was a kitschy cookie jar or a painting by Paul Klee. A tireless shopper, Warhol hit every kind of marketplace—flea markets, antique dealers, galleries, Saks Fifth Avenue. One of his favorite targets was Lamston's, the old Manhattan variety store, where he'd buy a 30-cent shopping bag and see how much he could cram in. At home, he'd lay out the contents on his bed and rub the prices off with Comet. "Then, the minute you've put all the stuff away," he wrote, "you want to go shopping again."

Andy Warhol Was a Hoarder

Plenty of people like to browse and buy, but Warhol's zealousness was unparalleled. The extent of his acquisitions became starkly apparent after his death in 1987. Hired to handle his estate, Sotheby's appraisers set up shop as best they could to document the goods in his home, a five-story brownstone he had moved to on East 66th Street. Staffers found rooms jammed with boxes and shopping bags. A Picasso was stashed in a closet; gems were found tucked away in the bed. There were heaps of cheap watches, dozens of perfume bottles, 175 cookie jars, as well as Tiffany lamps and paintings by Lichtenstein, Johns, and Rauschenberg.

The key feature distinguishing hoarding disorder from run-of-the-mill cluttering is that living spaces become so deluged with possessions they cannot be used for their intended purpose. A striking photograph of Warhol's dining room, taken shortly after he died, shows complete disarray with boxes piled high in front of a fireplace, paintings leaning against a wall, and a table laden with books, papers, bowls, and heaps of other objects. "There, in the spacious dining room, was a handsome Federal dining table, surrounded by a dozen Art Deco chairs. Underneath lay a luxurious carpet—obviously an Aubusson," writes biographer Victor Bockris in *Warhol*. "But entrance to the room was blocked. Occupying every inch of floor, table and sideboard space were so many boxes, shopping bags and wrapped packages—so much sheer stuff—that the appraisers could not penetrate further. This was not a room where anyone had dined, at least not in years." By the time Warhol died, he was living largely in his bedroom, where he stacked his wigs next to the TV and slept in a four-poster canopied bed.

What drove Warhol to amass such a monumental cache? Was he a compulsive hoarder? Or a collector with an appreciation for all things beautiful, no matter how mundane? In many ways, Warhol masterfully inhabited the role of both. "To me, it's a fascinating blurred line," says Dr. Carolyn Rodriguez, director of the Hoarding Disorder Research Program at Stanford University. Warhol amassed an astounding collection of art deco, American Indian artifacts, folk art, and works by Duchamp and Man Ray. And yet he made no effort to display his items in any organized way—one of the hallmarks that differentiates collecting from hoarding. Collectors delight in showing off their goods; hoarders keep their stuff under wraps. This was certainly true of Warhol, who was notorious for keeping visitors out. "Some of the stuff he bought was never unpacked," Sotheby's chairman John Marion told *New York* magazine after Warhol died. "The thrill of the chase was more interesting to him than presenting what he bought." When asked in a 1975 newspaper interview how he decorated his house, Warhol responded: "Just with junk. Paper and boxes. Things I bring home and leave around and never pick up."

The sheer number of items doesn't differentiate collecting from hoarding—what matters is whether or not there's any logic to the arrangement and how well the objects are maintained. A hundred shiny teacups in a glass cabinet constitutes a collection; a hundred bags filled with gum wrappers, paychecks, and newspaper clippings, a hoard. Warhol's Time Capsules are a prime example. They contain a jumble of rare photographs alongside suppository boxes. And he paid little attention to the condition of individual items. "Warhol threw things in the boxes without any regard for physical well-being," says archivist Wrbican. Since the museum began cataloging the Time Capsules, staffers have unfurled balled-up clothing and textiles and found cans of leaking Campbell's soup and desiccated pizza dough. A piece of decayed orange-nut bread, sent to Warhol by his niece, showed up in one box, as did his signature wigs, which one museum worker told *Carnegie* magazine "looked like road kill."

Andy Warhol Was a Hoarder

Warhol considered exhibiting the capsules in a gallery, and he toyed with selling them for as much as $4,000 each, but it never happened. Procrastination is a classic characteristic of hoarders, says Robin Zasio, a clinical psychologist who worked as a therapist on the TV show *Hoarders*. "They have great plans, but they never get to them because the hoard is so great and so overwhelming." Still, given Warhol's intentions and the historic value of the contents, the Warhol Museum considers the Time Capsules one continuous work of art comprising serial components that are an integral part of the museum's collection; several boxes have traveled to galleries abroad for exhibition. Even if their scrambled contents exemplify hoarding, the Time Capsules as a whole can be viewed as representing *something* artistically meaningful: a scrapbook of social history, a testimonial to consumerism, a celebration of the ordinary. "Warhol was endlessly in love with the day-to-day," says Wrbican.

He was not, however, always in love with his stuff. As much as he relished the hunt, a part of Warhol pined to be a neat freak. "I believe that everyone should live in one big empty space. It can be a small space, as long as it's clean and empty," he wrote. Distress is a key component of hoarding disorder, and Warhol seems to have experienced the feeling both when he was confronted with throwing something out and when he got fed up with his jam-packed surroundings. "I'm so sick of the way I live, of all this junk, and always dragging more home," he declared in *The Andy Warhol Diaries*. "Just white walls and a clean floor, that's all I want."

⌒

THE HUMAN IMPULSE TO HOARD is rooted in evolution and has lingered in our brains. "Since the caveman days, we've been hunting, gathering, and collecting," says Stanford's Rodriguez. "It's normal human behavior." It is a compulsion we share with a wide range of animals, from honeybees to the Barbados green monkeys. Wild rats, it turns out, collect not just food but inedible objects, too—stuff they ostensibly don't *need* to survive—which may help explain why "pack rat," the name for a bushy-tailed rat that drags anything and everything into its den, is used in reference to people, too.

A lot of us are bad at throwing stuff out. We hold on to movie stubs, shoe boxes, and magazines. Homework piles propagate on our kitchen tables. We stuff too many Band-Aid boxes into our medicine cabinets and hang on to old phone books—things we think might come in handy one day but that we don't really need. Although we pledge to be better organized, we never have the time or energy to do it. We may casually refer to ourselves as "hoarders," but in reality we'd probably qualify as midrange messy on a cluttering continuum that starts with what Zasio calls "clear and clean" and ends with borderline hoarding. The next step up, a diagnosable case of hoarding disorder, requires many more piles and much more life disruption than most of us will ever face. In extreme cases, hoarders' homes look like domestic war zones, with inhabitants navigating mountains of clothing, moldy newspapers, rotting sandwiches, and cat feces.

This level of hazardous hoarding was catapulted into the modern American consciousness by two reclusive Columbia-educated brothers, Homer and Langley Collyer. On March 21, 1947, an anonymous tipster called the New York City police to report a dead man inside a mansion on Fifth Avenue at 128th Street. The cops broke in and uncovered a shocking scene: rooms and hallways crammed with busted baby carriages, broken musical instruments, car parts, and rat-infested debris. Homer, who was blind and cared for by his younger brother, was found dressed in a ragged bathrobe. He had died from a heart attack and starvation. Three weeks later, after hauling more than 100 tons of possessions out of the home—including 14 pianos and a 2,500-volume law library—police uncovered Langley's partially decomposed, rat-chewed corpse under stacks of newspapers. He had triggered one of his own booby traps, set to deter intruders, and suffocated about ten feet away from his brother. Crowds gathered to watch work-men remove the belongings; newspapers published photographs of the squalor. It was mesmerizingly awful: two brothers from an upper-crust New York family, buried by their junk.

Hoarding, it soon became clear, could be anyone's problem: rich or poor, privileged or neglected, famous or unknown. Jackie Kennedy Onassis's aunt, Edith Ewing Bouvier Beale (known as "Big Edie"), and Beale's daughter, Edith (known as "Little Edie"), also started out with well-to-do upbringings in New York City. Big Edie was married at St. Patrick's Cathedral and aspired to a singing career. Little Edie attended private schools, made her society debut at the Pierre Hotel in 1936, and had a successful stint as a model. A cousin called her "the most beautiful Bouvier girl of them all." But health inspectors who raided the pair's broken-down East Hampton mansion in 1971, where they lived with dozens of feral cats, found a five-foot mountain of empty cans in the dining room, and human waste upstairs.

The women were spared eviction after Onassis offered to pay for a cleanup; later, they agreed to be the subjects of a documentary film made in 1975. The critically acclaimed *Grey Gardens*, which developed a cult following, exposed the Beales' bizarre living conditions. In one scene, Little Edie goes into what was once her brother's dingy room and sifts through some of his belongings. "I feel so strongly about mementoes and everything because of Mother that I'm never able to ever clean out these desk drawers and throw this stuff away," she says. In another clip, she sets out biscuits for raccoons that have infiltrated the attic.

It took several decades for hoarding to make its way from these astonishing cultural spectacles to the ranks of serious science. Until the early 1990s, little research existed, says Randy Frost, a psychology professor at Smith College and a pioneer in the field. At the time, Frost was teaching a seminar on obsessive-compulsive disorder, or OCD, when a student asked if there were any studies on hoarding, a condition that mental health experts then believed to be a subtype of OCD. The answer, Frost told her, was no. That inquiry prompted Frost to take a look at hoarding in its own right. He and his student posted ads in local newspapers seeking people who considered themselves to be "pack rats" or "chronic savers." They were surprised when they received more than 100 phone calls. Visits to their volunteers' homes revealed that hoarders didn't just hold on to old newspapers or sentimental stuffed animals, as many had long believed—they collected new items as well. Some still had their price tags attached. Frost discovered that people who hoard have deep emotional attachments to their items, no matter how ordinary. And he documented an important trend: Hoarding runs strongly in families, a finding that has since been confirmed by studies of twins.

Over the last 25 years, hoarding research has accelerated, and scientists have made several striking discoveries that have altered their earlier conception of the condition as a subtype or symptom of OCD. It turns out, says Frost, that many hoarders do not fit the diagnostic criteria for OCD, which includes a cycle of obsessive thoughts and compulsive actions. Most significantly, patients do not view their actions in the same way. People who struggle with OCD are almost always upset about their irrational behavior; hoarders, on the other hand, enjoy their shopping sprees, despite the inordinate mess they create. This realization, says Frost, "led people to say, 'This really does look very different.' "

Science is also beginning to uncover distinct visual clues about the inner workings of the hoarding brain. In a 2012 brain scan study, researchers including Frost asked compulsive hoarders to choose whether they wanted to keep a selection of paper items or get rid of them and have them shredded. Half of the items came from the volunteer's own home; the other half belonged to the investigators. Compared to a group of people with OCD and a group of healthy controls, the volunteers discarded far fewer of their own possessions and took slightly longer to make their decisions. They also reported more anxiety, indecisiveness, and sadness as they made their choices. Most fascinating, they registered different activity levels in areas of the brain related to decision-making, depending on whose stuff they were looking at. When the goods *didn't* belong to them, these brain regions didn't generate much excitement. When making choices about their *own* stuff? Fireworks.

This buildup of research has led to a more comprehensive understanding of hoarding as a distinct condition, and it is now listed as a separate but related disorder in the *DSM*. Researchers are beginning to sort out the most effective and acceptable treatment methods. Patients do not respond well to dramatic interventions like forced cleanouts, which can increase anxiety and depression as treasured possessions are hauled out to the trash. Preliminary data suggests that antidepressants may reduce hoarding symptoms, but many patients are averse to taking medications, and it can be difficult to keep track of them in cluttered homes, says Stanford's Rodriguez. Many patients prefer to attend support groups or individual therapy sessions, which can provide them with the skills to help them organize, discard, and make decisions about their possessions.

There is still much to nail down, including the factors that lead people to hoard in the first place. "In many ways, it's an exaggeration of normal behavior," says Frost. But what pushes normal to pathological? People with hoarding disorder often disclose stressful or traumatic events earlier in their lives, suggesting that the accumulation of stuff may serve as a distraction and even a source of security. Deprivation is also considered a factor, but views are shifting on the type of hardship that has an impact. It makes logical sense that an individual might hoard to make up for a lack of material abundance in childhood—a reality that Warhol experienced. And yet the research so far does not substantiate this theory—nor, for that matter, do the Collyer and Beale cases. Frost says emotional impoverishment may be more important. He has found that hoarders are much less likely to report growing up in a warm and supportive family, compared to people with OCD and to people who have neither condition. Hoarding may provide comfort to those who feel neglected.

One condition hoarding and OCD do share is anxiety. Hoarders get nervous about throwing things away; they worry that they might need their possessions, won't remember them if they're gone, or must hold on to them for sentimental reasons. By *not* getting rid of anything, they are able to ward off their uneasiness. Difficult life circumstances can make hoarders anxious, too—a death in the family, abuse, loss of a job. Feeling desperately overwhelmed, they turn to inanimate objects as a substitute for the unpredictability of life. "Hoarding affords many of its sufferers the illusion of control and replaces fear with a feeling of safety," Frost and his co-author Gail Steketee write in their book, *Stuff: Compulsive Hoarding and the Meaning of Things.*

In some cases, the emotional connections hoarders form with their stuff may signify trouble attaching to people. Warhol's entourages certainly kept him entertained. A regular at Studio 54, Warhol hobnobbed with everyone from Calvin Klein to Liza

Minnelli, and his Factory was filled at all hours with his minions making silk screens, filming movie scenes, playing music, and experimenting with drugs. An indefatigable gossip, he picked up the phone for his "checking in" routine each morning, grilling one friend or another on the juicy details of their love affairs and party-hopping. But these were snippets of others' lives. Warhol himself was a self-described loner who lived with his mother and, outside of a 12-year relationship with interior designer Jed Johnson, had few deep and lasting connections. On Good Friday in April 1981, Warhol noted in his diary: "Went home lonely and despondent because nobody loves me and it's Easter, and I cried."

Objects became a substitution for intimacy. "When I got my first TV set, I stopped caring so much about having close relationships with other people," he reflected. He had an "affair," as he described it, with his TV and then "married" the tape recorder he bought in 1964. For years, Warhol carried the device, which he referred to as his "wife," everywhere and recorded thousands of hours of conversations. This rabid collection of information is its own brand of hoarding (4,000 of Warhol's audiotapes are now archived at the Pittsburgh museum). But the tapes also served to distance Warhol from the complexities and turmoil of human interaction. "The acquisition of my tape recorder really finished whatever emotional life I might have had, but I was glad to see it go," he reported. His problems were no longer problems once they were transferred to tape, he explained.

In Warhol's case, "it would make a lot of sense that he would feel connected to his stuff, because he could not connect to other people," says Zasio. "The more stuff he had, the better he would feel psychologically—because he's connecting to something, and it fills that void."

ON JUNE 3, 1968, VALERIE SOLANAS, a bit player in one of Warhol's movies, stepped off the elevator at the Factory, pulled out a .32-caliber handgun, and shot Warhol, piercing his abdomen. Solanas, who had written a manifesto calling for the elimination of the male sex, blamed Warhol for losing a screenplay she had written. "He had too much control over my life," she was quoted as saying. Still conscious, Warhol was rushed in critical condition to Columbus Hospital on East 19th Street, where he spent five hours in surgery and almost two months recovering. He later posed for photographer Richard Avedon, showing off an elaborate maze of scars covering his torso.

In the years following the shooting, Warhol dreaded the thought of returning to the hospital. Despite being told in the 1970s that he needed gallbladder surgery, he put off scheduling the operation for years. Instead, he took painkillers and Valium and turned to crystal healing to give him energy. Not that he didn't worry chronically about his health; among other concerns, Warhol fretted that x-rays would give him cancer and that he might contract HIV. In early February 1987, the artist felt a sharp pain after eating dinner at a Japanese restaurant. "So now I'm throwing out all the junk food," he reported afterward in his diaries. "I guess it was a gallbladder attack." After a scan showed that his gallbladder was indeed severely infected and in danger of rupturing, the artist finally agreed to have surgery. The operation went smoothly, but Warhol died of a heart attack the next morning, on February 22, 1987. He was 58.

After appraisers completed the gargantuan task of sorting through Warhol's belongings, Sotheby's published a six-volume catalog, *The Andy Warhol Collection*, chock-full of almost 10,000 items. Their auction, held over ten days in the spring of 1988, drew standing-room crowds, which included international dealers who had flown in to buy up the famous goods. *Newsweek* declared the event, which raised $25 million, "the biggest garage sale ever." It was an ironic epilogue for the enigmatic artist who routinely dodged questions about himself ("The interviewer should just tell me the words he wants me to say and I'll repeat them after him," he once said) and kept his home and his hoard under wraps.

In perhaps the most famous quote attributed to him, Warhol said: "In the future, everyone will be world-famous for 15 minutes." For Warhol and his stuff, 15 minutes turned out to be forever.

Princess Diana

I T WAS, AS WE WERE ALL TOLD, a fairy-tale wedding. It certainly *looked* like one, anyway. There was Lady Diana Spencer sitting next to her father, Earl Spencer, in a horse-drawn Cinderella glass coach with red and gold trimming. As the coach made its way through the throngs of admirers lining London's streets, the cameras zoomed in on Diana's face, shrouded by a veil that tumbled across her lap like snow on a hillside. When she stepped out of the carriage at the entrance to St. Paul's Cathedral, all eyes were on the fresh-faced 19-year-old and her lavish silk taffeta gown, which had been kept a closely guarded secret and engulfed her slim frame in puffy sleeves and a 25-foot train. "If you asked a little girl to draw a princess, I think she'd draw a dress just like that, with tiny bodice, tiny waist, and a great big skirt," a BBC commentator said to an estimated 750 million television viewers around the globe.

Groom Charles Philip Arthur George had entered the church first, dressed in his naval commander uniform with gold braid, his white-gloved hand clutching a ceremonial sword. Now he awaited his bride on the steps of the dais under the cathedral's regal dome. After some initial fussing to tame her train, Lady Diana began her journey down the red-carpeted aisle on the arm of her father, past more than 2,500 VIP guests who had gathered to witness the much awaited royal celebration that 29th day of July 1981. The TV announcers, fueling the fairy-tale depiction, made dreamy pronouncements throughout the festivities. Underneath Lady Diana's veil, one of them said, "There is an air of mystery about her as she quietly takes this longest and happiest walk she will ever take."

At the altar, the archbishop of Canterbury presided over the couple's vows in his magisterial headdress. "This is the stuff of which fairy tales are made," he said. "The prince and princess on their wedding day." There was the memorable gaffe on Lady Diana's part: "I, Diana Frances, take thee, Philip Charles Arthur George," she said, mixing up the order of the groom's first two names. No matter. The rings were exchanged, the couple blessed, and the wedding concluded with traditional solemnity and pomp. The prince and princess, now married, were greeted by a fanfare of trumpets as they bowed and curtsied to Queen Elizabeth, then walked arm in arm down the aisle to exit the church. "Those who are married live happily ever after the wedding day if they persevere in the real adventure, which is the royal task of creating each other and creating a more loving world," the archbishop had said in his address to Charles and Diana. "That is true of every man and woman undertaking marriage. It must be specially true of this marriage in which are placed so many hopes."

Those hopes, harbored by the royal family, the nation, the monarchy, and the world, would deflate soon after the wedding cake was cut. From the start, the union of Charles and Diana was taxed by the expectations and demands of royalty, a rushed engagement with little history between them, the rash hunger of the paparazzi, and the most proletarian of problems: another woman, Camilla Parker Bowles. Princess Diana struggled to connect with her husband, live up to the requirements of Buckingham Palace, and handle the reality that "there were three of us in this marriage," as she famously said years later. Despite her popularity, her dazzling looks, and the accolades she earned for her sympathetic outreach to sick and dying people around the globe, Diana spent much of her time in the palace unhappy and even, at times, suicidal.

A princess is idealized as beautiful, glittery, and perfect, not prone to mental health disorders. Isolated and feeling gravely misunderstood, Diana found solace by turning inward. As she later admitted in a widely watched television interview with Martin Bashir, broadcast by the BBC in 1995, Princess Diana succumbed to self-injurious behaviors by cutting her arms and legs—and to the eating disorder bulimia nervosa, which she battled for years. She felt neglected, Diana said, at times when she needed support the most. She filled her stomach with food as a way to comfort herself. "It's like having a pair of arms around you," she later recalled.

Did Diana's troubled marriage and the extraordinary expectations thrust upon her trigger her mental health battles? Or was she destined to turn on herself at some point in her life, even if she'd never set foot in Buckingham Palace? We will never know. What is clear, though, is that mental illness does not discriminate. "For all the status, the glamour, the applause," Diana's brother, Earl Spencer, said at her funeral in 1997, "Diana remained throughout a very insecure person at heart, almost childlike in her desire to do good for others so she could release herself from deep feelings of unworthiness of which her eating disorders were merely a symptom."

⌒

THE DIANA-CHARLES FAIRY TALE WAS ROOTED in an age-old fantasy modernized and glorified by Disney: A girl from ordinary circumstances meets her Prince Charming, falls madly in love, and is swept off to a castle, where she is anointed with a glittering tiara and lives happily ever after. "She rides to St. Paul's as a commoner," one of the television commentators remarked as Diana made her way to the church on her wedding day, "and she comes back as the third lady in the land."

Diana, though, was no run-of-the-mill British citizen. Born on July 1, 1961, at Park House in Norfolk, England, Diana Frances Spencer was the third daughter of Frances Roche and John Spencer, both of whom came from upper-crust British families. Frances's father, Maurice, held the title of fourth Baron Fermoy, an honor dating back to his family's Irish heritage; he was a close friend of King George VI. Frances's mother was the daughter of a baron herself, and served as Queen Elizabeth's lady-in-waiting for more than 30 years. The Spencer family, meanwhile, crossed bloodlines with King Charles II and King James II and were leaders of the Whig aristocracy, which ruled England in the 18th and 19th centuries. Diana's father served as personal assistant to both King George VI and Queen Elizabeth early in his life, and he would later succeed his father as the eighth Earl Spencer, an honorary title dating back to 1765. When Frances Roche and John Spencer were married at Westminster Abbey in 1954, the queen topped their guest list.

Although Diana was born into great social status and wealth, her childhood was marred from the start. To begin with, she was a girl. By the time Frances became pregnant with Diana, she and Johnnie, as her husband was called, were under ample pressure to produce a male heir to inherit the Spencer title. The couple already had two daughters, Sarah and Jane, and they had recently lost a son, John, who died within hours of his birth. Diana, born just 18 months later, was declared a "perfect physical specimen" by her father, but she always believed her arrival to be a disappointment. They were "crazy to have a son and heir and there comes a third daughter," she said in one of the famed tape-recorded interviews she provided to British journalist Andrew Morton, which were later printed in his best-selling book, *Diana: Her True Story*. "What a bore," she imagined them saying, "we're going to have to try again." The biographer Sally Bedell Smith speculated that Diana's psychological struggles may have stemmed from her very existence. "The nub of Diana's insecurity," Smith writes in *Diana in Search of Herself: Portrait of a Troubled Princess*, "was her nagging belief that had John survived, she would not have been born."

The Spencers did, finally, succeed in having a son, Charles, who was born three years after Diana. But by then their marriage had begun to unravel. Theories abound about what contributed to the early stages of its demise: the pressure of producing a male heir; baby John's death; the ferrying of Frances to fertility doctors after Diana's birth to see why she was unable to produce a healthy boy; Johnnie's temper; Frances's restlessness with life in rural Norfolk. As with any relationship, there was likely a tangle of reasons. Both said later that they had simply drifted apart.

Within a few years, however, the marriage suffered irreparable damage. In 1966, Frances attended a London dinner party with her husband, where she met Peter Shand Kydd, a former sheep rancher in Australia and the wealthy heir to his father's wallpaper business. One year later, after a group ski vacation in Europe and a series of secret rendezvous with Kydd in a rented apartment, Frances admitted to an affair and asked her husband for a separation. In 1969, Frances and Johnnie were officially divorced on grounds of adultery, and Johnnie was granted custody of the children, who would visit their mother on weekends. A rotation of nannies hired to care for Diana and Charles (their two older sisters were off in boarding school) did not sit well with the youngsters. When they didn't like them, "we used to stick pins in their chair and throw their clothes out of the window," Diana later admitted. "We always thought they were a threat because they tried to take Mother's position."

There is no evidence that a single negative experience leads to an eating disorder, but adversity early in life can increase a child's vulnerability. Diana's youth was not devoid of joyful experiences. Park House, which was leased to Diana's grandfather Maurice by King George V, was a rambling estate in the country where the Spencer children fed trout in the lake, swam in the pool, played in a tree house, and rode horses, according to biographer Morton. But none of that could make up for the turbulent aftermath of her parents' breakup and the loss of her mother's love and nurturing on a day-to-day basis.

Diana, who was six when her parents separated, spoke openly about the anguish she suffered as a young girl. In the reminiscences she shared with Morton, she recalled hearing her brother, Charles, "crying for my mother" at night. Too terrified of the dark to get out of her bed, however, she was unable to help. Her father, whom a friend later described as "crestfallen" about the end of his marriage, according to biographer Smith, was never able to talk openly about the divorce with his children. Diana's mother, meanwhile, was often weepy, especially when it was time for Diana and

Charles to leave after their weekend visits. "I remember Mummy crying an awful lot and every Saturday when we went up for weekends, every Saturday night, standard procedure, she would start crying," Diana recalled. "What's the matter, Mummy?" Diana would ask, and her mother would say, "Oh, I don't want you to leave tomorrow," a response Diana described as "devastating" for a young child. "It was a very unhappy childhood," she said.

Like so many children of divorce, Diana felt jostled between her parents. She later described "the trauma of going from one house to another" during the holidays, and she worried about showing an uneven allegiance to one or the other. Even a seemingly minor fashion decision could erupt into an agonizing display of loyalty. When she was chosen to be a bridesmaid for a cousin's wedding, Diana recalled, her parents gave her two different dresses to wear to the rehearsal: a green dress from her mother, a white dress from her father. "I can't remember to this day which one I got in," she said, "but I remember being totally traumatized by it because it would show favouritism." She comforted herself with a menagerie of stuffed animals, which took up much of her bed. "That was my family," she said.

People with eating disorders often have low self-esteem, a feeling of unworthiness and incompetence, and this was clearly true for Diana. Although she was a talented athlete—she excelled in swimming and diving and hoped to become a ballerina, until she grew too tall—she often felt out of place and defeated by her inability to excel intellectually. She also felt "horribly different" early on in school, she later said, for being the only child with divorced parents. Diana was sent off to a preparatory school, Riddlesworth, at the age of nine; three years later, she was accepted at West Heath, an elite boarding school that her older sisters had attended in Kent, England. Although the school was not known for its intellectual rigidity, nor were students expected to pursue college degrees at that time, Diana felt insecure about her capabilities. "At the age of 14, I just remember thinking that I wasn't very good at anything, that I was hopeless," she said.

Diana did manage to acclimate, make friends, and enjoy many of her nonacademic pursuits, including tennis, piano, and visits with patients at a nearby mental health facility. But she could never live up to her siblings' academic achievements. Her sisters did well at school, and her brother, to whom she felt closest, was a high achiever. "I longed to be as good as Charles in the schoolroom," she said. Instead, Diana failed her O-level exams, the standard tests required for graduation, not once but twice—a shortcoming that the media delighted in sharing. She made fun of herself, too, once telling a young boy that she was "thick as a plank," a comment that reporters served up with fanfare and which she later said she regretted.

Before her transformation from teenager to Princess of Wales, Diana enjoyed a few fleeting years of happiness as a single girl in the city. In 1978, the year she turned 17, Diana began living in London, initially working in temporary jobs as a nanny and waitress and then as a kindergarten assistant, where she thrived being around young children. For the first time, she enjoyed the freedom of independence. She liked socializing at restaurants and dinner parties, and she reveled in the fun of sharing an apartment with roommates. "I loved that—it was great," she recalled. "I laughed my head off there." She did not, according to her accounts, indulge in serious romantic relationships with boys. "I had never had a boyfriend. I'd always kept them away, thought they were all trouble—and I couldn't handle it emotionally," she said. Whether or not her hesitation stemmed from her parents' divorce is impossible to know, but the instability she felt after their breakup may have made her anxious about relationships in general. And there was another reason for holding off. In her interviews with Morton, Diana said she believed that she was destined to marry someone important. As a result, she said, "I knew somehow that I had to keep myself very tidy for whatever was coming my way."

And what was coming her way? A prince, a castle, and a life that would exacerbate her emotional volatility and foster debilitating mental illness. A fairy tale combusted.

⁓

DIANA MET PRINCE CHARLES IN 1977, when she was 16 years old and he was turning 29. Diana's older sister, Sarah, was dating the prince at the time—the two families had known each other through aristocratic circles—and Sarah had invited him for a pheasant shoot on the grounds of the family home in Althorp, where the Spencers had moved from Park House several years earlier. "I remember thinking what a very jolly and amusing and attractive 16-year-old she was," Prince Charles later said in a formal television interview after their engagement. Diana's first thought about Charles: "pretty amazing." He was, after all, the most eligible British bachelor—heir to the throne, next in line to be King of England. In her later reminiscences, however, Diana's assessment was far more blunt, tempered by her sister's relationship with Charles and her own lack of confidence. "God, what a sad man," she recalled. "My sister was all over him like a bad rash, and I thought, 'God, he must really hate that.' I kept out of the way. I remember being a fat, podgy, no makeup, unsmart lady."

Diana's insecurities about how she looked, a running theme in her reminiscences, is a classic symptom of eating disorders. As a teenager, she was remembered for her propensity to get "podgy" and her ability to gobble up food. Diana recalled that at boarding school her classmates egged her on to demolish a big meal in the morning, and she readily complied. "I ate and ate and ate," she recalled. "It was always a great joke—let's get Diana to have three kippers at breakfast and six pieces of bread, and I did all that." One friend remembered Diana eating a one-pound bag of candy during a bridge game; another described her as a "nice country girl" who loved "sweets, chocolate, and biscuits." She was also known to "dash across the street to 'tuck into a good-sized chicken portion' " when she was tense, according to Tina Brown in her biography, *The Diana Chronicles*. While taking a cooking class, Diana recalled, she was tempted by whatever was on the stove: "My fingers were always in the saucepans."

These incidents might have been nothing more than a teenage girl's dalliances with the delights of food. Plenty of college-age kids report episodes of binge eating, a condition whose features include eating when not hungry and consuming excessive amounts of food until uncomfortably full. In most cases, the behavior does not become habitual. In people with an underlying vulnerability, however, bingeing can be a symptom of "disordered eating," as it is known in the psychiatric world, which can progress to a full-blown eating disorder. The typical age of onset for bulimia is adolescence or early adulthood, which is precisely when Diana said her problems began—just after her engagement to Charles, when she was 19 years old.

After their first meeting, Charles and Diana had become reacquainted at several events, including the prince's 30th birthday party at Buckingham Palace in 1978 and at a country house gathering in Sussex in 1980. By this time, Charles's liaison with Diana's sister was long over (less than a year after they began dating, Sarah had declared their relationship "totally platonic"), and Diana had matured from a 16-year-old teenager to a young adult. It was in Sussex, at a summer barbecue, that Charles and Diana connected at a personal level. Sitting next to each other on a hay bale, Diana expressed sympathy over the death of Charles's great-uncle Lord Mountbatten, with whom Charles had been very close. Diana noted how sad Charles had looked as he walked up the aisle at his great-uncle's funeral. "My heart bled for you when I watched," she told him. "I thought, 'It's wrong, you're lonely—you should be with somebody to look after you.'" The prince later said he was moved by Diana's concern.

Charles was also under enormous pressure to marry. He was 31 years old, and the British tabloids had been having a field day publishing photos of the polo-playing bachelor and his legions of dates, embarrassing him and irritating the royal family. Diana came from aristocratic lineage; she seemed unthreatening, bubbly, funny, and presumably a "tidy" virgin bride (a requirement under the monarchy's moral code). After a six-month courtship, the two became engaged on February 6, 1981, much to the delight of the media and a British public eager for happy news during times of economic despair. Charles and Di engagement mugs, tea towels, thimbles, and figurines flooded the streets. The queen announced the engagement "with greatest pleasure" from Buckingham Palace; Prince Charles said he was "delighted and happy and I'm amazed that she's been brave enough to take me on." Diana said, she was absolutely "delighted and thrilled, blissfully happy." When asked if they were in love, Diana quickly answered, "Of course," to which the prince responded, "Whatever 'in love' means"—a statement that would be rehashed repeatedly in later years as an ominous sign of future troubles.

Within days of the much celebrated news, Diana found herself missing her friends and deserted by her fiancé, who left for a five-week overseas trip soon after they were engaged. She felt isolated in a suite in Buckingham Palace without support. "I couldn't believe how cold everyone was," she said later. Above all, she was rattled by the shadow of Camilla Parker Bowles, Charles's former girlfriend. Diana stated that her bulimia started the week after her engagement when "My husband put his hand on my waistline and said: 'Oh, a bit chubby here, aren't we?' That triggered off something in me—and the Camilla thing. I was desperate, desperate."

Patients with anorexia nervosa severely restrict the amount of food they eat; those with binge eating disorder, by contrast, eat large amounts of food in a short period of time and feel a loss of control over how much they're consuming. Bulimia is characterized by a two-step pattern of binge eating followed by purging through self-induced vomiting, laxatives, enemas, excessive exercise, or fasting to avoid weight gain. Patients with bulimia commonly report that bingeing is self-soothing and numbing, allowing them to block out negative emotions, says Cynthia Bulik, founding director of the University of North Carolina Center of Excellence for Eating Disorders. Purging, meanwhile, can serve as a release from the physical discomfort of binge eating and the guilt and shame that often comes with it. The first time she made herself sick, Diana later recalled, "I was so thrilled because I thought this was the release of tension."

The impact of Diana's eating disorder became starkly apparent over the course of just a few months. Between February 1981, when she got engaged, and her wedding in July, Diana's waist decreased from 29 inches to 23.5 inches—the size of an average eight-year-old girl. "I had shrunk to nothing," she recalled. The evening before she and Charles were to be married, Diana had a particularly bad bout of illness. "I ate everything I could possibly find . . . I was sick as a parrot that night," she said. "It was such an indication of what was going on." The next morning, she was "deathly calm," feeling as if she was "a lamb to the slaughter." The "tiny bodice" and "tiny waist," described by the TV commentator on Diana's wedding day, were not the attributes of a princess but evidence of a serious sickness.

Diana's bulimia did not improve during the couple's honeymoon. Already, "her royal highness"—the title she would be stripped of after the couple's divorce—was overwhelmed by the role she had taken on as wife and public figure. She feared the unknowns that lay ahead, and she was demoralized by Charles's ongoing relationship with Camilla Parker Bowles. Just after their engagement, she had stood by when Camilla called to speak to Charles. "It just broke my heart," she recalled in the Morton interviews. Two weeks before their wedding, she discovered a gold bracelet. Charles planned to give it to Camilla as a farewell gift and token of gratitude for her support, according to the prince's biographer Jonathan Dimbleby. But Diana assumed the worst. "I was devastated," she recalled. On their honeymoon, the two fought over a pair of cuff links, given to Charles by Camilla. While at sea on a Mediterranean cruise, Diana was sick repeatedly. "By then the bulimia was appalling, absolutely appalling. It was rife, four times a day on the yacht," she remembered. "Anything I could find I would gobble up and be sick two minutes later . . . I remember crying my eyes out on our honeymoon."

Diana's pregnancy with William, the couple's first son, intensified her physical and mental strain. She endured both morning sickness and ongoing episodes of bulimia; constantly excusing herself in her evening dress to rush off to the bathroom, she found herself perceived as "a problem" by the royal family. After William's birth, in June 1982, she also suffered from postpartum depression, and soon became so noticeably gaunt that the British tabloids speculated that she had anorexia. A British journalist writing in *People* magazine pronounced Diana "not anorexic" ("She simply follows the axiom that has been attributed to the Duchess of Windsor:

'No woman can be too rich or too thin,' " the writer stated), but the story was illustrated with a photo of Diana dressed in a gown that exposed her exceedingly slender arms. Her backbone was so pronounced it appeared to be standing out in relief. Many people suffer from eating disorders in secret; Diana's illness played out on an international stage, adding to the mounting pressure she was already feeling to look good.

It must be said that Diana's reminiscences, published in Morton's book and shared by Diana in a 1995 BBC television interview, are a one-sided account told in reflection after unhappy times. Diana's descriptions of her suffering have been viewed by some as self-serving and by others as evidence of the hardships she endured. Diana linked her illness to the start of her life in the palace—and to her husband, whom she blamed for being unsympathetic and unsupportive. Even the birth of their second son, Harry, she said, was met with negativity, because Charles wanted a girl. At that point, she said, "the whole thing went down the drain."

Prince Charles's perspective has been revealed most extensively in Dimbleby's authorized biography, published in 1994. Dimbleby's account depicts the prince as an exhausted husband dealing as best he could with a troubled and demanding wife who was desperate for attention. The prince was unprepared and "perplexed" by Diana's initial weight loss before their wedding and by her sudden mood shifts, which he observed repeatedly during their honeymoon and their marriage. She suffered from "overwhelming feelings of boredom, loneliness and emptiness, futility and abandonment," Dimbleby writes, all of which put a terrible strain on the marriage. She was at times despairing, self-absorbed, jealous, and self-pitying. When she was unhappy, Diana sat with her head on her knees, and though the prince attempted to "soothe her back to cheerfulness," it was often impossible to help her.

Diana conceded that she was psychologically ill equipped to cope with the expectations and responsibilities thrust upon her so quickly. "One minute I was nobody, the next minute I was Princess of Wales, mother, media toy, member of this family, you name it—and it was too much for one person at that time," she said. It might have been too much for anybody, especially a young woman barely out of her teens married to a man in his early 30s. When it came down to it, the two had few interests in common (she wasn't a big fan of hunting, polo, or books by the South African philosopher Laurens van der Post) and little foundation on which to build a deep and nurturing relationship. On top of all that, Diana had no emotional scaffolding to grasp on to, and was plagued by her ongoing lack of confidence. "I hated myself so much I didn't think I was good enough. I thought I wasn't good enough for Charles, I wasn't a good enough mother—I mean doubts as long as one's leg," she said.

These insecurities seemed to contribute to a desperate, but futile, search for reassurance. Diana bemoaned a lack of encouragement from the royal family and complained that she never received a pat on the back for succeeding at her duties. When she attracted more attention than her husband—her glamorous looks, her smile, her openness lit up the crowds wherever they went together—he became jealous, she said. An effective speech won her no accolades. "Anything good I ever did, nobody ever said a thing—never said 'well done,' or 'was it OK?' " she said in her 1995 television interview. "But if I tripped up—which invariably I did, because I was new at the game—a ton of bricks came down on me." She coped, Diana said, by diving into bulimia as her "escape mechanism" and her "release valve." On a royal trip to Majorca, she said, "I spent my whole time with my head down the loo."

Andy Warhol Was a Hoarder

FOOD FIXATIONS, ESPECIALLY ACCOUNTS of willful starvation, date back hundreds of years. In medieval Europe, female saints were known to refuse food as a way of preserving their holiness. Some vomited when they smelled meat, others covered their faces around food, and some even starved to death. The most well known was Catherine of Siena, who lived in the mid-1300s. She "ate only a handful of herbs each day and occasionally shoved twigs down her throat to bring up any other food that she was forced to eat," writes historian Joan Jacobs Brumberg in her book *Fasting Girls: The History of Anorexia Nervosa*.

Over the last few decades, eating disorders have been invariably associated with a culture that glorifies thin bodies. Models are airbrushed to trim their thighs and arms. Diet ads saturate the airwaves, promising weight loss fast or your money back. The fashion industry indulges in "vanity sizing," in which designers slash size numbers so that women who might otherwise wear a 12 can gleefully buy an 8. In 2014, the clothing manufacturer J.Crew took this trend to a whole new level when they introduced a new size, 000, for women with a 23-inch waist—just the size Diana might have worn on her wedding day. Nutritionists and mental health experts decried the move, fearing that young women might resort to extreme dieting to squeeze into a size that would be unhealthy for all but the most petite among them.

Cultural pressure alone, however, does not cause eating disorders. Millions of people are subject to skinny fashion obsessions and unobtainable standards of "beauty" every day—but only about one percent will become anorexic, and 2 percent will develop bulimia over a lifetime. As scientists explore the psychological and biological roots of eating disorders, they are beginning to unravel a slew of contributing factors. Like other mental illnesses, eating disorders are triggered by a complex interplay of individual psychological characteristics, genes (probably hundreds), and environment. Studies have found that eating disorders are at least 50 percent "heritable," which means that you are more likely to develop an eating disorder if it runs in your DNA. Diana, it turns out, was not the only one in her family to suffer: Her sister Sarah battled anorexia in her 20s, at the very time that she was dating Prince Charles.

The significant influence of genes negates the oft-held judgment that people with eating disorders are solely responsible for their illnesses—that they make a decision to starve themselves or overeat. The reality is far more complex. "No one would choose to have an eating disorder," says researcher Bulik, who is conducting a global study to identify the genes involved in anorexia. "We need to emphasize the genetic and biological piece more, in order to dismiss old myths that eating disorders are somehow a choice."

Although anorexia and bulimia manifest differently, they share some key characteristics. A significant number of people experience "diagnostic flux," says Bulik, meaning they cross over from one disorder to the other, suffering from anorexia at one point in time and binge eating and purging at another. Eating disorders are far more common in women than in men; data suggest that the hormonal shifts associated with puberty may play a role in female vulnerability, says Marsha Marcus, a professor of psychiatry and psychology at the University of Pittsburgh School of Medicine. Anorexia and bulimia are also strongly associated with other mental health disorders. As many as 50 to 70 percent of patients with bulimia will suffer from depression at some point in their illness, and many will struggle with different forms of anxiety as well.

In many cases, mood disorders come first and are a pathway to illness. Once anorexia or bulimia set in, underlying symptoms of depression and anxiety can be perpetuated and even exacerbated.

Diana openly discussed her ongoing feelings of frustration, inadequacy, sadness, and fear—all symptoms of both depression and anxiety. It wasn't just the turmoil going on within the walls of the palace that challenged her. After her many visits to sick and dying people around the world—work she savored—she was often unable to soothe herself, and resorted to eating. "I'd come home and it would be very difficult to know how to comfort myself having been comforting lots of other people, so it would be a regular pattern to jump into the fridge," she said.

People with bulimia—officially classified as a mental health disorder in 1980—are especially likely to struggle with impulsivity, often resorting to risky behaviors without considering the consequences. This is evident in their inability to stop eating during a binge, but can also manifest as alcohol abuse, drug abuse, shoplifting, promiscuity, and self-injury. Princess Diana resorted to hurting herself multiple times; in interviews, she admitted to throwing herself down the stairs while pregnant with William, running around with a lemon knife with serrated edges, and intentionally cutting her arms and legs.

Patients may resort to cutting as a form of self-punishment or as a physical release of internal misery. Diana depicted her behavior as an attempt to make her anguish known and to be rescued from it. Unlike people with anorexia, who tend to look sick and skeletal, individuals suffering from bulimia can appear perfectly healthy from the outside. Diana did—and yet she wanted those around her to know what was happening below the surface. "You have so much pain inside yourself that you try and hurt yourself on the outside because you want help," she said. "So yes, I did inflict upon myself. I didn't like myself. I was ashamed because I couldn't cope with the pressures." One night, feeling rebuffed by her husband, whom she accused of being dismissive and abandoning her when she was most desperate, "I picked up his penknife off his dressing table and scratched myself heavily down my chest and both thighs."

Bulimia and self-injury together are associated with borderline personality disorder, a diagnosis that has been floated for Diana, who shared numerous characteristics of the disorder with Marilyn Monroe. Sally Bedell Smith makes an argument for a borderline diagnosis in her biography, citing Diana's mood swings, her feelings of emptiness, her impulsivity, and her struggle to find her identity. Diana openly acknowledged her experiences specifically with bulimia and self-injury, and both can exist independently of other diagnoses. At the same time, it is true that they can be features of other conditions or deeply intertwined with them. All of this underscores how difficult it can be to parse out diagnoses in every area of mental health, where behaviors and symptoms constantly bump up against each other, overlap, and merge.

In the case of bulimia, researchers are examining how one of these symptoms—impulsivity—manifests in the brains of patients. In one intriguing study, Rachel Marsh and colleagues at Columbia University scanned the brains of 20 women with bulimia and 20 without while they completed a task on a computer screen that required them to choose the direction of an arrow. In one version of the exercise, the arrows were situated on the logical side of the screen (left-pointing arrows on the left; right-pointing arrows on the right). In another version, the arrows appeared on opposite sides (left-pointing arrows on the right; right-pointing arrows on the left), making the exercise more challenging and requiring patients to think before they acted. The women with bulimia responded to the difficult task faster and also made more mistakes, suggesting that they had greater impulsivity. The scientists discovered that the frontostriatal circuits in the brain—areas responsible for mediating self-regulation and impulse control—were underactive in the women with bulimia. These regions of the brain may actually be smaller in people with bulimia, too, perhaps contributing to patients' inability to control their behavior. Although these findings are preliminary, they raise the tantalizing possibility that the brains of people struggling with bulimia are structurally different—either because the individuals were born that way, or because the illness changed their brains over time.

Eating disorders can lead to a host of devastating health consequences, including gastrointestinal issues, bone loss, heart abnormalities, hormonal and electrolyte disturbances, and, in the case of bulimia, a ruptured esophagus from forced vomiting. Death, by organ failure or suicide, is the gravest threat of all. The main treatment for bulimia is cognitive-behavioral therapy, which teaches patients how to change their thought patterns from negative ("I'm hopeless; I'm only going to be happy if I'm thin") to positive ("I'm a good person; my weight has nothing to do with who I am"). The therapy also provides tools for recognizing triggers and stopping the bingeing and purging cycle. Patients often receive antidepressants to treat accompanying depression and anxiety, as well as nutritional counseling, which helps reestablish healthy eating patterns.

Diana's treatment varied widely. Early on in her marriage, she was distrustful of psychiatrists, and angered when she was prescribed tranquilizers to calm her down. "She knew in her heart that she did not need drugs; she needed rest, patience and understanding from those around her," Andrew Morton writes in his biography. To de-stress, she tried hypnotherapy, acupuncture, and aromatherapy. It wasn't until well into her illness, as late as 1988, that she finally received the help she needed to treat her bulimia. An old friend, worried about Diana's health, had threatened to go public unless Diana confided in a doctor. It was the wake-up call the princess needed, pushing her to seek treatment from Dr. Maurice Lipsedge, the same prominent London doctor who had successfully treated her sister Sarah for anorexia years earlier. Dr. Lipsedge provided weekly counseling sessions and helped build back her self-esteem, Diana said. By 1990, her bouts of bulimia occurred just once every three weeks, down from four times a day. Her progress was "a big 'hooray' on my part," she recalled. When she was interviewed in 1995, Diana said her bulimia had lasted "a long time," but it was over. "I'm free of it now."

By then, her anguish was well known. Morton's tell-all book, *Diana: Her True Story*, was published in June 1992 and was met with a flurry of curiosity, shock, and controversy. Initially described as a collection of accounts by Diana's friends (it was only later revealed that the princess herself was the source), the book sold millions of copies and turned Buckingham Palace upside down. Diana said she relayed information about her marriage, life stresses, bulimia, and suicide attempts because "I was so fed up with being seen as someone who was a basket-case." As secrets were aired, royal watchers, historians, and the ever-present media speculated about the collapse of the marriage—and perhaps even the monarchy. The queen called 1992 her "annus horribilis."

In November of that year, Charles and Diana visited South Korea on their last official foreign tour together. A photograph captured them looking in opposite directions during a commemorative service to honor British soldiers killed during the Korean War—a symbolic representation of the distance between them. One month later, the British prime minister delivered the news: Prince Charles and Princess Diana were "amicably" separating. Diana heard the public report of their separation while she was at an event away from the palace and found it "just very, very sad," she said. "The fairy tale had come to an end." Within a few years, Diana and Charles would both admit to infidelity in separate television interviews beamed around the world; a final end to their marriage, once unthinkable, was now inevitable. In August 1996, one month after their 15th wedding anniversary, Charles and Diana were officially divorced.

⌒

DIANA'S DECISION TO TALK OPENLY about her bulimia allowed the world to peer through the gilded windows of Kensington Palace—and to appreciate the ubiquity of mental illness. "She was human, she was admitting to her frailties," says Arianne Chernock, an expert in modern British history at Boston University. Just as First Lady Betty Ford's openness about her breast cancer diagnosis increased screenings, Diana's candidness seemed to spur people with bulimia to seek help. A study of eating disorder trends in the United Kingdom, published in the *British Journal of Psychiatry* in 2005, found that new cases of bulimia jumped dramatically in the 1990s—even as anorexia cases remained stable—and then dropped again after Diana's death in 1997. The authors speculated that intense press coverage of Diana's experience might have contributed to the increase by raising public awareness about symptoms. "Identification with a public figure's struggle with bulimia might have temporarily decreased the shame associated with the illness," the study authors wrote, "and encouraged women to seek help for the first time."

Diana left a deep and lasting imprint on history. Although there was concern early on that her illness and the demise of her marriage to Charles would stain the monarchy, Diana's outspokenness about what went wrong may have helped guide the next generation to make wise choices from the start, Chernock theorizes. Prince William and Catherine Middleton did not marry until eight years after they started dating, giving them far more time to mature in their relationship. (Kate was 29 at their wedding in 2011; William turned 29 two months later.) Their long courtship also allowed them to become adept at managing the media. Indeed, as the queen celebrated her diamond jubilee in 2012, a record 69 percent of Britons said Britain would be worse off without a royal family—a level of support that Chernock believes must be credited in part to Diana. "The royal family is in such a stronger position now," she says. "You can't separate the success of today from Diana's contributions."

During her battle with bulimia and in the years following her recovery and her separation from Charles, Diana found solace in getting out of the palace and visiting with everyday people who had struggles of their own. Relaxed and friendly, she readily engaged in small talk and consoled others, even touching and hugging sick patients with AIDS at a time when most people stayed away out of fear. She could identify with those in crisis, she said, because she suffered herself. In her final interview before her tragic death in a car crash in Paris on August 31, 1997, she told the French newspaper *Le Monde*, "I am much closer to people at the bottom than to people at the top."

After Diana died, the editor of the *British Medical Journal* published a two-paragraph remembrance highlighting Diana's work with sick children, her fight against land mines, the many health concerns she campaigned for—AIDS, leprosy, drug addiction—and her honesty about bulimia. The editor, Richard Smith, acknowledged that it was unusual for the publication to mourn a public figure outside of the medical profession. This time, he felt it was the right thing to do. "She seemed to speak so well to and for the vulnerable because of the difficulties in her own life," Smith wrote. "Her life was full of glamour and opportunity, but her gift was to create a very special life—and an inspiration to many—from adversity." That recognition, a handful of words tucked away in an academic publication, could not compare to the pageantry of Diana's funeral at Westminster Abbey on September 6, 1997. In the end, though, it might have been the kind of tribute she would have appreciated most of all.

Abraham Lincoln

THERE ARE FEW FACES BETTER KNOWN than that of our 16th president. One hundred and fifty years after his death, Abraham Lincoln's famous visage remains ever-present, filling our children's piggy banks with pennies and gazing out from our five-dollar bills. He stands amid Civil War ruins at Rogers State University in Claremore, Oklahoma, and leans against a tree stump, a young boy cast in bronze, in Hodgenville, Kentucky. In the U.S. Capitol, he wears a bow tie and cloak. At the Lincoln Memorial, he looms 19 feet above us. At Mount Rushmore, in the Black Hills of South Dakota, he erupts dramatically out of granite.

With his prominent nose, bushy eyebrows, and stormy hair (he once tousled it deliberately after a photographer combed it flat),

Lincoln had a distinct and memorable look. After a political rival called him two-faced at a debate, the story famously goes, Lincoln quipped, "If I had another face, do you think I'd wear this one?" But what was going on beneath? What lurked in the depths of his mind and his spirit? It is a question Lincoln's contemporaries and historians have debated for more than a century. The president was often funny and sometimes even jovial. He was inarguably ambitious and enormously accomplished, writing some of the most memorable and elegant prose ever crafted by a politician, leading a country through the greatest internal strife it had known, and ending slavery.

What is less appreciated is that Lincoln was also deeply distressed and likely suffered from clinical depression. Throughout his life, he had endured numerous tragedies: watching his beloved mother die when he was nine years old; losing two young sons to infectious disease; and presiding over the nation's bloody Civil War, with its staggering death toll of more than 620,000 men—a far greater loss than the United States experienced in any other war, before or since.

But even beyond the external traumas life threw at him, Lincoln seems to have been wired for melancholy, both genetically and somewhere deep in his soul. He talked about his "nervous temperament" and, stunningly, his desire, at times, to end his life.

Historical records are filled with Lincoln's contemporaries describing a notable gloom that seeped out from within. William Herndon, Lincoln's law partner, observed that "his melancholy dripped from him as he walked." Another man, after seeing Lincoln for the first time, made note of his long, pale face and his enormous hands and feet. But what struck him most of all, he said, was the look in Lincoln's eyes: "Lincoln had the saddest eyes of any human being that I have ever seen."

Abraham Lincoln

LINCOLN'S EARLY LIFE WAS A MIX of happy sojourns in the woods and family tragedy spurred by the difficult times in which he lived. Born in a log cabin with a dirt floor near Hodgenville, Kentucky, on February 12, 1809, he was an enthusiastic learner, an avid reader, and a decent farmhand, wielding his ax proficiently and harvesting corn for the family. The deaths in his family were sudden—but, sadly, not uncommon. There were, of course, no antibiotics to treat infectious diseases in the 19th century; women died regularly during childbirth; and many children never lived to see their fifth birthdays, succumbing to poor nutrition and disease spread through contaminated milk and water.

Lincoln's father, Thomas, a carpenter and farmer, would live to be 73 years old. But in 1818, when Lincoln was nine, his mother, Nancy, contracted "milk sickness," an illness believed to be caused by a poisonous plant toxin that tainted milk. For days, she writhed with fever and chills before summoning her children to her deathbed to tell them to be "good and kind" to their father. She was just 34 years old. Nine years later, Lincoln's older sister, Sarah, died after delivering a stillborn baby. A neighbor saw Lincoln bury his face in his hands as the "tears slowly trickled from between his bony fingers and his gaunt frame shook with sobs."

It is almost certain that these traumas had a deep impact on Lincoln—possibly even influencing his later onset of depression—but they did not eviscerate his spirit. He emerged from his teenage years a likable, friendly, and good-natured young fellow. His contemporaries took special delight in his extraordinary gift for storytelling. Ida Tarbell, the muckraking journalist, interviewed a man named John Roll who remembered meeting Lincoln when he was 22 years old in the old town of Sangamon, Illinois, near the Sangamon River. Tall and lanky by then (he would reach the then unusual height of six feet four inches), Lincoln had come to build a flatboat—and, as it turned out, to entertain other laborers during rest time.

In Tarbell's account, published in *McClure's Magazine* in 1895, she describes workers assembling on a long log to whittle, talk, and listen to Lincoln's "irresistibly droll" yarns. His stories were so funny, Roll said, that "the boys on the log would whoop and roll off" repeatedly, leaving the wood polished up like a mirror. "It took four weeks to build the raft, and in that period Lincoln succeeded in captivating the entire village by his storytelling," wrote Tarbell. Long after Lincoln left Sangamon—the county he would later represent in the Illinois state legislature—"Abe's log" was preserved in his memory until it finally rotted away.

Depression often strikes in early adulthood. In the summer of 1835, when Lincoln was 26 years old, grave concerns about his emotional health began to surface, according to journalist and biographer Joshua Wolf Shenk, who presents a meticulous case for Lincoln's depression in his book *Lincoln's Melancholy: How Depression Challenged a President and Fueled His Greatness*. By then, Lincoln had been elected to his first term in the Illinois state legislature, and was studying law as a means to a full-fledged profession and income. He threw himself into his legal studies so exhaustively that he lost weight and alienated himself from his friends. Lincoln's closest companions "were afraid that he would craze himself—make himself derange[d]," one acquaintance in the area recalled.

It was the death of a young woman named Ann Rutledge, whom Lincoln had met at her father's tavern and boardinghouse, that seemed to send him into the depths of true desperation. To this day, the extent of their relationship is unclear. Were they friends? In love? Engaged? Nobody knows for sure, but Lincoln clearly had strong feelings for her. When Rutledge became ill with "bilious fever," most likely typhoid, and died at the age of 22 in

August 1835, Lincoln suffered what Shenk describes as his first major depressive episode. He isolated himself, took to wandering off into the woods alone with his gun, and was so overwrought that even a bout of cold, rainy weather sent him into a tailspin as he worried about Rutledge's grave getting wet. "The effect upon Mr. Lincoln's mind was terrible," one of Rutledge's brothers wrote at the time. "He became plunged in despair." Most worrisome, Lincoln began talking about suicide, prompting his anxious friends to rally around him to be sure he stayed safe. "That was the time the community said he was crazy," one neighbor recalled.

One could legitimately speculate that Lincoln was simply grieving, a state that can look like depression. But even after seeming to recover from Rutledge's death, he continued to wrestle with misery. Robert L. Wilson, a fellow politician who served with Lincoln in the Illinois state legislature in 1836 and 1837, later recalled Lincoln telling him that "although he appeared to enjoy life rapturously, still he was the victim of terrible melancholy." When he was alone, Lincoln told Wilson, "he was so overcome with mental depression, that he never dare[d] carry a knife in his pocket."

In the winter of 1840, five years after Rutledge's death, Lincoln would succumb to another bout of deep anguish, even though nobody had died. In the days and months leading up to this second breakdown, he was saddled with professional and personal turmoil. It was a particularly trying time in his career. By the late 1830s, Lincoln had become a respected and popular politician, winning reelection to the state legislature three times. But after supporting a program that derailed the state's economy, he almost lost his bid for a fourth term in 1840, shaking his confidence. At the same time, Lincoln had campaigned exhaustively and unsuccessfully for a political ally, adding to an already heavy workload, with multiple cases to be argued before the state supreme court.

Lincoln's love life was in disarray as well. He had broken his engagement to Mary Todd, the woman he would later marry, because of significant misgivings that the two were ill suited. But severing the relationship affected him at a profoundly moral level, and he was troubled by his decision. Lincoln's old friend and closest confidant, Joshua Speed, said he was so worried about his friend that he "had to remove razors from his room—take away all Knives and other such dangerous things."

Over the first few weeks of January, in 1841, Lincoln failed to attend legislative sessions and missed numerous political votes. "By this time, Lincoln's illness was the talk of the town," Shenk writes, and a local newspaper "poked fun at his indisposition." Lincoln was confined to bed, though he did manage to seek treatment for "hypochondriasis," a term used then to describe a milder form of melancholia that had the potential to get worse. Around this time, Lincoln wrote to one of his law partners, saying, "I am now the most miserable man living." In a note to his friend Speed, Lincoln mused, "if what I feel were equally distributed to the whole human family, there would not be one cheerful face on the earth."

Tragedy and misfortune do not define a person's mental health, nor do they determine a diagnosis. You can grieve without needing Prozac. You can be miserable without being depressed. Even today, it can be difficult to accurately assess depression—and of course, we cannot sit Lincoln down for a 21st-century screening test to determine how often he experienced poor appetite, low energy, and hopelessness. Never? Sometimes? Always?

Nevertheless, the symptoms Lincoln suffered during his two initial breakdowns are consistent with today's definition of depression. Key features include a depressed mood for at least two weeks, a loss of interest or pleasure in everyday activities, weight loss or gain, fatigue, feelings of guilt, indecisiveness or worthlessness, and thoughts of death or suicide. One bout of the blues does not add up to clinical depression, says Dr. Nassir Ghaemi, director of the Mood Disorders Program at Tufts Medical Center in Boston. But "if it recurs repeatedly, it's a disease."

Depression, like autism, addiction, and other mental health conditions, exists on a continuum. The severity of the disorder can be gleaned in part from the number of episodes a person suffers and the intensity of each. Most people fall into the mild to moderate range, says Ghaemi, and he believes that Lincoln's depression would qualify as moderate. Lincoln's first two episodes, when he was suicidal, were clearly debilitating. Later bouts appear to have been less overwhelming and shorter in duration; nonetheless, they had a profound impact on his outlook and behavior.

Accounts of Lincoln's penetrating melancholy are abundant and consistent throughout his life. Herndon, Lincoln's law partner and early biographer, kept extraordinarily detailed notes and described a man often overtaken by misery. In the course of a single day, Lincoln's mood could shift from cheerful and good-natured to "a sad terribly gloomy state," Herndon reported. During these periods, Lincoln often rested his chin on the palm of his left hand and gazed off into the distance. Some mornings, Herndon would find Lincoln lying on the couch looking up toward the sky or sitting in a chair with his feet on the windowsill, so completely withdrawn that he failed to acknowledge his colleague's arrival. Herndon's "good morning" was received with nothing more than a grunt. "I at once busied myself with pen and paper, or ran through the leaves of some books," Herndon wrote, "but the evidence of his melancholy and distress was so plain, and his silence so significant, that I would grow restless myself." At these moments, Herndon would find an excuse to leave the office for a while, he recalled, "and before I reached the bottom of the stairs I could hear the key turn in the lock, and Lincoln was alone in his gloom."

Much has been made of Lincoln's marriage and the impact it had on his mental health. He eventually did marry Mary Todd, on November 4, 1842, and the couple settled into a cottage in Springfield. Over the next 11 years, they produced four sons: Robert, Edward (Eddie), William (Willie), and Thomas (Tad). The two were not completely mismatched—they shared a love of poetry and humor, and Mary Lincoln supported her husband's political ambitions. Correspondence between them, written in the late 1840s while Lincoln was living in Washington serving a term in Congress and Mary and the children were at home in Illinois, shows affection and a desire to be together. But emotional volatility plagued their union much of the time. Mary had a hot temper (the president's White House secretaries nicknamed her the "Hellcat"), suffered from intense mood swings, and was famous for her outlandish behavior, especially her exorbitant buying sprees. (She once acquired 84 pairs of kid gloves in less than a month.) The mental health of Mary Lincoln, whose eldest son helped commit her to a mental institution ten years after her husband's death, has been itself the subject of great debate. Did she suffer from schizophrenia? Bipolar disorder? Or was she the victim of unspeakable grief after witnessing her husband's assassination and the deaths of three of her four sons?

Lincoln had his own challenges as a husband. Unable to handle his wife's tempestuous fits, he often chose to ignore her and leave the house rather than sort out what was wrong. And his tendency to veer into dark places and disappear into a solitary funk greatly upset his wife. She found his moodiness "profound and troubling," according to biographer Daniel Mark Epstein. "He could be—especially in company, at the dinner table where he had an audience—full of high spirits, his eyes twinkling, taking as much pleasure in telling his jokes and yarns as in hearing her laughter," Epstein observes in *The Lincolns: Portrait of a Marriage*. "But he could sink into fits of melancholy that could drain the light from a room. More often, it was his silence that worried or exasperated her. He sat staring into space as if he were dead or time traveling— who knew?—in a trance or catatonic state. She could not reach him though he sat within a few feet of her."

The tragic deaths of their children affected the Lincolns individually and, most certainly, as a couple. In 1850, three-year-old Eddie died, probably from tuberculosis. Willie, who was most like his father in personality, succumbed to typhoid fever at the age of 11 in 1862, during Lincoln's second year in the White House. The "idolized" child in the family, as Mary described him, Willie brought particular joy to the president with his intelligence and bright spirit. Mary took to her bed, inconsolable. Willie's death brought the president to his knees. Elizabeth Keckley, a former slave who worked as Mary's assistant and dressmaker, said Lincoln's body "convulsed with emotion" when he saw his son's body. "I never saw a man so bowed down with grief." (The couple's youngest son, Tad, died at 18—probably from pneumonia—six years after Lincoln was assassinated.)

As president, Lincoln's personal traumas were compounded by the horrific battles and losses of the Civil War. After the governor of Pennsylvania described a battlefield slaughter to Lincoln, the president "groaned, wrung his hands and showed great agony of spirit," Lincoln scholar Michael Burlingame writes in his biography *The Inner World of Abraham Lincoln*. A War Department telegraph operator who had taken messages from Lincoln during that battle reported, "When it was learned that over 13,000 men were killed, the calamity seemed to crush Lincoln. He looked pale, wan and haggard. He did not get over it for a long time—and, all that winter of 1863, he was downcast and depressed. He felt that the loss was his fault." Following a Union defeat in the summer of 1864, Lincoln said, "I was as nearly as inconsolable as I could be and live."

Over the course of his life, Lincoln sought relief through various treatments. He was believed to have taken "blue mass," a mix of mercury and several other ingredients. Today, the pills would be considered highly toxic, but they were commonly prescribed in Lincoln's day to treat a variety of health problems, including toothaches, constipation, and melancholia. The president found his most comforting refuge in words, stories, and humor. He loved poetry and Shakespeare's dramas, which he would read late into the night. His gift for oration and the passion with which he delivered his tales delighted his audience and lifted his spirits. "If the day was long and he was oppressed, the feeling was soon relieved by the narration of a story," said a judge who knew him. "His countenance and all his features seemed to take part in the performance. As he neared the pith or point of the joke or story every vestige of seriousness disappeared from his face. His little gray eyes sparkled; a smile seemed to gather up, curtain like, the corners of his mouth; his frame quivered with suppressed excitement; and when the point—or 'nub' of the story, as he called it—came, no one's laugh was heartier than his."

Laughter was Lincoln's trusted antidote, healing his anguish with light. His humor was "as natural as his melancholy," Tarbell wrote. "It bubbled up through things like one of those warm springs that one sometimes comes upon in a rugged, rocky field." Medical studies now confirm that humor can reduce stress, cut pain, and lighten one's mood. Lincoln seemed to know this instinctively. He told Herndon, his law partner, that "if it were not for these stories—jokes—jests I should die: they give vent—are the vents of my moods & gloom."

⌣

DESPITE THE ENORMITY OF DEPRESSION—the illness affects at least one in ten Americans and is the leading cause of disability worldwide—researchers still don't fully understand what causes it. It is clear that mood disorders run deep through family lineage. Twin studies show that if one twin suffers from depression, the other is at a significantly higher risk of developing the illness as well; if your parent or sibling has depression, your chance of developing it is two to three times greater than average. "Risk" is the critical word here. You inherit certain physical characteristics from your mother and father—for example, curly hair, brown eyes, attached or unattached earlobes. The development of mental health conditions depends on a far more complex mix of genes, life circumstances, and environment. While the DNA passed on by your parents may increase your susceptibility to depression, there's no certainty that you'll actually develop it.

The mental health history of Lincoln's family is impossible to fully determine, but his parents were said to be somewhat doleful. Descriptions of Lincoln's mother very often referred to her as "sad," a word Lincoln used about her himself. His father, known to be a storyteller and jokester, also had a "somber streak," Shenk notes, and would routinely suffer glum periods, spending hours alone in the fields or the woods. A neighbor said he "often got the blues." Lincoln's paternal uncle, Mordecai, had mood swings, and his three sons all exhibited depressive characteristics. The daughter of another cousin was committed to the Illinois State Hospital for the Insane. "His melancholy was stamped on him while in the period of gestation," a fellow lawyer said about Lincoln. "It was part of his nature."

"Stamped on him" is an elegant and prescient description of what we know now about the power of DNA and its role in transmitting predispositions for illness from one generation to the next. It also speaks to the discoveries being made today about the impact of environmental factors in a mother's womb on her growing fetus. Research suggests that a baby developing in an anxious or depressed woman may be exposed to stress levels and hormones that alter its brain development, possibly making it more susceptible to later mental health conditions. After birth, other influences may push a person who is genetically vulnerable to depression over the edge. A turbulent early childhood involving sexual or physical abuse and emotional neglect appears to be especially consequential. So does the death of a parent when a child is young.

Lincoln's mother, Nancy, died quickly, within a week of contracting milk sickness. Decades later, Lincoln told a friend how lonely he felt after she died. Burlingame, the Lincoln scholar, describes Nancy's death as "the most important cause of Lincoln's depression." Lincoln also had an unhappy and distant relationship with his father, who was known to be cold and harsh. Thomas Lincoln, who never learned to read, had little tolerance for his son's keen enthusiasm for books. A cousin reported that he would sometimes "slash" or whip Abe when he caught him reading instead of doing chores or working in the fields. After his wife's death, Thomas left ten-year-old Abe and his older sister Sarah, then 12, alone for months while he traveled to Kentucky to bring back a new wife. Upon their return, Lincoln's stepmother, Sarah Bush Johnston, found the children "wild—ragged and dirty." Years later, Lincoln declined to visit his father on his deathbed and did not attend his funeral in 1851. His father's lack of support and empathy "may have hurt as much as the sudden shock of his mother's death," Burlingame writes.

These early traumas likely laid the groundwork for depression in Lincoln—and it is possible that the emotionally wrenching events he suffered as an adult activated memories of prior loss. What's intriguing is the way in which depression changes the brain over time. Studies have found that the hippocampus, the brain's hub for learning and memory, shrinks in patients who have had multiple episodes of depression, making them more susceptible to a lifelong struggle. Among people who experience one bout of depression, more than half will suffer another in their lifetime. Every episode increases the risk of an additional occurrence— by the time you have three, your chances of having a fourth are 90 percent. Scientists call this the "kindling" effect; the brain is waiting and ready to catch fire.

First episodes are often triggered by a specific life experience, as appears to have been the case with Lincoln. But later ones may strike simply because a person's brain has been primed to feel down. Plenty of people get divorced, lose their jobs, and care for sick parents, but most do not become clinically depressed as a result; instead, they become lonely, angry, frustrated, and sad. They move on. People with major depression, on the other hand, are wired for despondency. Even when life seems to be chugging along fairly well, minor mishaps will touch off symptoms, which sometimes seem to strike like sudden turbulence on a smooth airplane flight.

At its worst, depression is a debilitating, suffocating, and isolating experience. The novelist William Styron described the anguish he suffered as a "veritable howling tempest in the brain." In his memoir *Darkness Visible: A Memoir of Madness*, Styron said he felt that his brain was under siege and that his thoughts "were being engulfed by a toxic and unnameable tide that obliterated any enjoyable response to the living world." Depression saps every ounce of joy, every morsel of optimism. "It is hopelessness even more than pain that crushes the soul," Styron wrote. "So the decision-making of daily life involves not, as in normal affairs, shifting from one annoying situation to another less annoying—or from discomfort to relative comfort, or from boredom to activity—but moving from pain to pain. One does not abandon, even briefly, one's bed of nails, but is attached to it wherever one goes."

Over the centuries, the concept of depression has undergone enormous transformation. Early on, it was thought that people who experienced sadness and negative thinking were possessed by some external demonic force that required excision. Hippocrates and the ancient Greeks believed that mental problems were the result of an imbalance of four bodily fluids, or humors: blood, yellow bile, black bile, and phlegm. Melancholia was linked to an excess of black bile, which had to be purged from the body through bloodletting. Early Christianity viewed depression as punishment for temptation by the devil and the depravity of sin. Great thinkers of the Renaissance, on the other hand, saw an upside to depression as a possible catalyst for genius, fueling literary and artistic creation. By the time Lincoln was born in the early 19th century, a distinction had been made between melancholia, which was defined as all-encompassing despair, and the melancholic temperament, which made people gloomy but also imbued them with sensitivity and keen analytic reasoning.

Although Lincoln clearly experienced depressive episodes, not everybody agrees that he had full-blown clinical depression. One of the greatest sticking points revolves around the balance between Lincoln's moods and his accomplishments. How does a man suffering from depression preside over a country in strife, write the Gettysburg Address, quash slavery, and still seem to retain a rich sense of humor and even gaiety at times? Depression and productivity do seem an unlikely match. Skeptics assert that Lincoln could not have succeeded as president and been chronically depressed at the same time. "It is impossible to reconcile this debilitating disease with the Lincoln who labored tirelessly and effectively during his demanding presidency," Harold Holzer, a leading Lincoln scholar, has written. Without treatment, Holzer argues, many depressed people who lived during Lincoln's era went mad or committed suicide: "Clinically depressed people often can't get out of bed, let alone command an army."

All true. But the key feature of the condition is that depressive episodes come and go, like an ocean wave that crashes with intensity then recedes into foamy calm. It does not plague people every minute of every day. "There's not a single piece of commentary in one thousand years of description of depression that says it does," says Tufts's Ghaemi. "It's much briefer, it's episodic." Depression does not have to be incapacitating to qualify as depression, he says, and mild to moderate cases "are fully consistent with being a productive person." Even somebody who burrows under the covers and closes the shades during a severe depressive episode can be fully functional weeks later, performing surgery, giving TED talks, writing literary and musical masterpieces. Goethe, Schumann, Luther, and Tolstoy all battled depression, and yet their accomplishments are legendary. "Some people suffer mild depression and are totally disabled by it; others suffer severe depression and make something of their lives anyway," writes Andrew Solomon, who experienced a breakdown during the final stages of writing *The Noonday Demon: An Atlas of Depression*, his National Book Award winner. He managed to finish it anyway.

Anthony Storr, a 20th-century British psychiatrist, described recurrent depression as a "spur," propelling people to achieve great acts even in their more dire states because they are desperate to escape the morass of despondency. Lincoln's experience is consistent with this observation. In a letter, he advised his friend Joshua Speed to "avoid being idle" and "engage in some business" at times of despair. Winston Churchill was also a dark man driven to action. Churchill referred to his own depression as his "black dog." It was a constant companion, so overwhelming at times that he worried he might succumb to it completely. "I don't like standing near the edge of a platform when an express train is passing through. I like to stand right back and if possible to get a pillar between me and the train," he told his physician. "I don't like to stand by the side of a ship and look down into the water. A second's action would end everything. A few drops of desperation."

Storr believed it was Churchill's own experience with depression that afforded him the conviction to stand firm during the Battle of Britain in the summer of 1940, as the Germans incessantly attacked England's Royal Air Force. Any rational leader might have concluded that the end was near, Storr wrote in his book *Churchill's Black Dog*. "Only a man who knew what it was to discern a gleam of hope in a hopeless situation, whose courage was beyond reason, and whose aggressive spirit burned at its fiercest when he was hemmed in and surrounded by enemies, could have given emotional reality to the words of defiance which rallied and sustained us in the menacing summer of 1940," he continued. "Churchill was such a man: and it was because, all his life, he had conducted a battle with his own despair that he could convey to others that despair can be overcome."

Could being depressed, as Storr seems to argue, make you a better leader? Nassir Ghaemi thinks so. In his book *A First-Rate Madness*, Ghaemi argues that depression and other mood disorders infused such leaders as Churchill, Gandhi, and Martin Luther

King, Jr., with positive attributes, including empathy, creativity, resilience, and realism—all of which inspired exceptional leadership during times of crisis. Indeed, the notion of "depressive realism," dating back to the late 1970s, has launched a whole branch of science, which argues that depressed people view the world more realistically than their more upbeat peers who may be irrationally optimistic. In Lincoln's case, Ghaemi says, the president's level-headedness allowed him to advocate for ending slavery without alienating opponents, and to face the Civil War with full appreciation of its worst outcomes in a way that was more perceptive than many of his advisers. "Lincoln was not overly optimistic," Ghaemi says, "and did not assume a win would be easy."

The notion that depression comes with positive attributes is controversial, given the severity of the illness and the risk of suicide. But a host of depression memoirs confirm that many people who suffer terribly also say they value the magnitude of emotional depth they experience. In the last paragraph of his book, Solomon concludes that his depression has allowed him to discover his soul—"a part of myself I could never have imagined," until "hell came to pay me a surprise visit. It's a precious discovery."

Evidence shows that depression and even joy can coexist without negating each other. Indeed, it is not at all unusual for two dueling qualities to create a kind of psychological oxymoron in the same person. Great performers suffer from stage fright. Doctors have horrible hypochondria. Pulitzer Prize winners battle self-doubt. There may be no better example of this than Robin Williams, the funny man who made the world laugh while suffering a cancerous misery inside. "Lincoln is only one example of a person whose enormous vitality, effectiveness, humor, empathy—all these characteristics we associate with the best of human existence—run hand in hand with terrific pain," says Shenk.

Andy Warhol Was a Hoarder

The notion that depression is inextricably linked to positive qualities raises intriguing questions about whether combating the condition with medication will dampen the soul while lessening the despair. Psychotherapy, along with lifestyle changes like regular exercise, can alleviate depression. But antidepressants are rampant in today's fix-me-fast society, with one in ten Americans now taking them. Some are mildly affected but want to take the edge off daily stress and turmoil. In severe cases, the medications can help significantly, especially in combination with psychotherapy. Many clinicians argue that the real problem is undertreating people who need help but never seek it.

It's impossible to know if Lincoln would have benefited from Prozac, or if treating him might have quelled the deep qualities—sensitivity, empathy, insight—that contributed to his greatness. It's also hard not to wonder. A cartoon published in the *New Yorker* several years ago depicted this question with the kind of humor Lincoln might have enjoyed. Titled "If they had had Prozac in the nineteenth century," it featured images of Karl Marx, Friedrich Nietzsche, and Edgar Allan Poe. Marx declares, "Sure, capitalism can work out its kinks!" Nietzsche says, "Me too, Mom. I really liked what the priest said about all the little people." Poe, looking at a black raven, chirps, "Hello, birdie!"

✎

APRIL 14, 1865, GOOD FRIDAY, was a cool, gray day in Washington, D.C. That afternoon, the president and Mary Lincoln went for a ride in their open carriage past the Capitol to the Navy Yard, where Lincoln wanted to see the warships. Navy officers and sailors saluted, and although the war was not yet over, the president told his wife that he considered it ended. "During the drive he was so gay," Mary Lincoln later recalled, "that I said to him, laughingly, 'Dear husband, you almost startle me by your great cheerfulness.'"

A few hours later, the Lincolns set out for Ford's Theatre to see the British farce *Our American Cousin*. Clara Harris, a New York senator's daughter whom Mary Lincoln had invited to accompany them, remembered the president's happy mood, too. "He laughed & joked & he was evidently bent on having a jolly evening." Upon their arrival, the audience applauded and the orchestra played "Hail to the Chief." At around ten p.m., an actor took to the stage with a laugh line. And then—the unthinkable. John Wilkes Booth opened the state box door, took aim, and shot President Abraham Lincoln in the head. "Awful Event," the *New York Times* headline read the next day. "President Lincoln Shot by an Assassin."

One week later, a train carrying Lincoln's coffin departed from Washington, D.C., bound for Springfield, Illinois, the president's final resting place. Young Willie's coffin was also on board, exhumed from its plot in the capital so that he could be buried next to his father. Over the course of its 1,600-mile journey, "The Lincoln Special" traveled through seven states and almost 200 cities, where grieving citizens wept and paid tribute to their righteous president.

"Not often in the story of mankind does a man arrive on earth who is both steel and velvet, who is as hard as rock and soft as drifting fog, who holds in his heart and mind the paradox of terrible storm and peace unspeakable and perfect," the writer and Lincoln biographer Carl Sandburg said on the 150th anniversary of Lincoln's birth in 1959. The young farm boy from Kentucky, the storyteller, the jokester, the strategist, the deeply loving father, the president of exceptional character. Steel and velvet, melancholy and mirth.

Christine Jorgensen

I T WAS MAY 1, 1950, a rainy day in New York harbor, when 23-year-old George William Jorgensen, Jr., embarked on the ocean liner *Stockholm* with a few hundred dollars and a one-way ticket to Copenhagen. Before the ship set sail on its ten-day journey, George celebrated with family and friends in his stateroom. They serenaded the young adventurer with a round of the old Norse drinking toast, "Skoal!" They talked about the relatives he should visit—George's grandparents had emigrated from Denmark to the United States in the late 1800s—the places he might see, the photographs he would take.

Andy Warhol Was a Hoarder

George played along enthusiastically, indulging requests to deliver personal greetings and reassuring everyone that he'd be a good European tourist. "Yes, I'll write often," he told them. "No, I didn't make a return reservation, because I don't know how long my money will last. Yes, I'll remember. No, I won't forget."

On the surface, the atmosphere was lighthearted and anticipatory, but George was harboring a secret more momentous than anyone could have imagined. He was not heading to Denmark to discover his family roots, eat pickled herring, and visit the famed Rosenborg Castle with its Dutch Renaissance architecture. George Jorgensen, a former Army private first class, was going to Europe to transform himself into a woman.

George set sail that May day sporting short hair and a man's overcoat. Almost three years later, after undergoing hormonal treatment and sex-reassignment surgery, Jorgensen returned to the United States with a new look, a new gender, and a new name: Christine. George was quiet and unassuming; Christine became an instant media sensation. The *New York Daily News* had been tipped off about Jorgensen's transition and published a scoop in advance of her arrival, which set off a flurry of additional stories and a hunger for more. When she arrived at New York International Airport wearing lipstick and a fur coat with matching cap, Jorgensen was greeted by a throng of shoving journalists—a scene that was "more like a battlefield," she would later recall, "with flash-bulbs popping, photographers shouting instructions, and reporters lobbing questions from the firing line." Sweating under the blinding lights, Jorgensen was rattled by the onslaught of queries: "Where did you get the fur coat?" "Do you expect to marry?" "How about a cheesecake shot, Christine?"

At a time of prudish sexual mores and widespread sexism in 1950s America, Jorgensen's stunning metamorphosis was front-page news, with headlines reading "Ex-GI Becomes Blonde Beauty" and "Bronx 'Boy' Is Now a Girl." Journalists tracked her every move, including how she tossed off a Bloody Mary and teetered in her heels. Some even accused her of being a fake. Americans were shocked, intrigued, and confounded all at once. How could a man become a woman? And why would he want to? Over the next months and years, Jorgensen's case would shake up rigid assumptions about the immutable nature of gender, precipitate a debate over its definition, and become one of the most transformative developments in the history of sex in America and the world.

Today, Jorgensen would be diagnosed with gender dysphoria, a condition characterized by a "marked incongruence" between the gender somebody is deemed at birth and the gender he or she identifies with and yearns to be. Untangling the coiled intersection of body and mind is an important goal of scientists in every field of medicine and psychology; nowhere is that crossroads more pronounced than in the fraught world of sex and gender. Was George Jorgensen's body wired to be a woman from birth, as predetermined as long eyelashes or a throaty laugh? Or was he suffering from a mental health problem that needed to be fixed? Christine Jorgensen had plenty to say about both.

⌒

IN MANY WAYS, GEORGE JORGENSEN had a happy and unencumbered childhood. His parents, George Sr. and Florence, met at a social hall in the Danish-American community in New York City, and were married in 1922. George Sr. served in the Coast Guard and then formed a construction company with his father and brother. Florence stayed at home to take care of Dolly, the couple's first child, and George, who was born on May 30, 1926. His birth, which landed on Memorial Day that year, was marked by street parades and the clattering of brass bands.

The tight-knit Jorgensen family lived in the Throggs Neck section of the Bronx, where George grew up surrounded by dozens of aunts, uncles, and cousins. Every year, Grandma Jorgensen, the matriarch of the family, who had silvery hair and a passion for African violets, hosted a joyous Scandinavian Christmas. Young George always looked forward to marching hand in hand around the tree, singing carols, eating turkey drumsticks, and searching for the sole almond hiding in the rice pudding.

Although he was secure in the warm embrace of his family, George Jorgensen never felt at home with himself. A delicate and shy child, he could not reconcile his own feelings and interests with the social rules for boys. "A little boy wore trousers and had his hair cut short," Jorgensen later wrote in a best-selling autobiography. "He had to learn to use his fists aggressively, participate in athletics and, most important of all, little boys didn't cry." But young George had no stomach for fighting and ran away instead. At times, he *did* feel like crying, and he liked "girly" toys, too. When he was five, he prayed for a beautiful doll with golden locks for Christmas. He got a red railway train instead.

The difference between George and his male peers was palpable from an early age. He preferred his sister's games of jump rope and hopscotch to rough-and-tumble sports. He liked Dolly's dresses and her long blonde hair. He felt more at home at her camp than at Camp Sharparoon, where a piercing whistle moved campers from one activity to the next, and George was compelled to join in with the other boys—a requirement he dreaded, because he knew he would stand out and be teased. At Dolly's camp, by contrast, "the girls didn't call me 'sissy' or ask me if I was really a girl dressed in boys clothes, like the boys at Camp Sharparoon did," Jorgensen recalled.

One of George's most painful childhood experiences occurred at school, where he kept a treasured piece of needlepoint in his desk drawer. He liked to reach in and touch it or, if no one was looking, take it out and admire it secretly. "I didn't display it openly, probably sensing the derision that might result," Jorgensen recounted. After recess one day, George, then about eight, was heartbroken to discover that his needlepoint had disappeared from his desk. His teacher called the class to order, then summoned George and his mother, whom she had sent for without telling George, to her desk. As his classmates watched, the teacher held George's precious fabric up just out of his reach and asked if it belonged to him. "Yes," George said, his face hot, his eyes stinging with tears. "Mrs. Jorgensen," the teacher said, "do you think that this is anything for a red-blooded boy to have in his desk as a keepsake? The next thing we know, George will be bringing his knitting to school!" His classmates snickered.

Jorgensen remembered feeling "upset and puzzled" by the line drawn between "masculine" and "feminine." What was wrong with enjoying needlepoint? Why *couldn't* a boy have long hair and wear dresses like his sister? One day, George posed his problem to his mother. "Mom, why didn't God make us alike?" he asked. "My mother gently explained that the world needed both men and women, and that there was no way of knowing before a baby was born whether it would be a boy or a girl. 'You see, Brud,' she said," referring to George by his nickname, " 'it's one of God's surprises.' 'Well,' I replied, 'I don't like the kind of surprise God made me!' "

⌒

It is not unusual for young children to be captivated by toys, colors, or clothing that are stereotypically considered masculine or feminine. Plenty of boys enjoy playing with dolls and kitchen sets, and many girls prefer short haircuts and action figures. And why shouldn't they? Most parents accept this when their children are toddlers; many even encourage it and are relieved when their daughters stick up their noses at pink dresses and princesses or their sons shun trucks and superheroes. The majority of these children will move through childhood with the usual bumps and bruises, and then tussle with adulthood as we all do. Along the way, they'll face their share of personal and spiritual quandaries—Do I want to be a parent? Am I really cut out to be a lawyer? Do I believe in God?—but they will never question the most fundamental essence of their identity: Am I male or female?

This was a predicament that haunted George Jorgensen. It wasn't just that he preferred the company of girls or liked the way they looked; it was that he felt he was meant to *be* a girl. It was a conviction that was deeply rooted, knotted up in the core of his being, and it did not diminish as he aged. By puberty, it was clear that George did not fit the masculine mold, either physically or emotionally. He was, as Jorgensen later reflected, "extremely effeminate" and continued to identify with classically "feminine" interests. Although he had plenty of friends who were girls, he was not interested in dating any of them. As a teenager, "I recall that I was even more keenly aware that I was different from other boys," Jorgensen wrote. "Once I overheard one of them say, 'George is such a strange guy.' At other times, they didn't have to say it; I could read the thought in their attitudes."

By all accounts, George Sr. and Florence Jorgensen were supportive during their son's growing-up years (Florence remembered both her kids as "model children," according to Jorgensen's account). But Jorgensen knew it could not have been easy having a child who didn't fit in and acknowledged this as one of the reasons Army service was appealing. Although George failed his first two draft physicals for being underweight, he passed in the fall of 1945, the year he graduated from high school. With the fighting phase of the war over, he was assigned to process paperwork for thousands of U.S. soldiers returning home. The Army gave George the opportunity to serve his country, and his parents the chance to boast about their son.

George viewed his military experience, which lasted 14 months, positively overall. But, once again, it reinforced the gulf between him and his peers. His fellow servicemen wanted to get married and have families; George didn't know what he wanted, other than to retreat further into his "protective shell." One day after he was discharged, he aired his confusion with two female friends. "Maybe you'll think I'm insane," he said, "but did either of you ever look at me and think that I might not be a man at all, but a . . . woman?" His friends were bewildered. "But George, you're made like a man, aren't you?" one of them asked. Yes, his body was male, although underdeveloped, he told them. But as far back as he could remember, he had felt "the emotions of a girl." Although attracted to men, George admitted, "I notice them, not as a man, but as a woman might. I just don't know what category to put myself in." According to later reports by Jorgensen's doctors, George felt that "nature had made a mistake," and he attempted, early on, to right it himself as best he could. He secretly dressed in women's clothing to relieve "the psychic pressure" he felt in men's clothing; he shaved his pubic hair in a way that made him appear more feminine and gave him "inner satisfaction," according to his physicians. On the outside, however, he had no choice but to do his best to appear and act like a man.

It is not surprising that George Jorgensen initially wondered if he was gay. At the time he was coming of age, in the 1930s and early

1940s, there was little popular understanding, let alone knowledge, of what we know now as transgender: "persons whose gender identity, gender expression or behavior does not conform to that typically associated with the sex to which they were assigned at birth," as the American Psychological Association defines it. A small cadre of medical experts in the United States had consulted with patients who felt out of sync with their sex; as George would soon learn, several European doctors had initiated experimental treatments with hormone therapy and surgery. But there was not yet an appreciation of transgender as a distinct condition. The term "transvestism," a catchall grouping at the time, included people like Jorgensen but was also used more broadly to describe cross-dressers—those who got pleasure out of dressing up in male or female clothing not their own. The notion that people could or would undergo a physical transformation from man to woman, or woman to man, would have been as unthinkable as landing on the moon.

Being gay, on the other hand, was a known quantity, lambasted from pulpits everywhere for centuries. At the time Jorgensen was growing up, the mainstream medical establishment was busy trying to convert patients from gay to straight by subjecting them to hysterectomies, castration, shock therapy, and even lobotomy. At the same time, sexual behavior had become a niche research subject with scientists attempting to understand what Americans were doing and who they were doing it with. This was the era of Alfred Kinsey, the famed sociologist who interviewed thousands of Americans about their sexual practices and preferences. His first major report, published in 1948, concluded that homosexuality among men was far more common than believed. No matter what the clergy said or the doctors did or the sex researchers published, it wasn't going away. Indeed, gay culture was beginning to flourish in nightclubs and cabarets, from San Francisco to Chicago to the streets of lower Manhattan, not far from where Jorgensen grew up.

Despite his own sensibilities, George perceived being gay as religiously objectionable and immoral. But he could not deny his attraction to boys. When he was a teenager, George got to know a boy named Tom during annual summer visits to a farm in upstate New York. The two became fast friends, corresponding back and forth during the off-season. One day, Tom wrote a letter raving about a girl he'd met; George's immediate reaction was jealousy. In the library, he had read about "sexual deviation" in a book about human relationships. Now that he realized he had developed feelings for his friend, George could not help but ask himself: "Was this the same thing I felt? Was I one of those people?"

In his quest for answers, George scoured books and news articles about human behavior and sexuality. The more he read, the more he began to suspect that his condition might be related to hormones. One day in October 1948, he came across a newspaper story about a well-known endocrinologist in New Haven who was conducting hormone experiments on animals—"the masculinization of a female chicken and the return to vigor of a castrated rooster," as Jorgensen later recalled. After mustering up the courage to make an appointment, George told the doctor about his history of feeling girlish and living a life as what he dubbed a "sexual mix-up." He had tried to live and feel like a man, he said, but he had failed. Could it be that he was suffering from some kind of chemical imbalance?

George assumed the doctor would do a medical exam, but he wrote down the name of a psychiatrist instead. At the time, the prevailing view was that emotional and behavioral turmoil, however it manifested, was triggered by early childhood experiences— often parental neglect or abuse. Psychoanalysis was seen as the answer, and there was little else the doctor could offer. Dejected, George went to see the psychiatrist, who prescribed a series of sessions to guide him away from his "feminine inclinations." He declined.

If there was a moment that changed everything, it was when George stumbled across a book called *The Male Hormone*, published in 1945. Author Paul de Kruif, a well-known science writer of the day, described a series of experiments in which testosterone injections had cured sexual impotence, increased muscular endurance, and even eradicated depression. The overarching message was that sex hormones played a decisive role in differentiating men and women. Jorgensen later described the book as "salvation in my hands"; it reaffirmed George's belief that he was suffering from a hormonal, not a psychological, malfunction and provided hope that changing the chemical balance in his body might solve his problem. Soon after, George learned about the treatments being performed in Europe, where research into gender and sexuality was far more progressive, and made his pivotal decision to set sail for Copenhagen. "To my friends and family, then, I was merely planning a tourist jaunt," Jorgensen wrote, "but the Old World was to be the point of no return as George Jorgensen."

In Denmark, George met with Dr. Christian Hamburger, an eminent endocrinologist who agreed to take him on as an experimental patient, free of charge. As Hamburger would later recount in an article published in the *Journal of the American Medical Association*, George presented as a man fully determined to become a woman: He "felt a pronounced distaste toward his own genitals and toward his male physical features" and "felt it impossible to continue life as a man." Hamburger was exceedingly interested in the role of hormones, so he had a scientific interest in George's case. He was also compelled by the level of anguish George revealed, which included thoughts of suicide. Hamburger concluded that it was his responsibility, along with his colleagues, to help. "We clearly pointed out to him that any irrevocable step should be taken only after careful consideration. But on the other hand we did not think we were in the position—despite all difficulties—to decline an attempt at giving the patient medical aid."

Initially, Hamburger suggested that George consider taking testosterone to make him feel more masculine, but George refused. Instead, he began a steady course of estrogen, which added weight to his hips, stimulated breast development, and softened his face. He had electrolysis to prevent beard growth and grew out the hair on his head. Throughout his care, George underwent a series of psychiatric evaluations to be sure that he was not harboring any deep-seated emotional turmoil that might be clouding his judgment. Ultimately, his doctors were confident that their patient was mentally stable and that his conviction to be a woman was deep and sincere; they approved his request for castration. In two operations, George's genitalia were removed—the last vestiges of his male body.

In May 1952, just before Jorgensen's 26th birthday, the newly transformed American donned a beret and went to visit the U.S. ambassador to Denmark to request a change of name on his, now *her*, passport. The application was approved. George Jorgensen was now Christine, a name chosen in honor of Dr. Christian Hamburger. Before returning to the United States, Jorgensen sent the most important letter of her life, explaining to her family what she had really been doing in Europe and revealing her gender transformation for the first time. "I have changed, changed very much, as my photos will show, but I want you to know that I am an extremely happy person and that the real me, not the physical me, has not changed," she wrote. "Nature made a mistake, which I have corrected, and I am now your daughter."

⌒

ARE SOME PEOPLE DESTINED to be transgender? Is it steeped into their hormones? Imprinted on their brains? Or are they suffering, instead, from a deeply rooted psychological problem or mental illness that can be diagnosed and treated? Jorgensen's transformation from George to Christine catapulted these questions into the American consciousness. As news accounts focused on the minute details of Jorgensen's appearance—her gestures, her figure, her pearl earrings, her "smooth, low-pitched voice"—people who had never before questioned the essence of gender began to wonder: What constitutes man and woman? Does anatomy define identity? What is gender, anyway?

Jorgensen had become public fodder on December 1, 1952, when the *New York Daily News* published a story about her case while she was still recovering from surgery in Copenhagen. Who tipped the reporter off is unclear—it might have been a lab tech in the Danish hospital or a family friend—but it touched off a media frenzy. Reporters lit up the hospital switchboard, clamoring for interviews; publishers offered thousands of dollars for exclusives. Even today, transgender revelations elicit huge interest; in 2015, 17 million viewers tuned in to the ABC News show *20/20* to watch the gold-medal Olympian then known as Bruce Jenner reveal that "my brain is much more female than it is male." Several weeks later, Jenner announced her new identity as Caitlyn on the cover of *Vanity Fair* and then thanked her supporters on Twitter after amassing one million followers in a record speed of just four hours.

In Jorgensen's day, the news was far more shocking, because so few people had ever heard of anyone changing his or her sex. Wary of the media's salacious curiosity, Jorgensen accepted a $20,000 contract with *American Weekly* magazine to tell the story on her terms in a five-part series. The first installment was timed to appear just as Jorgensen deplaned in New York on February 12, 1953.

After her case became public, Jorgensen and her doctors received hundreds of letters from other people desperately seeking care for their own gender identity issues. The outpouring prompted Jorgensen's physicians to take a stand. In the account they published in the *Journal of the American Medical Association* in May 1953, Hamburger and his colleagues laid out their patient's medical history and made a plea for supporting, rather than thwarting, patients. Psychotherapy, they argued, had failed to "fix" people; it was time for doctors to better understand the condition, so that they could help their patients achieve productive lives. "It has been an exceedingly depressing experience to learn the degree to which these persons feel they have been let down by the medical profession and by their fellow men," Hamburger and his colleagues wrote. "In loneliness and misery they have had to fight their own tragic fate."

Jorgensen's personal transformation was a lightning rod, triggering heated debates that would ultimately require the medical and mental health community to define—and then refine—what gender and biological sex really are. There were loud voices arguing against surgery. In response to Hamburger's report, one doctor wrote a letter to the editor, no doubt emblematic of others' views, which suggested that Jorgensen showed "masochistic traits" and may have been schizophrenic. The patient's "sexual perversion" might have benefited from a more intensive psychotherapy, the doctor advised. "With all due respect for the surgical skill of

Dr. Hamburger and his associates," he wrote, "one can hardly maintain that the psychiatric indication for this procedure was sound."

By the 1960s, however, specialists had begun to disentangle the concept of gender identity from sexual orientation and cross-dressing. The endocrinologist Harry Benjamin, who became an advocate for transgender patients and treated many in the United States, pronounced in his 1966 book, *The Transsexual Phenomenon*, that attempting a cure through psychotherapy was a "useless undertaking." Around the same time, the first American medical center to officially offer sex-reassignment surgery opened its doors at the renowned Johns Hopkins Hospital in Baltimore, staffed by psychiatrists, surgeons, and other specialists. Even then, most mainstream medical practitioners did not support hormone treatment and surgery for patients they deemed to be psychotic or delusional. But at a 1966 press conference announcing their first two successful male-to-female surgeries, the chairman of Hopkins' Gender Identity Clinic said: "If the mind cannot be changed to fit the body, then perhaps we should consider changing the body to fit the mind."

The terminology around transgender has changed over time and even now it continues to evolve. In Jorgensen's day, individuals who sought out surgery were known as "transsexuals," a term used to distinguish them from "transvestites"—men who dressed in women's clothing but didn't necessarily want to change their bodies. Today, "transgender" is used broadly to describe people whose gender identity is different from their biological sex. The language around a clinical diagnosis has changed, too, from "gender identity disorder" to its most recent incarnation: "gender dysphoria." A diagnosis of gender dysphoria requires that a person's feeling of incongruence with his or her assigned gender at birth persists for at least six months. Above all, the diagnosis requires that the condition causes "clinically significant distress or impairment," according to the *DSM*.

This latest name change has powerful significance. Prior use of the word "disorder" struck many as judgmental, as if something were mentally wrong with people who felt their bodies were out of sync with their gender. Some transgender advocates argued to eliminate the condition from the *DSM* altogether, echoing the heated history of homosexuality, which was designated a "sociopathic personality disturbance" in 1952 and then removed in 1973, when the medical establishment resolved that it was not a pathological disorder. But sexual orientation and gender dysphoria differ in at least one critical way: You don't need hormones or surgery to be gay. You do if you want to transform your body. In the end, the diagnosis was kept so that patients could seek clinical care, but the name was altered to reduce stigma. "Dysphoria," which the dictionary defines as a state of feeling unwell or unhappy, was chosen to refer specifically to the distress that might be associated with the condition. But as the American Psychiatric Association puts it, "gender nonconformity is not in itself a mental disorder."

Nobody knows why certain people feel so strongly at odds with their sex. There are a number of theories about physical causes. One leading contender: If a fetus is exposed to atypical levels of sex hormones in the womb—perhaps because the mother was prescribed hormones for medical reasons—a boy's brain may end up "feminized" and a female's brain may be "masculinized." Genetic glitches may also contribute. In one study, scientists found that transgender adults who had transitioned from male to female were more likely to have a variation in a gene that mediates testosterone levels, which may result in less testosterone reaching the developing brain. Identical twins are more likely to both be transgender than are fraternal twins or siblings, suggesting a possible hereditary link. And intriguing studies have found that a region of the brain's hypothalamus, which is involved in regulating sex hormones, is smaller in male-to-female transgender patients than it is in typical males, and much closer in size to typical females. The research so far, however, is preliminary at best. "At the moment, there are a lot of theories with very little evidence," says Dr. Peggy Cohen-Kettenis, a pioneering transgender researcher and a psychologist at VU University Medical Center in Amsterdam.

What is evident, however, is that many transgender people feel a strong conviction from a very early age. Jan Morris, the widely read Anglo-Welsh travel writer who transitioned from James to Jan when she was 46 years old in 1972, remembers identifying as a girl while sitting underneath a piano in her family home at the age of three or four. "It became fashionable later to talk of my condition as 'gender confusion,' " Morris writes in her memoir. "But I think it is a philistine misnomer. I have had no doubt about my gender since that moment of self-realization." Her feelings were so powerful, she continued, that if she had to do it again, "I would search the earth for surgeons, I would bribe barbers or abortionists, I would take a knife and do it myself, without fear, without qualms, without a second thought."

Chaz Bono, who began transitioning from female to male in 2008, has been outspoken about how firmly he believes his condition is physical, not psychological. Bono, who was born a girl named Chastity in 1969 to the famed pop music duo Sonny and Cher, told a reporter that he has felt male for as long as he can remember. Bono said he fared pretty well in early childhood, when it is almost always easier for girls to be tomboys than for boys to like dresses and dolls. But when he hit puberty, he felt as if his body was betraying him. "There's a gender in your brain and a gender in your body. For 99 percent of people, those things are in alignment," Bono said. "For transgender people, they're mismatched. That's all it is. It's not complicated, it's not a neurosis. It's a mix-up. It's a birth defect, like a cleft palate."

There is no one-size-fits-all treatment today for gender dysphoria. Some transgender individuals choose not to physically change their bodies. Others seek hormone therapy to alter their sexual characteristics: testosterone to promote hair growth and a deeper voice for a female-to-male transition; estrogen to increase breast development and decrease muscle for a male-to-female transition. Still others will opt for surgery, which might include breast augmentation and vaginal construction for male-to-female patients (Jorgensen underwent plastic surgery to create a vaginal canal and female genitalia after she returned to the United States) and breast reduction and creation of a penis or "phalloplasty" for female-to-male patients. Reliable data is hard to come by, but male to female sex-reassignment surgery is more common than female to male— in part because women who receive hormone treatments may feel satisfied with their transition without undergoing the pain and expense of a difficult operation.

The most controversial debate by far is how young is too young to begin treatment. Jorgensen was in her 20s when she set out to seek a medical solution in Europe. Bono and Morris transitioned in their 40s; so did Renée Richards, the professional tennis player who was born Richard Raskind in 1934. Caitlyn Jenner went public at 65. But today, children as young as five are pleading with their parents to let them become boys or girls. Many of them are being taken to pediatricians, psychologists, and, in some cases, hormone specialists to assess their strong desires.

Clinicians, not to mention the public, vary dramatically on what they believe is appropriate, and clinics differ on the treatments they provide. On one extreme are medical experts who believe that early treatment is appropriate and even crucial in some cases; it may save children from their own internal angst, compounded by teasing or bullying from peers, and even death. In a survey of transgender and "gender nonconforming" Americans, a staggering 41 percent reported that they had attempted suicide, nearly nine times the national average. Doctors who believe in early treatment do not want to see that statistic edge any higher. They encourage parents to allow their children to dress in the gender they identify with and to change their names. Medical treatment starts with puberty blockers, drugs that are prescribed shortly after the onset of puberty to stop the development of male and female sex characteristics. The effects of the drugs are reversible, so children who stop using them resume ordinary development. Those who continue, however, would be spared the torment of maturing physically in the "wrong" sex. As older teenagers, they could then take hormones of the opposite sex (testosterone or estrogen), allowing them to embrace the gender they identify with more seamlessly.

Experts at the other end of the spectrum believe it is unethical to diagnose and treat children who are still too young to understand what gender means. Their goal is to attempt to uncover the potential psychological roots of the child's atypical gender identity. Parents are counseled to help their children feel comfortable with the gender that matches their biological sex rather than endorsing a shift. They should not call their daughter "David," for example, and let her socialize only with boys, nor should they allow their son to wear a ponytail and play solely with dolls. Above all, these experts caution, children should not be treated with hormones, which can have immediate and long-lasting side effects, including an increased risk of heart disease and cancer. The most outspoken critics—one of them a Johns Hopkins psychiatrist who helped halt sex-reassignment surgery there in the 1970s—argue that giving hormones to children borders on child abuse.

Both sides stand strong in their convictions. An accurate diagnosis is the most critical step. Clinicians must have in-depth discussions with the child and his or her parents, assessing the intensity of behaviors and feelings (some children will talk specifically about wanting to cut off their penis or grow breasts) and how long they have endured. Studies so far show that only about 15 to 20 percent of children who report strong transgender feelings early in life turn out to be what clinicians call "persisters," meaning they have a gender dysphoria that will not disappear after puberty has started. The rest, "desisters," will lose those feelings over time; many of them, it turns out, will grow up to be gay or bisexual. Differentiating between the two is not always easy, which is why researcher Cohen-Kettenis has staked out something of a middle ground. Although children should be allowed to pick their friends and their toys early on, she says, parents should not accommodate requests for name changes—nor should they call their daughter "he" when she's really a "she."

Research shows that when gender dysphoria does persist through adolescence, it is likely to endure into adulthood. Cohen-Kettenis, who has been studying and treating transgender children, adolescents, and adults since the 1980s, believes cautious intervention during the early stages of puberty is appropriate for the right candidates. She and her colleagues pioneered the use of puberty blockers in children starting at around the age of 12. This is a time, she says, when early desires crystallize one way or the other, and when persisters usually make their wishes very clear. "Their impression is that they didn't have a choice," she says. "This was the only way to go." In these cases, Cohen-Kettenis and her colleagues believe that the benefits of careful treatment outweigh the risks.

In a study of 70 adolescents who received puberty blockers, she and her team reported that symptoms of depression and emotional and behavioral problems decreased during treatment, and day-to-day functioning improved, making their quality of life comparable to non-transgender youth.

How will they do over the long term? It's too early to say. Alice Dreger, a bioethicist who has written extensively about sex and gender, advises parents to be wise consumers and strong advocates for their children. "The shape love should take is often unclear," she writes, "but love is what we as parents must shape out of our fears, anxieties, desires, and hopes."

THE TRANSGENDER WORLD HAS EVOLVED dramatically since Jorgensen shipped off to Copenhagen in 1950. Jorgensen broke new ground at a time when transgender had no face; she fought a very personal battle when even the experts had little information to offer. Today, with a mobile device in hand, trans men and women can instantaneously connect for meet-ups, figure out where to get hormone therapy, and map out gender-neutral bathrooms on college campuses. Guidance on options that would have been inconceivable just a few decades ago—such as how to freeze eggs or sperm before transitioning from female to male or male to female—is now readily available with just a click of the mouse.

As *Time* magazine recently declared on its cover, the transgender movement is "America's next civil rights frontier." Advocates are pushing to remove long-standing requirements stipulating that the only way to change gender on official documents, like driver's licenses, is to show proof of a surgical sex change. Many states require this, but the American Medical Association adopted a new policy in 2014, saying that provision should be eliminated for birth certificates since surgery is not considered essential to living as male or female. The State Department has removed a similar requirement for passports. Transgender proponents are pushing for changes in the health care arena, too, where they are lobbying insurance companies to pay for treatment. In one landmark case, a 74-year-old Army veteran who was born male, but had been living as a woman for many years, filed suit against Medicare for denying coverage for sex-reassignment surgery. An appeals board ruled in her favor. "Ever since the first story about Christine Jorgensen came out, I knew that's what I needed to do," she told the *New York Times.* "[I] want congruence between what I am as a human and my body."

Transgender men and women are gaining footholds in art, culture, and entertainment. Chaz Bono was the first transgender contestant to appear on *Dancing with the Stars,* where he tangoed to "The Phantom of the Opera." "I came on this show because I wanted to show America a different kind of man," Bono said in front of a standing ovation after he was voted off the season. "If there was somebody like me on TV when I was growing up, my whole life would have been different." Laverne Cox was bullied as a child in Mobile, Alabama; she grew up to be a star on the hit drama *Orange Is the New Black* and the first transgender person featured on *Time*'s cover. In a breakthrough ad campaign, Barneys New York produced a spring catalog featuring trans men and women wearing clothes from high-end designers like Balenciaga and Manolo Blahnik, shot by celebrated fashion photographer Bruce Weber. "What is between my legs is not thoroughly who I am," says one model. "If gender is black and white, I'm gray."

Transgender individuals often lead fairly conventional lives. Jennifer Finney Boylan, who transitioned from male to female in her 40s during her tenure as a popular English professor at Colby

College in Maine, has written extensively about her life as both James and Jennifer. With a sharp wit, she has shared her ups and downs, including the impact of her transformation on her wife—to whom she has remained married for more than 25 years—and her two sons. In a column she wrote for the *New York Times*, Boylan described her fear that her transition, which took place when her boys were under the age of ten, would affect them negatively. So when her son Zach summoned his parents to tell them he had made two important decisions, she was filled with trepidation. The big news: Zach wanted to be a pacifist, and he'd decided to switch from tuba to Irish fiddle. In a television interview several years later, Zach championed his parents. "If normal is a family that has a mom and a dad and two kids and a white picket fence, then no, I don't live in a normal family," he said. "But if a normal family is one where everyone treats each other as equals and with love, then yeah, I live in a normal family."

One of the most dramatic evolutions of the last 50 years is how people think about gender. In Jorgensen's day, it was viewed as two distinct categories: male and female. If you strayed from one or the other, you were categorized as gay. Today, gender is viewed on a spectrum. You can be "genderqueer" (you identify as neither male or female), "gender fluid" (your gender identity shifts over time), "cisgender" (your gender aligns with your sex), and any number of other delineations. Facebook offers these and dozens of other gender options in its drop-down menu, from "androgynous" to "gender questioning." In her memoir *She's Not There*, Boylan put her finger on this changing conceptualization: "The line between male and female turns out to be rather fine. Although we imagine our genders as firm and fixed, in fact they are as malleable as a sand castle."

AFTER HER RETURN TO THE UNITED STATES in 1953, Jorgensen reunited with her family and built herself a house in Massapequa, Long Island. Early on, the press and the public could not get enough of her. Not everyone approved—far from it—and there were plenty of tasteless jokes. Journalists described her as "mankind's gift to the female species" and the "latest thing in blonde bombshells." Jorgensen, who dressed elegantly and spoke straightforwardly, did her best to present herself as a thoughtful but determined human being, rather than some kind of sexualized freak. It helped that most of the thousands of letters she said she received from people around the globe were supportive and encouraging. Her parents, who lived with Jorgensen in her new home, stood by her. "She's ours and we love her," she remembered her father telling the press.

In the 1950s, Jorgensen created a life on the stage, launching a nightclub act that took her from the Copa Club in Pittsburgh to venues in Detroit, Philadelphia, New York City, and even Cuba. She was, after all, a celebrity, whether she liked it or not. Dressed in sophisticated gowns, Jorgensen entertained her audiences with a mix of singing, dancing, and banter. Some clubs refused to book her on moral grounds, but others promoted the new star, happily filling their seats. She was derided by certain reviewers—the British press ridiculed her act before she even appeared—but lauded by others. Through it all, she retained a sense of humor. One night while dining with friends at a Manhattan restaurant, Jorgensen noticed the celebrity specialties on the menu—the Bing Crosby sandwich, the Frank Sinatra dessert. "I said casually, 'All these items named after famous people, and there's not even a mixed salad named after me,' " Jorgensen recounted in her memoir. "There was a shocked silence at the table. I didn't realize what I'd said, until suddenly there was a great shout of laughter from my friends."

Jorgensen later appeared in theater, taking on a variety of roles including the character of Miss Western in the theater adaptation of Henry Fielding's 18th-century novel *Tom Jones*. In 1967, more than a decade after her return from Denmark, she published her autobiography, which sold almost 450,000 copies in paperback. Jorgensen was engaged to men twice but never married. One engagement was called off. The other, to a labor union statistician, was stymied when New York's marriage license bureau rejected the couple's application on grounds that Jorgensen's birth certificate listed her as "male." Jorgensen went on to lecture about her experience and spoke out on behalf of transgender people and their rights. She lived the last two decades of her life in California, where she was diagnosed with bladder and lung cancer. Jorgensen died on May 3, 1989, in San Clemente, three weeks short of her 63rd birthday.

Jorgensen's celebrity status has faded over the decades, but her legacy has not. In her pioneering quest to embrace her true identity, Jorgensen forged a path for millions of other people. Although she was accused many times of masquerading as a female, "the real masquerade would have been to continue in my former state. That, to me, would have been living the lie," she wrote. "I found the oldest gift of heaven—to be myself."

Frank Lloyd Wright

I N JUNE 1943, FRANK LLOYD WRIGHT received an invitation he could not possibly pass up: his first commission in New York City. Hilla Rebay, longtime art adviser to businessman and collector Solomon Guggenheim, had sent the famed architect a letter asking him if he would design a new museum for Guggenheim's expansive collection of modern art, including abstract paintings by Chagall, Delaunay, Kandinsky, and Klee. "I need a fighter, a lover of space, an originator, a tester and a wise man," Rebay wrote. "I want a temple of spirit—a monument, and your help to make it possible."

In many ways, Wright was the ideal man for the job. Then 76, the flamboyant architect had been rousing the design world with his bold and innovative buildings for more than 50 years. His artistic vision of "organic" architecture had produced breathtaking structures that melded with nature in a way never seen before. While others erected high-rises ambushing the sky, Wright built light-filled sanctuaries hugging the hills. Everything was novel. In his first independent commission, the Winslow House, built in River Forest, Illinois, in 1893, Wright defied the vertical bent of the time, building a horizontal home that would become an integral element of his trademark style. With Fallingwater, the dramatic retreat he constructed in Pennsylvania's Allegheny Mountains in the late 1930s, Wright accomplished the unthinkable: stretching a 5,330-foot residence over a 30-foot waterfall.

But as Guggenheim and his staff would quickly discover, Wright's extraordinary talent was intertwined with a supreme narcissism that played out in myriad ways with his clients. Rooted in nonconformity, the maverick architect pursued his artistic convictions with little concern for the utilitarian matters of stability, practicality, and cost. Organic simplicity and aesthetics mattered above all else, and Wright pushed the limits, using nontraditional materials and unusual designs to achieve his ideals. His buildings were notorious for their physical defects, including inadequately heated rooms and drooping beams. Leaky roofs, an unwelcome feature of his flat-topped buildings, were practically an architectural insignia. Even Wright's most resolute admirers could not help but pay homage to the depths of what sociologist and architecture critic Lewis Mumford described as Wright's "colossal self-admiration."

Wright's ego did not wane as he aged—and indeed, took center stage throughout the planning and construction of the Guggenheim, exasperating everyone from Guggenheim himself to the contemporary artists whose works would be displayed. The architect's early designs violated building codes and prompted ongoing feuds over excess expenses. It was Wright's conception of the museum, however, that fueled the greatest aggravation. Wright had made it clear that he wanted to "do away with the stilted, pretentious grandomania of the old-fashioned 'art exhibit,' " as he put it in a letter to Guggenheim. But his new-fashioned design was its own brand of grandomania. Rather than prioritize the art, Wright's plans required that the paintings be displayed at an angle to accommodate his dramatic and predominant spiral walkway. The project soon raised a fundamental question about what the museum would be showcasing: modern art or Wright's ego?

In December 1956, shortly after construction began, 21 artists, including Milton Avery, Willem de Kooning, and Robert Motherwell, signed a letter stating that Wright's design indicated "a callous disregard" for adequate viewing of works of art. Ever confident, Wright paid little heed to his critics. "Somebody said that the museum out here on Fifth Avenue looked like a washing machine," he told Mike Wallace in a television interview a year later. "But I've heard a lot of that type of reaction, and I've always discarded it as worthless. And I think it is."

Frank Lloyd Wright was one of the most self-promoted and celebrated architects in history. Impertinent, pioneering, and dramatic, Wright embraced his ego throughout his life, used it to get ahead, and promoted it to the world without an ounce of modesty. Plenty of people are narcissistic. Wright's behaviors line up with a far more deeply entrenched mental health diagnosis: narcissistic personality disorder. "Early in life I had to choose between honest arrogance and hypocritical humility," he famously said. "I chose the former and have seen no reason to change."

Andy Warhol Was a Hoarder

FRANK LLOYD WRIGHT UNABASHEDLY fiddled with the truth—
how he got his jobs, how much his buildings would cost, even
the date of his birth. Records show that he was born on June 8,
1867, but Wright later declared the year to be 1869, presumably
because he wanted to appear younger in his elder years. His birth-
place was Richland Center, a Wisconsin farming town. But Wright
was vague and often tight-lipped about the location, most likely
because it betrayed his humble beginnings; to this day nobody is
sure of the precise address. The architect even altered his middle
name, changing it from Lincoln to Lloyd, a tribute to his mother's
family, the Lloyd Joneses, who had emigrated over stormy Atlantic
waters from Wales to America in the 1840s.

Wright's father, William Carey Wright, was a widower with
three young children when he married Anna Lloyd Jones in the
1860s. Charming and well liked, William was "one of life's dar-
lings," according to his son's biographer Meryle Secrest. He was
admired for his many talents and avocations—singing, playing the
piano, practicing law (despite having no degree), and preaching.
Highly skilled as an orator, he even gave a eulogy for Abraham
Lincoln in Lone Rock, Wisconsin, in April 1865. Anna, a school-
teacher in her mid-20s and one of ten children, was a headstrong
woman who took pride in her lineage of stoic and hard-working
farmers. She strode like a man, Frank later wrote in an autobiography, refused to wear corsets, read Lowell and Longfellow to her
children, made pie without peeling the apples, and cherished the
beauty and sanctity of nature.

William Wright was more than a decade older than his second
wife; Anna, at five foot eight, was taller. Those were the least of
the couple's incongruities. Raised in New England, he was a Bap-
tist with English roots; she was born in Wales and came from a
long line of religious radicals who had formed their own brand

of Unitarianism. But it was their progeny that set them apart the most. Anna seems to have been overwhelmed by her sudden role as a caregiver for three small children, and the marriage grew more stressful with the births of Frank and his sisters, Mary and Maginel. Now there were six mouths to feed, a challenge exacerbated by William's habit of abandoning jobs and recklessness with money. With William's instability and Anna's frustration, there was little room for companionship. Some accounts suggest that Anna vied with her stepchildren for her husband's attention. Her stepdaughter Elizabeth Wright Heller, especially, did not harbor good memories. "I never could please her," Heller wrote in a memoir, "no matter how hard I tried."

One child, however, did please Anna over all the rest: Frank. Enamored of her firstborn, Anna doted on him to the exclusion of everyone else. "William Wright and his daughters were left in no doubt that the son was the mother's favorite," according to Brendan Gill, another biographer. Wright's memories of his father are less than loving. Although he was proud of his father's preaching and shared his deep appreciation for music, Frank was also afraid of the man who rapped his knuckles during piano practice and didn't seem wholly invested in his son. "He never made much of the child," Wright recollected in his detached third-person reminiscence. "Perhaps the father never loved or wanted the son at any time." Young Frank turned to his mother for solace. Anna's worship of her son, her "extraordinary devotion," as Wright described it, disturbed her husband and tainted the couple's relationship. "The differences between husband and wife," he later wrote, "all seemed to arise over that boy." The portrait that emerges is one of two fused allies: mother and son against husband and father.

Anna's relationship with Frank went beyond just favoritism, however. In his autobiography, Wright depicts his mother in almost mythic proportions, as both his loyal protector and overseer of his destiny. He was, according to his reminiscences, his mother's great hope, "a means to realize her vision," and she was single-minded about the path he would take. Even before he was born, she determined that he would become an architect. His mother's conviction was so strong that she hung a series of framed wood engravings of old English cathedrals on Frank's nursery walls. "The boy," Wright recollected, "was to build beautiful buildings."

Given his talent for masterfully reshaping the past, Wright's autobiographical recollections have been scrutinized by biographers. Gill, a friend of Wright's in his later years, called the architect a "hypnotist" who glorified his mother and diminished his father to elevate his own auspicious beginnings. In his biography, Gill picks apart the smallest details of Wright's account, including the portrayal of his room (how would there have been space for a separate nursery for Frank in the Wrights' small house?) and the engravings hung by his mother (Anna's family attended religious services in simple meeting houses and eschewed religious adornment). Wright's autobiography, according to Gill, is "an extended apologia—a fabrication that takes the form of a bittersweet romance, with Frank Lloyd Wright as its hero." It is not, however, surprising. Rewriting one's past is characteristic of narcissistic people, who become adept at embellishing life stories to enhance their self-image. What matters is that Wright's account is the truth that he fashioned and wished others to believe.

Narcissism—a blend of conceit, self-centeredness, and rude behavior—pervades every facet of society, from the bleachers of Little League ("My kid should be pitching!") to the highest positions of law, medicine, government, and business. Being narcissistic, however, is not the same thing as a clinical case of narcissistic personality disorder, one of ten personality disorders contained in the *DSM*. A diagnosis is made when a patient exhibits at least five out of nine symptoms: a grandiose sense of self-importance; a pre-occupation with fantasies of unlimited success, power, brilliance, beauty, or ideal love; a belief in one's own special status, which can only be understood by other people in the same esteemed orbit; a need for excessive admiration; a sense of entitlement; exploitive behavior in relationships; a lack of empathy; an envy for others or a belief that others are envious in return; a demonstration of arrogant and haughty behaviors and attitudes.

Since narcissistic personality disorder first appeared in the *DSM* in 1980, the condition has been hotly contested. Plenty of confident, powerful people who might qualify for a diagnosis are doing just fine, thank you. Or at least *they* think they are. Why stick a label on them? Narcissism may even be necessary for survival in a society that ranks individual achievement higher than communal success. Just a few years ago, a brouhaha erupted over narcissistic personality disorder's very existence as its own clinical diagnosis. One group of experts tried unsuccessfully to eliminate it as a distinct condition in the *DSM*—in part because its symptoms so often overlapped with features of other personality disorders, like borderline.

Over the decades, a more nuanced definition has emerged. Narcissism has long been associated with an overarching grandiosity, but it isn't always rooted in confidence. This has led to the theory that narcissism may exist in two forms: grandiose or "overt" narcissism and vulnerable or "covert" narcissism. Overt narcissists are easier to spot, because they display their behaviors publicly with aplomb. Covert narcissists exhibit many of the same feelings—they dislike sharing credit, they're caught up in themselves, they're hypersensitive to criticism—but they are also likely to be anxious and introverted. Some narcissists may have characteristics of both.

Andy Warhol Was a Hoarder

Frank Lloyd Wright would have made an exceptionally strong candidate for an overt form of narcissistic personality disorder. The childhood narrative he relayed in his reminiscences—whether factual, fantastical, or somewhere in between—reads as a case study for several key factors linked to the development of the condition. Early interactions between parent and child are especially significant, and are often rooted in neglect. In some cases, a parent may be cold or unavailable. But the neglect may also emerge out of an overindulgence that results in a disregard for the child's own sense of self, says Elsa Ronningstam, an associate clinical professor of psychiatry and narcissism expert at Harvard Medical School. A parent might, for example, assign a specific role to a child—he or she will be a great actress, a doctor, or, in Wright's case, an architect—which ends up disrupting healthy development. Heaped with expectations, a child thinks, "If I don't follow this path, I don't exist," says Ronningstam.

Often, this destination is set by a parent whose own quest for greatness is never brought to fruition and who may harbor narcissistic traits of his or her own. Anna Wright believed that she was capable of far more than she was able to achieve, according to biographer Secrest, and this was "clear evidence that she had transferred to Frank her unfulfilled ambitions." Frank's sister Maginel later recalled that her mother did not view Frank as a typical child: "He was her protégé, her legacy. He would accomplish what she and her husband could not." Such presumptions can fuel a child's tenacious determination to succeed. But they can also spawn deep levels of insecurity. In some cases, the bravado and bluster of narcissism may mask an underlying vulnerability or lack of self-esteem, says Ronningstam. As Secrest notes, Wright may have believed that "he was not lovable for who he was, but only for the person Anna wanted him to be."

Anna clearly cherished her son, but too much adulation can backfire. A spoiled or "golden" child may develop a sense of entitlement, believing that he is better than everyone else and deserves special treatment—one of the core characteristics of narcissistic personality disorder. Often, a parent indulges a child by stepping in to save him from disagreeable circumstances (an argument with a friend) or from defeat (questioning a judge at a musical competition). The problem is that overindulgence can interfere with a child's ability to build resilience in response to the normal bumps and pitfalls of life. This is how vulnerability can be spawned. Instead of building healthy self-esteem, these children develop a kind of helplessness because they have not learned to integrate the pluses and minuses in their life, says Ronningstam. "They're not prepared for a rainy day."

One of Wright's childhood memories flawlessly illustrates his mother's indulgence. When he was about 11, he concocted a party for his three country cousins. There would be surprises and presents for the boys, he told them, and "the possibilities grew as he talked until expectations were boundless." The boys rushed home, changed clothes, and arrived early for the festivities, not realizing that the party existed solely in Frank's imagination. Although initially surprised, his mother quickly came to her son's rescue, providing the children with molasses candy, popcorn, and ginger cookies. She even unearthed a few presents and convinced her husband to play "Pop Goes the Weasel" on the violin. Later, when Anna asked Frank why he wanted to fool his cousins, he turned the blame on them, accusing the boys of ruining all the fun by believing him in the first place. "And Mother understood," Wright asserted. "Nobody else."

By the time Frank was 18, his parents' marriage was over. Anna stopped sharing her husband's bed, moved him into the coldest room in the house, and told him she hated the "very ground" he walked on; William reported that he had suffered "violence, indignity and abuse" for years, described his wife as "violently angry," and left. By all accounts, father and son never saw each other again.

Determined to pursue the architectural path he and his mother had mapped out, Wright began working part-time as a junior draftsman for a civil engineer and took classes at the University of Wisconsin–Madison. But he bridled at the rules and regulations of conventional schooling; although he claimed to make it halfway through his senior year, records reportedly show that Wright completed only two semesters. His real education, he would later state, came from the wooden blocks and brightly colored strips of paper he played with as a child, made by the renowned childhood educator Friedrich Froebel, and the summers he spent on a Lloyd Jones family farm near Spring Green, Wisconsin. It was there, where he milked cows, hauled wood, dodged hornets, and got sore, that Wright would learn the merits of strenuous labor—and there that he would inhale the delights of nature: the milkweed blossoms, the deep blue of the nighttime sky, the feel of mud between his toes.

To pursue his calling, Wright knew that he needed to live in a place where architects worked. In early 1887, he pawned the books his father had left behind (including a favorite copy of Plutarch's *Lives*) and the mink collar his mother had sewn into his overcoat. He bought a train ticket to Chicago. It was time to fulfill his destiny.

⌒

NINETEEN-YEAR-OLD FRANK LLOYD WRIGHT arrived in Chicago at an opportune time. A massive fire had eviscerated much of the downtown in 1871, and the city was undergoing rapid new development. Still, Wright was not overly impressed. Hurrying from one office to the next as he looked for a job, he showed contempt for the work of other architects and was not ashamed to say so years later. The Palmer House looked like "an ugly old, old man whose wrinkles were all in the wrong place," he wrote in his autobiography; the Chicago Board of Trade was a "thin-chested, hard-faced, chamfered monstrosity"; the Interstate Exposition Building, a "much-domed yellow shed on the lake front." The cityscape had nothing to offer, Wright concluded, but rank-and-file monotony.

As he worked his way up from apprentice to virtuoso, Wright showed a flair for ingratiating himself with people who could help him, then moving on when they had nothing left to offer—a classic trait of narcissistic personality disorder. Despite his lack of an academic degree, he landed his first job with Joseph Lyman Silsbee, a prestigious architect who was designing a high-end subdivision in the city—and, conveniently, a new church for one of Wright's uncles, Jenkin Lloyd Jones. Wright claimed that Silsbee did not know the family connection when he hired him, but historians dispute this, chalking it up to yet another one of Wright's historical tweaks. By then, Wright had also developed some drawing skills at his part-time job back home. Either way, his interactions with Silsbee illustrated Wright's sense of entitlement, which would infuse every aspect of his behavior throughout his life.

Just a few months after he started, Silsbee gave Wright a raise, bumping him from $8 to $12 a week. But Wright wanted more. When Silsbee refused, Wright quit on the spot, got himself a job at a competing firm, quickly decided that the new place didn't suit him, and informed his new boss that he was going back to Silsbee. Wright later acknowledged how his behavior must have come off to his employer. "I think he thought me a young coxcomb," he wrote in his autobiography—but his own advancement mattered more. As is the case for any narcissist, the ultimate question is not "What is my obligation here?" but instead "How can I profit from this situation?"

And profit he did. Silsbee agreed to take him back, increased his pay, and allowed Wright to take on his first commission, designing a school for two of his maternal aunts who had inherited their father's farmland in Wisconsin. But once again, Wright set his sights elsewhere, this time on the firm of Dankmar Adler and Louis Sullivan, which had received a commission to build Chicago's tallest building, a 17-story tower with offices, shops, a theater, and a concert hall designed to rival the Metropolitan Opera House in New York City. Wright would make as much use of Sullivan, a brilliant young architect, as Sullivan made of him. Within just a few months, Wright managed to get his boss to agree to a five-year contract and a loan so that Wright could build a home in the Chicago suburb of Oak Park for himself and his new bride, Catherine Tobin, the daughter of one of Uncle Jenk's parishioners. The two men developed a close relationship—Wright would later refer to Sullivan as his *lieber Meister*, or beloved master—but that did not stop him from betraying Sullivan's trust. Despite the fact that his contract explicitly forbade moonlighting, Wright started building his own "bootleg" houses, enraging his boss. A few months before his contract expired, Wright recollected, "I threw my pencil down and walked out of the Adler and Sullivan office, never to return."

Wright's personal relationships were similarly fractured and scarred. Narcissists feed on admiration and expect it from the people around them. Catherine Tobin, a tall lively redhead, was just 18 when she married Wright on June 1, 1889; he was one week shy of his 22nd birthday. Kitty, as she was called, may have adored Wright early on, but her devotion would not last. The couple's six children arrived in rapid succession: three boys and two girls in the first eight years and a final baby boy in 1903. As a father, Wright was entertaining at times, but he could also be remarkably detached. He built his children a playroom with a fireplace and a barrel-vaulted ceiling and filled it with toys and colored balloons. He played the piano and entertained guests. The couple's second son, John Lloyd Wright, remembered his father throwing him in the air and tickling his toes. "He was an epic of wit and merriment that gave our home the feeling of a jolly carnival," he wrote in a memoir. But Wright was also unencumbered by fatherly devotion. He described watching another son, a toddler at the time, stuck in a mud puddle and gasping for air as a sprinkler doused him with water. " 'All right,' I thought cruelly. 'Let's see what stuff he's made of!' " Wright recalled in his autobiography. "I let him lie there half drowned, literally, to see what he would do."

Impatient with the constant hubbub of children, Wright made it clear that any "father-feeling" he had was for his work, not his offspring. "The children were their mother's children," he wrote. "I hated the sound of the word papa." Architecture consumed him. Having honed his skills working for others, Wright began building his own architectural practice while Kitty dedicated herself to raising and educating their children. Her husband took on bold new design projects, including his famed prairie houses with their horizontal lines, low-pitched roofs, open floor plans, and centrally located hearths, which he began building at the turn of the century to blend in with the flat midwestern landscape. Kitty, meanwhile, developed her own interests in social causes and literary groups. The two, inevitably, grew apart. The dissolution of a marriage is always complex, but Kitty's shift in allegiance away from Wright and toward their children could not have satisfied a man who demanded attention. Middle-aged by then, he was also restless.

In the fall of 1909, 42-year-old Wright abandoned his wife and children and set sail for Europe with Mamah Cheney, a married client and a friend of Kitty's with whom he was having an affair. Mamah, who had left her husband and two children to be with

Wright, was highly educated and fluent in French and German. The two were soul mates, the architect declared. Wright departed quickly one night, his son John recalled, and "didn't even say goodbye." He did, however, leave his family with something to remember him by: an unpaid $900 grocery bill.

Wright seemed to have no compunction about abandoning his commitments of matrimony and fatherhood. Conventional rules didn't apply to him. As biographer Ada Louise Huxtable put it, "he simply created his own moral code." When Wright returned from Europe in the fall of 1910, he found that the denizens of his hometown, Oak Park, would have none of his scandalous affair; neighbors shunned him, clients abandoned him. Kitty refused to grant her husband a divorce, insisting that they would reunite. But none of this stopped Wright from creating a new life with his mistress, who followed him back to the States the following summer.

Wright now needed a retreat, a place to build the next phase of his personal and professional life. His mother, Anna, had conveniently acquired a plot of land in Wisconsin, near the Hillside Home School that Wright had helped build for his aunts. Throughout his life, Wright juggled his finances like the overseer of a three-ring circus—requesting advance payments from clients, using a prized Japanese print collection as collateral for loans, and borrowing from creditors. With land now in hand, Wright called on wealthy businessman Darwin Martin, a client and one of his loyal moneymen, to help finance construction of a home for him and Mamah.

Initially, Wright claimed that the residence would be for his mother. Martin agreed not only to provide a loan but to help finance the mortgage payments Wright owed on the Oak Park home where Kitty lived with their children. This is almost impossible to fathom. But it speaks to the beguiling effect narcissists can have on others. Exceedingly alluring and charismatic, they effectively seduce the people who serve them. This was certainly the case for Wright, whose creditors continued to lend him money despite his bombast and his debts. "The fact is that he was a confidence man of infinite charm," writes biographer Gill, "and nobody could refuse him anything for long."

It is mind-boggling that a man who asked to borrow money to build a home for his mother would dream up what amounted to a kingdom in the hills for himself and his mistress. But as always, Wright's grandiosity and fantasies of unlimited success played out in full. Even when money was tight, he refused to waver from the "organic" architectural vision that would drive him throughout his life.

Steeped in Ralph Waldo Emerson's view of nature as spiritual expression, Wright's vision required that man-made structures meld harmoniously with the trees, hills, water, and sky that surrounded them. "I knew well that no house should ever be *on* a hill or *on* anything. It should be *of* the hill," he wrote. "Belonging to it. Hill and house should live together each the happier for the other." Emerson's tenets of nonconformity, combined with the religious dissenters in Wright's mother's family, fueled the architect's approach to his work. Indeed, the Lloyd Jones family motto, "Truth Against the World," could not have been better scripted for Wright's weighty ideals. "The sort of expression we seek," he wrote, "is that of harmony, or the good otherwise known as the true, otherwise known as the Beautiful."

This dogma inspired Wright's vision for his Wisconsin estate and studio, which he named "Taliesin" after the Welsh bard whose name translates as "shining brow." In his autobiography, Wright laid out his grand conception of a house built atop a hill overlooking expansive vineyards and fruit trees. He envisioned apple and plum trees, bushes with their "necklaces of pink and green gooseberries," asparagus and melon, honey hives, cows, sheep, and horses. "I looked forward to peacocks Javanese and white on the low roofs of the buildings or calling from the walls of the courts," he wrote. There would be no gutters so that icicles could drip and beautify the look. "Taliesin in winter was a frosted palace roofed and walled with snow, hung with iridescent fringes."

In the fall of 1911, Wright and Mamah moved into Taliesin. Their scandalous relationship did not, however, go unnoticed. On Christmas Day, after articles about the couple's cohabitation appeared in the papers, Wright held a press conference at his home. He told reporters that he had married too young and that his marriage had unraveled; he hoped to fulfill his life as an artist with Mamah. Wright may have intended his remarks to be an honest account for an inquiring public, but they were infused with righteousness. "The ordinary man cannot live without rules to guide his conduct," Wright said. "It is infinitely more difficult to live without rules, but that is what the really honest, sincere, thinking man is compelled to do." In the end, the relationship would not last, ending tragically in the summer of 1914, when a deranged servant set Taliesin afire and murdered Mamah, her two children, and several other guests while Wright was working in Chicago. Wright filled Mamah's coffin with flowers and, in despair, set out to rebuild Taliesin. "Her soul has entered me," he wrote in a letter to his neighbors, "and it shall not be lost."

Wright's personal tumult continued after the Taliesin calamity. Soon after Mamah's death, a condolence note from a sculptress named Miriam Noel caught Wright's attention—she, too, had suffered in love, she told him. Could they meet? Conspicuous and spirited, Noel matched Wright's sartorial style. He carried a walking stick and wore flowing capes and a porkpie hat; she draped herself in necklaces, capes, and turbans. Within days of their meeting, she addressed him in a letter as "Lord of my Waking Dreams!" Wright, still struggling to recover from Mamah's death, was taken in by what he called Miriam's "enlightened companionship." But their relationship was tumultuous from early on. Miriam, Wright would soon discover, was a morphine addict and may have suffered from schizophrenia. Still, after nine years together, the two were married in 1923 (one year after Kitty Wright finally granted her husband a divorce). Wright hoped that marriage would improve their relationship; instead, as he later wrote, it "resulted in ruin." Within months, Miriam walked out, and the two were officially divorced several years later.

It didn't take Wright long to move on. In 1924, a Montenegrin dancer, Olgivanna Lazovich, caught his eye at a performance of the Russian Ballet in Chicago. She was 26; he was 57. Neither was divorced when they began living together, and they would soon have two children to care for—Olgivanna's own young daughter and an out-of-wedlock baby girl of their own. In 1926, Wright, along with Olgivanna and the children, spent two nights in jail for committing adultery and violating a law that prohibited the transport of women over state lines for any "immoral purpose."

Wright's professional trespasses were no less astounding. Worshipping his aesthetic design ideal above all else, he showed little concern for the most basic structural mishaps. Stories about the notorious leaky roofs he designed are as entertaining as they are confounding. As historian William Cronon recounted in an essay published by the Museum of Modern Art, water poured onto the heads of congregants during the first High Holy Days celebrations at the Beth Sholom Synagogue outside of Philadelphia in 1960. The roof of the Johnson Wax building in Racine, Wisconsin, held up by 21-foot-tall "lily pads"—slender columns that spread into circles at the top—dripped so frequently that workers kept five-gallon buckets on their desks to catch the splashes. And then there's the famous dinner party story. One night, Herbert F. Johnson, of Johnson Wax, called Wright from the middle of a soiree at his elegant 14,000-square-foot home, which the architect had also designed. As Cronon described it, the party "had been interrupted by a steady drip onto Johnson's bald head." Wright suggested that "the irate owner solve the problem by moving his chair."

Wright's clients were expected to feel grateful to dwell in one of his rarefied homes, no matter the inconveniences, and they needed to embrace his aesthetic vision. The architect equipped some of his houses with custom-designed wooden furniture as part of his plan for "organic simplicity," making it challenging for people to bring their own. Artwork and decoration were unwelcome with the exception of his Japanese prints, which Wright savored as the purest form of art. Clients were not supposed to tinker with any of it. Even gardening required his approval. If the ceilings were low—he claimed to be five feet, eight inches, but may have been shorter— so be it. Not enough closet space? Time to get rid of excess. As his son John described it, Wright "builds a romance about you, who will live in it—and you get the House of Houses, in which everyone lives a better life because of it. It may have a crack, a leak, or both, but you wouldn't trade it for one that didn't."

Wright's encounter with Arthur Miller and Marilyn Monroe is a classic example of the architect's self-serving vision. In 1957, the couple invited Wright to design a home for them in Roxbury, Connecticut. Wright climbed to high ground to take in a view of the hills that stretched out from their old farmhouse. "He took one look and then peed and said, 'Good spot,' and we walked down the hill," Miller recounted in a letter to one of Wright's apprentices many years later. The couple wanted a place where they could live simply, not entertain, but Wright took little interest in their needs. When his plans arrived, they featured a circular living room with stone columns, a conference room with 12 chairs, and a stone swimming pool. Sleeping space? Not much. It was a house fit "for a corporation and not two people in the country," wrote Miller. "He simply had us all wrong." Not only that, Wright "had no actual idea" what the house would cost, Miller reported. "He said something about $250,000, which was absurd even in the mid-Fifties for that kind of construction."

Hardly surprising. Wright was perpetually irresponsible with money, both his own and his clients'. It was no secret that he lured in commissions with lowball estimates and then unabashedly upped the price. A church Wright promised for $60,000 rang in at more than $200,000. The price of Fallingwater, the vacation home he built for department store owner Edgar Kaufmann and his family, soared from $35,000 to $155,000. He routinely requested advance payments, then neglected to put them toward the project. Instead, he might buy a grand piano—there were 11, he claimed, at Taliesin—or another Japanese print to add to his vast collection. Money didn't have value, other than getting him what he wanted, his son John later reflected in his memoir. "He carried his paper money crumpled in any pocket—trousers, vest, coat or overcoat. He would have to uncrumple a bill to see its denomination. He never counted his change," John wrote. "He either paid too much or too little for everything."

Although quick to spend, Wright was delinquent about paying back, whether it was a grocery bill or taxes owed on his estate. "This love for beautiful things—rugs, books, prints, or anything else made by art or craft or building—especially building—kept the butcher, the baker and the landlord always waiting," Wright confessed. "Sometimes waiting incredibly long." John, also an architect, experienced this firsthand when his father hired him with the promise of a regular salary. Wright would take him out for a meal and stuff a $20 bill in his pocket every now and then, but he never followed through with a paycheck. When John raised the issue, his father looked at him reproachfully. "He then proceeded to figure out what I had cost him all during my life, including obstetrics," John wrote. "Whatever the amount was, which I could not comprehend, if I never received salary from him for the rest of my life it would still be too much, and he would be justified in the matter." John continued working with his father, even traveling to Tokyo, where Wright would live for four years while he built the famed Imperial Hotel. When a client's payment arrived, John took the opportunity to deduct the amount he was owed. He received a cable from his father the next day: "You're fired! Take the next ship home."

Despite this behavior, Wright continued to attract admirers. In 1932, they began flocking to Taliesin, where Wright had launched the Taliesin Fellowship for young architects—and a kingdom of his own. The program was conceived out of monetary necessity during the Great Depression. The 1920s had been especially rough on Wright's finances: His commissions had dried up during his tenure in Japan, a second fire had destroyed the living quarters at Taliesin, and he had barely managed to hold on to his estate after failing to pay his mortgage. Olgivanna, whom Wright married in 1928, was his staunchest defender and a true devotee. It was she who helped dream up the program—a moneymaking venture—in the name of education. As biographer Ada Louise Huxtable describes it, "out of ingenuity and desperation, a brilliant scheme was formed to turn penury into profit."

Wright, then in his mid-60s, and Olgivanna, in her mid-30s, touted the fellowship as hands-on living and learning in a working cooperative. Appalled by conventional colleges, which he charged were churning out "creatively impotent" and sedentary students, Wright was adamant that his apprentices engage in physical labor.

At Taliesin, apprentices took part in running the day-to-day operations of the 200-acre estate with its fruit trees, vegetable garden, and artificial lake stocked with fish. They hoed the fields, tended the manure pit, cooked meals, did laundry, hauled stones, cut trees, and built their own lodging. There was no formal instruction; instead, apprentices were awarded the opportunity to work alongside Wright in his studio. The annual price tag for this privilege was steep. Initially set at $650—more than Ivy League tuition—it quickly grew to $1,100. Wright had no trouble filling his spots.

Depending on whom you asked, the Taliesin Fellowship was either "a clever con game serving Wright's total self-interest, or a profound preparation for a life in architecture," as Huxtable put it. Many apprentices, tasked with everything from making homemade Christmas gifts for the Wrights to preparing Russian stews under Olgivanna's watchful eye, left in the first few years, frustrated that Wright was providing little architectural training. His harshest critics viewed the fellowship as a cult with Wright as its leader, and Olgivanna as domineering matriarch. But others appreciated the labor—not to mention the concerts, films, and lectures that were a required part of their cultural education—and stayed for years. Some became loyal acolytes, even working with Wright on later projects.

None, however, would ever gain the stature that Wright achieved and that Olgivanna glorified for eternity. "He stands as a giant among the generations of men," she wrote in a book about her husband published one year after his death. "His projection left on earth will speak for thousands of years to those who understand."

꒰꒱

THE WORD "NARCISSISM" COMES from a Greek myth about a beautiful hunter, Narcissus, who scorns those who love him. One day,

Narcissus is followed into the woods by a nymph named Echo, who tries to embrace him. Narcissus throws Echo to the ground, rejecting her; she flees the woods and dies of a broken heart. Only her voice, her echo, remains. Narcissus, meanwhile, is lured to a pool by Nemesis, the goddess of revenge, where he becomes mesmerized by the exquisite face he sees in the water, not realizing it is his own reflection. Transfixed, but unable to obtain the object of his desire, Narcissus dies.

It is difficult to track narcissistic personality disorder with any kind of precision. Most people who exhibit characteristics of the disorder aren't rushing in for treatment; in general they see nothing wrong with their behavior, nor do they recognize its impact on others. If one does happen to land in a therapist's office, it's almost always because he or she is there for a coexisting condition, like drug dependence, or because a spouse or a boss has given an ultimatum: Shape up or you're out of here. The best estimates for a clinical case of narcissistic personality disorder show that it affects up to 6 percent of the general population.

Everyday narcissism is far more widespread and, according to some researchers, on the rise. Anybody living in 21st-century America knows that there are plenty of self-absorbed people out there. The standard assessment tool for garden-variety narcissism is a questionnaire called the Narcissistic Personality Inventory, which consists of 40 statements, each written in two very different ways: "I prefer to blend in with the crowd" or "I like to be the center of attention"; "I like to do things for other people" or "I expect a great deal from other people"; "The thought of ruling the world frightens the hell out of me" or "If I ruled the world it would be a better place." Respondents are asked to pick the best match, and scored according to which option they choose. College students have been administered this test for decades, and a recent study found a striking 30 percent increase in narcissism levels between 1979 and 2006.

The study's authors speculated on a number of social causes, including an emphasis on boosting self-esteem starting in preschool. Brad Bushman, a professor of communication and psychology at Ohio State University and one of the investigators, says parents' efforts to build self-esteem by making their kids feel special can backfire. In a later study, published in 2015, Bushman and his colleagues found that when parents view their children as "more special and more entitled," the children internalize these inflated views and are more likely to develop narcissistic traits. Parents who express affection and appreciation, by contrast, nurture healthy self-esteem. For children, "it's really important that feedback is contingent on behavior rather than blanket praise," says Bushman.

Social media can also foster narcissism. Technology has certainly made it a whole lot easier to *act* like a narcissist. Among celebrities, who score higher than the general population on the Narcissistic Personality Inventory, reality TV stars are the most narcissistic of all. Today, anyone with a computer or mobile device can perform in her own reality show. Where once we might have talked about a promotion over coffee with a friend, we can now share the news with hundreds of admirers who laud our every move with "like" clicks—and expect similar ovations for their own status updates. Technology is making it easier than ever to self-promote in the guise of sharing. Just when the selfie seemed to be as vainglorious as it could get, crafty marketers added the attachable pole to give iPhone photographers a better angle on their double chins. No wonder it has been dubbed the "narcissistick." One can only imagine what Wright might have done with Instagram.

Charming, charismatic, and richly endowed with self-esteem, narcissists are often well rewarded, too. Charles O'Reilly, a professor at Stanford Business School, found a direct correlation between how employees rated their CEOs at 32 high-tech firms in Silicon Valley and the executives' total compensation. The most narcissistic bosses, whom colleagues described using adjectives such as "arrogant," "boastful," "conceited," and "egotistical," earned higher wages, owned more stock, and showed the biggest gap in pay compared to CEOs who ranked lower on the narcissistic scale. Confidence and power are vital components of leadership, but narcissistic bosses cross the line. "When you talk to people who work for them," says O'Reilly, "you find out that they're typically abusive and manipulative."

Like Wright, Steve Jobs was one of the world's greatest innovators, turning characterless technology into elegant, user-friendly works of art. Jobs was adopted as a baby, and his parents made him feel special, he told his biographer Walter Isaacson: "They said, 'We specifically picked you out.' " The truth was that another couple had turned him down first because they wanted a girl. Jobs knew that. But he *was* special in his signature black turtleneck, guiding his disciples through Apple's latest innovations—from the 13 "flavors" of the iMac (where else could you get a blueberry desktop?) to the sleek, palm-of-your-hand iPod and iPhone. Jobs's creative genius, however, was coupled with a thorny personality. He had a reputation for bullying some of his employees until they cried, twisting the truth, blaming others for his faults, and cheating his friends out of money. His sense of entitlement was legendary. A longtime girlfriend told Isaacson that she believed Jobs met the criteria for narcissistic personality disorder. "Expecting him to be nicer or less self-centered," she said, "was like expecting a blind man to see."

Political rulers are narcissistic almost by necessity. A slew of American presidents, from Chester A. Arthur to Bill Clinton, have earned the moniker. Dictators, especially, tend to be narcissistic; you can't rule with an iron fist without thinking you're better than everyone else. A litany of world leaders have exhibited the worst kind of hubris over the years, from Napoleon to Adolf Hitler, Idi Amin to Chiang Kai-shek. Men have no monopoly on narcissism; Madame Chiang Kai-shek, the despotic ruler's wife, exhibited plenty of her own. Wellesley-educated and elegant, she could be charming at one moment and ruthlessly insensitive the next. One night at a dinner party, President Franklin Roosevelt asked her how the Chinese government would handle a labor dispute. "She never said a word," Eleanor Roosevelt later reported, "but the beautiful small hand came up very quietly and slid across her throat—a most expressive gesture."

It has long been thought that an effective treatment for narcissism is hard to come by, given the inflexible nature of symptoms. There's no pill to make people more amiable, and traditional therapy won't work if a patient doesn't show up or has no interest in participating. One of the biggest sticking points is lack of empathy. A recent study found an intriguing clue about how people with narcissistic personality disorder may differ in this realm at a biological level: Compared to a control group, highly narcissistic people had less gray matter in the left anterior insula, a part of the brain linked to empathy.

But empathy may not be as all or nothing as it seems. People with narcissistic personality disorder are capable of turning it on when they're motivated to do so for self-serving reasons. The novelist Ayn Rand, who abided by a philosophy of "rational selfishness," was known to be ruthless, dismissing people she had no use for, including a long-lost sister. (Howard Roark, her lead character in *The Fountainhead*, is said to have been modeled after Wright; when asked about it, Wright famously retorted: "I deny the paternity and refuse to marry the mother.") And yet at times, she appeared to care when it was a matter of self-interest. A friend once said that Rand "could be immensely empathetic if she saw things in you that were like her. But if she didn't see herself in some aspect of you, she didn't empathize at all. You weren't real to her."

Rather than view it as present or absent, empathy should be seen as a skill that needs to be nurtured in people with narcissistic personality disorder, says Harvard's Elsa Ronningstam, who is pursuing this approach as a new way of conceptualizing the condition. Several small studies indicate that empathy may be more malleable than previously believed, and that actively guiding people to identify with others can alter behavior. In one report, scientists found that when female narcissists were prompted to "imagine how [she] feels" while watching a video documenting a woman's experience with domestic violence, they reported higher levels of empathy than they had without prompting. In another, prisoners given a similar test actually showed more empathic activity in their brains.

A more discerning view of empathy could open new avenues for treatment. If empathy actually exists under the narcissist's bombast, therapists might be able to unearth it—and maybe narcissists can become less self-absorbed and more compassionate people.

⌐⌐

WRIGHT SPENT THE FINAL YEARS of his life overseeing construction of the Guggenheim in New York City, where he set up camp at the Plaza Hotel. Never wavering from his aesthetic ideals, the architect overhauled his suite, which he named "Taliesin East," with velvet curtains, Japanese gold wallpaper, and, of course, a grand piano. A *Saturday Review* writer who interviewed him there in 1953 described the 84-year-old architect pacing about in a gray robe, beaded green slippers, and an orange-blue scarf, his long hair flowing. In a booming voice, Wright grandstanded about his favorite subjects—the poetic elegance of Japanese art, the debacle of

American architecture ("Look at the U.N. Building—a great slab in a great graveyard"), and his ongoing efforts to "wake my people up" to the fact that without worthy architecture, there would be no culture. "They'd call that arrogance, wouldn't they?" Wright quipped. "Well, I suppose it is."

The Guggenheim, one of Wright's most iconic achievements, would take 16 years to build, from start to finish. On April 9, 1959, just six months before it opened, Wright died at age 91 in a Phoenix hospital, where he had been transported after suffering an intestinal obstruction at Taliesin West, a winter home he built in the Arizona desert.

The Guggenheim's debut that fall was met with both acclamation and disdain. By then, numerous tweaks had been made, including the addition of metal rods that allowed the paintings to be hung vertically instead of tilted back against the sloping walls. In a review in the *New Yorker* that December, Lewis Mumford extolled Wright as "a true artist, one of the most richly endowed geniuses this country has produced" before skewering his design. The color was dull, the concrete "sullen" and fortress-like, and then there was the building's "ruinous" interior, commandeering both painting and viewer. "If the outside of the building says 'Power'— power to defy blast, to resist change, to remain as immune to time as the Pyramids," Mumford wrote, "the interior says 'Ego'—an ego far deeper than the pool in which Narcissus too long gazed."

It is impossible to disentangle Wright the architect from Wright the boy, the husband, the father, the philanderer, the tyrant, the innovator, the narcissist, the visionary. He was all of these, driven by his unique tangle of circumstances and experiences. In the end, Wright drove his people into the ground and he woke his people up. In so doing, he created a towering legacy that lives on in the breathtaking structures he created—and the beauty he fashioned from nature.

Betty Ford

O N Saturday, April 1, 1978, former president Gerald Ford sat his wife, Betty, down on a green-and-white couch in their living room in Palm Springs, California. Gathered in a semicircle around the former first lady were the Fords' four grown children, Mike, Jack, Steve, and Susan; Mike's wife, Gayle; two doctors; a nurse; and a couple of close friends. When the kids had first arrived at the house, Mrs. Ford assumed that they'd come for a family visit, and she was delighted to see them. But she quickly realized that there was nothing joyous about this gathering; nor would it turn out to be an April Fool's prank, much as she might have wished it to be. Instead, the Ford family had joined forces with medical experts to stage an intervention in which they confronted Mrs. Ford about her dependence on alcohol and prescription drugs. "Mother, we've got something to talk to you about," Betty Ford remembered her husband telling her, "and we want you to listen, because we love you."

It was a stunning turn of events. Not even two years earlier, the 38th president of the United States had been serving out his term in the White House, where First Lady Betty Ford had gained national prominence as an outspoken advocate for women's rights, a warm and lively host (she once danced the hora after a state dinner for Prime Minister Yitzhak Rabin), and a beacon in the fight against breast cancer after she went public with her own diagnosis in 1974. Now, just as she was trying to adjust to a more ordinary routine outside of the Washington spotlight, her celebrated life was collapsing. For months, the Ford kids had watched as their mother's decades-long habit of mixing prescription drugs and alcohol sabotaged her behavior and her health. It was Susan, then 19, who decided the situation was dire enough to warrant an intervention. "I was scared to death," reflects Susan Ford Bales, but she knew something had to be done. Her mother was not pleased. "I'd never heard of an intervention, and I would just as soon have kept it that way," Mrs. Ford recalled in *Betty: A Glad Awakening*, her forthright and revealing 1987 memoir. "I didn't want to hear *any* of what my family was telling me."

But tell they did. Mike, the eldest, acknowledged the many pressures and demands of political life in Washington, but said that his mother's behavior was now harming relationships with family and friends. Gayle reported that she and Mike were planning to start a family, but they wanted their children to know their grandmother as a healthy and loving person. Jack talked about never wanting to bring friends home: "I was always kind of peeking around the corner into the family room to see what kind of shape Mother was in." Steve described his mother turning down a special dinner he had cooked one weekend. "I'd gone to the store, done the shopping, put the silverware on the proper sides of the plates, and she went and got another drink," he remembered. "I was hurt." Susan told her mother that she had always admired her as a dancer, but now she was "falling and clumsy, and she just wasn't the same person." The former president told his wife of 29 years that she'd become slow, as if she was "in second gear," and it had become "increasingly difficult to lead a normal life."

Betty Ford's initial reaction was resentment, anger, shock, and denial. "My makeup wasn't smeared, I wasn't disheveled, I behaved politely, and I never finished off a bottle, so how could I be an alcoholic?" she thought. "And I wasn't on heroin or cocaine, the medicines I took—the sleeping pills, the pain pills, the relaxer pills, the pills to counteract the side effects of other pills—had been prescribed by doctors, so how could I be a drug addict?" She collapsed into tears, but she listened. After everyone had spoken, the lead doctor in attendance, Joe Pursch, asked Mrs. Ford if she would be willing to go into treatment. She agreed. That night, the family sat down to a pot roast dinner. One week later, after detoxing at home and celebrating her 60th birthday with friends, the former first lady checked herself into Long Beach Naval Hospital's Alcohol and Drug Rehabilitation Service.

Within a few days, Betty Ford went public with the news that she was battling two substance abuse problems. "I am not only addicted to the medication I have been taking for my arthritis, but also to alcohol," she said in a statement released at a press conference. Reporters pressed Robert Barrett, a former White House aide and close family friend who was overseeing the announcement, for more details. "We've never had too much success in keeping Mrs. Ford's mouth shut," Barrett told them, according to the *New York*

Times. "Somewhere along the line she'll be saying what she wants to when she wants to."

Before long, she did. "Hello, my name's Betty Ford," she would tell others struggling with addiction, "and I'm an alcoholic and a drug addict."

⌒

WELL BEFORE BETTY FORD took her first drink, swallowed her first pill, or, for that matter, became first lady of the United States, she was a spirited tomboy growing up in Grand Rapids, Michigan, with two older brothers and a German shepherd named Teddy. Elizabeth Ann Bloomer, also known as Betty, or sometimes Bet or Bets, was born on April 8, 1918, the third child and only daughter of Hortense Neahr and William Stephenson Bloomer. By the time Betty came along, Mrs. Bloomer was in her mid-30s, and Betty's brothers, Bill and Bob, were seven and five. Betty Ford always assumed she was an accident; Hortense Bloomer liked to say that her daughter had "popped out of a bottle of champagne."

Betty Ford's recollections of her youth, recounted in her first autobiography, *The Times of My Life*, are largely witty, lighthearted, and endearing. Every summer, the Bloomers trooped off to their family cottage at Whitefish Lake, about 30 miles north of Grand Rapids, where her father fished ("we were served fish and fish and fish until I hoped I would never see fish again," Mrs. Ford recalled) and the kids played, swam, and ate. Betty Ford described her mother as attractive, her father as good-looking, and herself as "a fat little kid." At the summer picnic grounds, she would toddle from table to table collecting cookies, cake, and ice cream. "I just got fatter and fatter until finally my mother hung a sign on my back," she remembered. "It said, PLEASE DO NOT FEED THIS CHILD."

Betty's father, a traveling salesman for a rubber company, spent a lot of time on the road; at home, he was an early radio enthusiast who loved tinkering with his simple receiver. "Wow! I got Chicago, I got Chicago, come listen to it," he'd shout, and the Bloomer kids came running. Mrs. Ford remembered her mother as loving and supportive, but also a perfectionist who insisted on formal manners—young Betty had to wear a hat and white gloves on shopping expeditions. This did not stop her, however, from roughhousing with the boys. Football, ice hockey, wrestling—she was determined to try it all. "When they got to rolling on the floor, I'd be trying to pull off the one who was on top," Mrs. Ford later recalled. "I was a terrible tomboy and the bane of my big brothers' existence."

It was an innocent childhood, as she described it, filled with playful antics and goofy mishaps. Young Betty and her friend Mary Adelaide Jones invented a fun game at sleepovers: They would stand in the shower and "stick our bottoms under the hot water, to see who could outlast the other and get her fanny reddest," Mrs. Ford recalled. There was "garbage night" on Halloween, when the kids tipped over their neighbors' trash pails, whitewashed their porches, and soaped their windows. An avid dancer, Mrs. Ford remembered one disastrous early recital when she dropped a sand bucket while skipping around on stage, much to the delight of the audience. And then there was her first kiss, in fifth grade: John Sears, the culprit, pecked her on the cheek under a blanket on the way to a school picnic.

The earlier a person begins to drink alcohol, the more likely he or she is to develop an addiction problem later in life. Betty Ford's initial experiences were fairly typical. She first tasted liquor when she was 12 or 13 at a girlfriend's house. "Three or four of us kids tried it, said, 'Oh, how awful,' and went our ways," she recalled. In her late teens and early adulthood, she drank to be social and to be accepted by her peers, she wrote, but she suffered toxic reactions on several occasions—episodes that might have served as red flags. When she was 19, her mother found her moaning in the bathroom after drinking a rum and Coke at a hotel in Grand Rapids. At another time, she blacked out after downing a "purple passion" (most likely grain alcohol mixed with grape juice), and she once got sick after having a Manhattan with a cherry on top. "Now, with the 20/20 vision of hindsight, I can see alcohol did not agree with me," Mrs. Ford later recalled, "but in those days, we didn't even know alcoholism was a disease or that it might be inherited."

Researchers have demonstrated that addiction is heavily influenced by genes, which account for about 50 percent of a person's risk. Alcoholism, it turned out, had a hold on the Bloomer family, something Betty first discovered when her father died suddenly from carbon monoxide poisoning while working on his car in the garage. It was after his funeral that Betty, then 16, was told he had been an alcoholic. Because her father drank on the road, Betty's mother had been able to shield her children from the effects. She could not, however, protect them from the disease: In her autobiography, Mrs. Ford disclosed that two of the Bloomer kids, she and her brother Bob, would struggle with alcoholism later in life.

After William Bloomer's death, the family soldiered on with classic midwestern grit. Betty, popular with the boys, enjoyed a busy teenage social life with the requisite rounds of spin the bottle. But her true passion was dance. Most transformative were summer classes at the Bennington School of the Dance in Vermont, where she met the legendary dancer and choreographer Martha Graham. "I worshiped her as a goddess," Mrs. Ford later recalled. "To this day, I feel that shiver of awe and delight when she comes on the scene." Soon, Betty was studying with Graham in New York City and performing in New York shows, including *American Document* at Carnegie Hall.

Being a Graham protégé was a formidable accomplishment, but it soon became clear that Betty, who was also modeling and socializing with friends, was too distractible to commit herself to professional dance. "You can't carouse and be a dancer, too," she remembered Graham telling her. Betty was homesick, as well, and couldn't resist her mother's pleas for her to move back to Michigan. There, she got a job in fashion at Herpolsheimer's, a Grand Rapids department store, and became reacquainted with Bill Warren, an old classmate who had taken Betty to her first school dance when she was 12. Now all grown up and in the insurance business, Warren was a good dancer, a decent tennis player, and, Ford later wrote, "unlike some of the men I dated, he wasn't a bit stuffy." The two were married in the spring of 1942, when Betty was 24 years old.

It did not take long, however, for Betty to realize that they were ill suited. She wanted a house and a family; Warren was more interested in hanging out with his pals at the local hot spot. "No matter how many somersaults I turned," Mrs. Ford wrote, "it wasn't enough to keep him home." Their relationship became enormously strained, especially after Warren, who had diabetes, became severely ill and spent months recovering. As soon as he was better, Betty started divorce proceedings; the marriage was officially over in September 1947, after five tumultuous years.

It was that very same fall that Betty met Gerald Ford, former Eagle Scout, former linebacker for the University of Michigan football team, former lieutenant commander in the Navy. At 29, Betty was more than eager to settle down for good, and Gerald Ford—"good-looking, smart, and from a fine family," as Mrs. Ford later described him—was a much prized bachelor. In her memoir, Mrs. Ford makes no mention of how Gerald viewed her divorce, which was relatively uncommon at the time. But his own parents had divorced when Jerry was just a baby, and Betty's status did not appear to impede their relationship at all. (Mrs. Ford later recalled that when a *People* magazine reporter asked her why she had never told anybody about her divorce—which went public after Jerry Ford was named vice president—she responded: "Well, nobody ever asked me.") The two became fast companions, and within just a few months, he popped the question. "He's a very shy man, and he didn't really tell me he loved me; he just told me he'd like to marry me," Mrs. Ford wrote. "I took him up on it instantly, before he could change his mind." The two were married on October 15, 1948, at Grace Episcopal Church. Betty wore a blue satin dress and carried red roses; Jerry sported a gray suit, a carnation in his buttonhole, a handkerchief neatly folded into his breast pocket—and a pair of brown shoes covered in dust.

He had a good excuse. The groom was campaigning for his first seat in Congress and had forgotten to change his shoes after shaking hands at a farm earlier in the day. Against all odds, Ford had won the Republican primary several weeks before the wedding. Now, he was a viable political hopeful, leaving little time for anything other than canvassing for votes. Their "farce of a honeymoon," as Betty Ford later described it, was marked by an unromantic lineup of activities: one Northwestern–Michigan football game; one freezing Saturday night sitting in football bleachers in Owosso, Michigan, to hear New York governor Tom Dewey campaign against President Harry Truman; one Sunday morning spent traipsing around newsstands to collect the political headlines; and one car ride home to Grand Rapids during which Jerry asked his bride if she could fix him a quick dinner, because he needed to dash out to a political meeting. "A fantasy of me in a hostess gown, soft music on the radio, icy martinis, the smell of a delicious roast filling the apartment," Mrs. Ford recalled, "died a-borning." Instead, she made him a cheese sandwich with a can of tomato soup.

On November 2, 1948, 35-year-old Gerald Ford won his seat representing Michigan's fifth district in the U.S. House of Representatives. The newlyweds whisked themselves off to Washington, where they would live for the next three decades. During that time, Gerald Ford's unexpected career elevated him from congressman to House minority leader to vice president and, finally, to president of the United States. Betty Ford, meanwhile, juggled the ups and downs of political life and the demands of four young children. Despite her charm, ambition, and fortitude, Mrs. Ford would soon find herself reeling from the hurdles of daily life, combined with her own feelings of inadequacy. While her husband gallivanted off to Congress and traveled the country, Betty Ford stayed home, shuttling the kids to Sunday school and Scouts and soothing herself with a pernicious mix: prescription drugs and alcohol.

ON JULY 6, 1957, MRS. FORD WOKE UP "swollen and sweaty" and very pregnant with the couple's fourth and youngest child. She was miserable and cried so hard, she recounted, that she went into labor. Gerald Ford rushed his wife off to the hospital, but didn't stick around. He and their young sons had a critical engagement with Mickey Mantle at Griffith Stadium, the old D.C. ballpark, where the Yankees were playing the Washington Senators. The baby was cooperative, Mrs. Ford recalled, making her debut during the seventh-inning stretch. By the time her husband returned to the hospital later that day (the Yanks won, 10–6), Mrs. Ford was sitting up and looking smug. Having delivered the couple's first baby girl, "I thought I had accomplished the impossible," she recalled.

Susan's arrival meant that Betty and Jerry, who was then serving his fifth term in the House, were now the parents of four children under the age of eight. Although they had full-time help at home, Betty Ford was determined to be a hands-on mother. The family home, situated in a tree-lined neighborhood in Alexandria, Virginia, just over the Potomac River from Washington, was filled with marbles, Tinkertoys, and energetic kids. Mrs. Ford was a den mother, a PTA mom, a Sunday school teacher at the local Episcopal church, and a self-proclaimed "zookeeper," overseeing a menagerie of gerbils, rabbits, praying mantises, fish, chickens, turtles, and a bird. For a time, there was even an alligator living in the backyard, fed by the Ford kids decked out in boxing gloves. One cold fall day, Mrs. Ford purposely decided to let nature take its course; much to her relief, the reptile froze to death and was buried with a cross over its head.

From the outside, life at the Ford house seemed "like a Norman Rockwell illustration," Mrs. Ford recalled. But inside, Betty Ford was becoming increasingly dependent on alcohol. Like so many alcoholics, she was unable to pinpoint the moment she morphed from a social drinker into somebody "preoccupied with drinking." It happened gradually in a town rife with political fund-raisers, lobbyist bashes, and official dinners. "If you go to enough cocktail parties, you start anticipating cocktail parties, and then when you aren't going to a cocktail party, you want the same kind of lift at home," she later recalled. Alcohol helped smooth the prickly edges of Washington politics both on the Hill and at home, where Mrs. Ford encouraged her husband to have a beer or a martini after work to loosen up. She served guests cocktails before dinner, too, "because it made for more successful parties, or so I thought," she wrote. And when Jerry was on the road, which was often, Betty

Ford poured a five o'clock drink with a neighbor—or without—and topped it off with a nightcap after the kids went to bed. Alcohol became a soothing elixir, so much so that she would sometimes add a tablespoon of vodka to a hot cup of tea.

People who suffer from low self-esteem are especially vulnerable to substance use. Despite her dexterity in juggling Republican National Conventions with trips to the pediatric ER to fix broken bones, Betty Ford struggled with her self-worth and her rank in the Washington hierarchy. She was the classic 1950s woman sacrificing her own yearnings—and much of her identity—for her husband's high-powered career. Although proud of his political achievements, Mrs. Ford was bitter about his constant travel, and she resented the accolades heaped upon him when she was the one keeping the family afloat back home. "On the one hand, I loved being 'the wife of'; on the other hand, I was convinced that the more important Jerry became, the less important I became," she wrote in her memoir. "And the more I allowed myself to be a doormat—I knew I was a doormat to the kids—the more self-pity overwhelmed me. Hadn't I once been somebody in this world?"

Betty Ford's self-pity was fueled by deep insecurities. She was self-conscious about being "uneducated"—she did not have a college degree—and she doubted her own maternal fortitude compared to her indomitable mother, who always managed to bear her problems alone. "She was my strongest role model, so when I couldn't shoulder my problems, I lost respect for myself," Mrs. Ford later recalled. "No matter how hard I tried, I couldn't measure up to my own expectations."

Betty Ford's inner fragility would soon be taxed by physical anguish—a noxious mix for somebody vulnerable to addiction. It began around 1964, when she landed in the hospital with a severe pinched nerve, possibly the result of stretching too far over a kitchen counter to open the window. She endured agonizing pain and excruciating physical therapy to restore full function in her left arm. The bigger problem, however, turned out to be the drugs she received to manage her discomfort. She took the medication consistently and often. It was a different era, her daughter says. "Doctors were God and you did what doctors told you to do." When she got used to the analgesic effects, her doctors never failed to prescribe more. "I hated feeling crippled, I hated my body's rebellion, I hated that I was hunched over and had to go to bed at night in traction, so I took more pills," Mrs. Ford recalled.

In the 1990s, a movement to eliminate needless suffering and the advent of powerful new drugs—including super-potent opiate pain killers—spawned a surge in prescription drug addiction and overdoses, which have now reached epidemic proportions, according to the Centers for Disease Control and Prevention. But in Betty Ford's day, the problem was still in its infancy. This was, after all, the 1960s—the era of drugs as remedy for everything from boredom to birth control. While teenagers experimented with marijuana, doctors wrote millions of prescriptions for Librium and Valium, often for women who struggled with the tribulations of marriage and child rearing. (The Rolling Stones 1966 hit "Mother's Little Helper" included the lyrics "Mother needs something today to calm her down / And though she's not really ill, there's a little yellow pill.") Soon, Mrs. Ford was routinely mixing alcohol with prescription medications—not just painkillers but tranquilizers, too. In 1965, the year her husband became House minority leader, her resentment, frustration, and insecurities came to a head. Betty Ford, in her own words, "snapped" and sought the help of a psychiatrist, whom she saw for about a year and a half.

It was Gerald Ford's unexpected ascension to the White House that bolstered his wife's confidence in a way neither one of them could have anticipated. In September 1974, less than two months after Ford was sworn in as president to replace Richard Nixon, Betty Ford was diagnosed with breast cancer and underwent an immediate mastectomy. From the start, the first lady was forthcoming about her illness at a time when few people talked openly about cancer—especially breast cancer. The public reaction was profound: Within days, women across the country scheduled appointments for mammograms (including Happy Rockefeller, the wife of Vice President Nelson Rockefeller, who learned that she, too, had cancer). Betty Ford, the independent, strong-minded woman, had found a public forum as well as an outpouring of support. "It was great for my self-esteem," she said in a television interview. "I was kind of amazed that I was this important person."

The first lady's newfound status allowed her to speak out in support of some of the most controversial and critical issues of the day, including the Equal Rights Amendment and the legalization of abortion. Her candor became her greatest asset, even when it shocked her audience. During a legendary *60 Minutes* interview with Morley Safer, the first lady was asked what she would do if she found out that her daughter was having an affair. "Well, I wouldn't be surprised," she said. Many of her views clashed with her own Republican Party, and she was criticized for being too outspoken— so much so that some party loyalists blamed her for Gerald Ford's loss to Jimmy Carter in 1976. Still, the first lady's honesty, wit, and mettle appealed to a large swath of Americans, and her approval rating climbed as high as 75 percent. Many people were more impressed by Betty Ford than by her husband, and wore campaign buttons touting their allegiance: "Betty's Husband for President," "Keep Betty in the White House," and "Betty Ford for President."

Although Mrs. Ford recovered successfully from breast cancer, her problems with addiction lingered throughout the two and a half years that she and her husband occupied the White House. By then, she was dependent on painkillers, which she continued to take to combat her neck pain and a painful case of osteoarthritis. She claimed that she "did not drink alcoholically" in the White House—"there was too much at stake," she wrote in her memoir—but she might have a drink before bed or at Camp David on the weekends. It was the combination of medication and alcohol that caused noticeable unsteadiness, at times even making her visibly woozy and garbling her speech. Sheila Rabb Weidenfeld, Betty Ford's press secretary, recalled watching the first lady mispronounce and slur words during a 1976 speech at a bicentennial event at a Mesa, Arizona, schoolhouse. "Reality" became "relality" and "society," "socíciety," Weidenfeld writes in her memoir, *First Lady's Lady*. She even stumbled over the Declaration of Independence. The first lady had ingested a vodka tonic and a pill on the plane, Weidenfeld remembered; "Could that be it?" A reporter asked what was wrong. Weidenfeld's response: "She hates making speeches and the sun is in her eyes and she's tired."

Denial and enabling are common features of addiction. Betty Ford was able to justify and more readily acknowledge her dependence on prescription drugs, which ultimately included painkillers, tranquilizers, and sleeping medications, because they were given to her by doctors for legitimate reasons. "Pills are infinitely preferable to alcohol if you're trying to convince yourself you're an innocent victim," she later wrote. "Doctors prescribe pills, you don't have that excuse with alcohol." Doctors enabled her because of her status. "They didn't say no to her," says her daughter. "They didn't confront her, because of who she was." Friends and family enabled her because they didn't realize how dire her situation was, or weren't sure how to help. Gerald Ford later admitted that while he worried about his wife's substance use, he never saw it affect her ability to carry on her duties, certainly not as first lady. "I was what they call an enabler," he told Larry King in a 2001 interview. "I really didn't recognize it."

After her husband's loss to Carter, Betty Ford found herself in a vulnerable place in California, both physically and emotionally—a ripe time for an addiction to intensify. She was upset about the election; she was no longer performing her first lady duties and receiving the adulation that had boosted her self-esteem; she was an empty nester with all four children out of the house; and she was often alone as her "retired" husband traveled around the country lecturing, teaching, and consulting. Pills and alcohol helped console her, and they were readily available. "I had a gourmet collection of drugs—I did a little self-prescribing; if one pill is good, two must be better—and when I added vodka to the mix, I moved into a wonderful fuzzy place where everything was fine, I could cope," she recalled. At times, she was taking as many as 25 pills a day.

In the fall of 1977, Betty Ford's substance use problem became acute in a very public way. She had been invited to narrate the *Nutcracker* ballet for NBC television in Russia. Anxious about performing on camera, she took pills beforehand, presumably tranquilizers, and appeared sluggish on the air. One journalist called her performance "sloe-eyed and sleepy-tongued." Later, back home in California, she felt as if she were in a "fog," and a companion described her as "kind of a zombie" during board meetings at a local hospital. Her friends got frustrated when it took her half an hour to finish half a sandwich. Soon, she began turning down social invitations, and her husband made excuses. "I'd tell people you had the flu," he later told her.

It was after a tense Christmas that year that the Ford family decided it was time to take action. The intervention took place just two weeks after the Fords moved into a new home in Rancho Mirage, where Mrs. Ford had been unpacking boxes. She recalled kidding her daughter, Susan, about the timing. "You waited till I got the whole job done, and then you sent me off to the hospital. Don't you have a twinge of guilt?" she asked. Her daughter didn't hesitate: "You needed to go. You were sick."

ALCOHOL AND DRUGS HAVE LONG HAD a double-edged reputation—good at certain times, bad at others. Over the centuries, alcohol has been regarded as medicinal panacea and religious offering as well as ceremonial drink and social lubricant. In the 1800s and early 1900s, medicinal compounds now deemed dangerous were welcomed as miracle cures. In an infamous 1884 essay, "Über Coca," Sigmund Freud rhapsodized about the merits of cocaine, which he used himself, recommended to friends, and prescribed to patients for depression and sexual impotence. Around the turn of the century, cocaine syrups and lozenges were marketed to treat a variety of ills, including headaches and seasickness. Bayer cough suppressants contained heroin. Mothers gave five-day-old babies a spoonful of medicine spiked with alcohol and opium to calm them down. And Mrs. Winslow's Soothing Syrup, which contained morphine, was sold as a tonic for teething.

Today, our perception of alcohol and drugs has changed dramatically with the knowledge that these substances can be highly addictive and fatal. The CDC estimates that the harmful effects of alcohol are responsible for about 88,000 deaths and 2.5 million collective years of "potential life lost"—lives cut short when Americans die prematurely from excessive drinking. Prescription drug addiction, meanwhile, has become an urgent concern among public health officials as Americans swallow too many pills to dull their physical and emotional pain, or crush and snort the medicines to get a quick high. Overdoses of opiate painkillers like Vicodin and OxyContin, the most commonly abused category of prescription drugs, now kill more than 40 people a day in the United States—more than heroin and cocaine combined. The problem has increased most dramatically among women. Between 1999 and 2010, the death rate from painkiller overdoses among women quadrupled (it rose two and half times among men); a staggering 48,000 women died, most of them unintentionally.

All told, 40 million Americans aged 12 and over struggle with addiction. That beats the number of people battling heart disease, cancer, or diabetes. Yet the public's conception of the illness is rooted in bias rather than science. It has been more than 250 years since addiction was first described as a disease, not a moral failing, says Dr. Samuel Ball, president of the National Center on Addiction and Substance Abuse at Columbia University (CASAColumbia). But because the initial act of drinking or using drugs requires a conscious decision, and because addiction directly affects a person's behavior and judgment, it continues to be viewed as willful and dishonorable. Even today, people struggling with alcohol and drug dependence are dismissed as drunks, lushes, druggies, and crackheads. They are seen as weak, manipulative, self-absorbed, and lacking willpower. And they appear to make bad choices over and over again with no regard for the lives of their loved ones.

Researchers are busy trying to shift this common misconception to an understanding that they believe is more in line with modern science: addiction as a chronic brain disease. Evidence for this dates back to the early 1990s when scientists began to harness the power of brain-scanning technology to unravel addiction at its roots. What they found is that some people are biologically primed to become dependent on alcohol and drugs, and, at the same time, these substances can alter the brain. At a most basic level, alcohol and drugs act on the same part of the brain that modulates many of our desires. This "reward system," as it has come to be known, works by flooding the brain with neurotransmitters, including brain chemicals related to pleasure, such as dopamine. This serves a critical survival purpose: ensuring that humans desire food and sex so that we stay alive and procreate. The problem, however, is that this same circuitry can become overloaded with substances that cause harm—multiple glasses of wine, a handful of painkillers, an injection of heroin.

The brain's reward network is paired with circuitry that controls our behavior, and together they provide an elegant "stop" and "go" system. "Go" responds to cues (the sight of a vodka tonic) and anticipated rewards (relaxes me, liquefies my problems). "Stop" is responsible for processing the consequences of indulging (too much is bad for me). Scientists are now learning more about the exceedingly delicate balance between "stop" and "go," and they have discovered that it varies across individuals, says Anna Rose Childress, director of the Brain-Behavioral Vulnerabilities Laboratory at the University of Pennsylvania's Center for Studies of Addiction. Some people are better at controlling their urges than others, possibly because they were born with well-regulated reward and behavioral-control systems, allowing them to distinguish what they want from what's actually good for them. Others, however, start out with unstable circuitry from birth, weakening their ability to "stop" when they should. In either case, positive childhood experiences can enhance the balance of this system, while stressful experiences, including poverty, violence, and abuse, can undermine it. "We are at the mercy of our biology and our environment," says Childress.

Viewed this way, addiction is not a choice but a matter of how our brains work at a most fundamental level. Biological and environmental risks also help explain why many people fail to stay sober. Relapse is the great nemesis for people struggling with addiction; it is exceedingly common (rates range from 30 to 70 percent for alcohol and as high as 85 percent for opiates) and is tremendously difficult to overcome. That's because alcohol and drugs, like food, become ingrained in the brain as a powerful and pleasurable memory, which is triggered by cues—a favorite bar, a pill bottle. These cues are so potent, Childress has discovered, that they can register in the brain sight unseen. In a landmark study, Childress and her colleagues showed a series of drug-related images, including crack pipes, to a group of patients addicted to cocaine. The pictures were visible for just 33 milliseconds, far too fast for the patient to consciously see them, and yet the images stimulated activity in the brain's reward system. In patients struggling with addiction, Childress explains, the "go" system was engaged long before "stop" could say, "Wait a minute! What about the consequences here?"

Alcohol and drugs are especially alluring to people suffering physical or mental anguish, both of which plagued Betty Ford. In some cases, the best way to prevent substance abuse or manage addiction is to properly identify and treat commonly co-occurring mental health conditions like depression, anxiety, bipolar disorder, and schizophrenia as early as possible—before they fester untreated and people self-medicate. Once addiction sets in, many people find their way to Alcoholics Anonymous, the long-running support group founded in 1935 by an Akron, Ohio, surgeon and a New York stockbroker, both of whom struggled with alcoholism. The program, rooted in faith and abstinence, views alcoholism as "a progressive illness that can never be cured." Members, who attend meetings all over the world, must attempt to follow 12 steps, which include admitting to being "powerless" over alcohol and seeking a spiritual awakening. Opinions about AA and other groups like it, including Narcotics Anonymous, are complex and mixed. Some people claim that AA has saved their lives through fellowship; others drop out, often because they are uncomfortable with the religious undertones or unable to commit.

Methadone has been used for decades to reduce cravings and suppress withdrawal in people addicted to opioids, such as heroin and prescription painkillers. Other treatments reduce highs, cravings, and symptoms of withdrawal. The use of medications to treat addiction remains controversial, however, because many providers in the field insist that recovery should be a "drug-free" process, despite scientific evidence that medicines can help. Childress is most excited about therapies that might one day interfere with the biological mechanics of the reward system itself, stopping the urges dead in their tracks. Her research has shown that a common muscle relaxant called baclofen clamps down on the "go" system in patients addicted to cocaine, preventing the brain from reacting to cues, both visible and unseen. The ideal treatment would work on the "stop" system as well, strengthening a patient's ability to resist the pull of a drink or a drug altogether. "It would be great to have both going at the same time," says Childress.

Today, the best approach to treatment is often a combination of medication, therapy, and support groups, says CASAColumbia's Dr. Samuel Ball. Given the complexity of the illness, however, there is no easy fix. It can be challenging for clinicians to tease out addiction from symptoms of other mental illnesses and to know which condition to treat first. Many people struggling with addiction never even have a chance at recovery: Only about 10 percent receive treatment at all, in part because mainstream doctors are still not adequately trained to identify the problem or they overlook its impact. And then there are the most stubborn barriers to care: shame, secrecy, stigma. "The denial piece of this disease is so powerful," says Ball.

Relapse is most wrenching of all. Watching a child, sibling, parent, or spouse become sober and then regress leaves family members feeling raw and helpless. Addiction, as everyone in the field will tell you, is a family illness. George McGovern, former senator and 1972 Democratic presidential nominee, described this eloquently in a memoir about his daughter, Terry, who battled both depression and alcoholism. During the last four years of her life, Terry was admitted to a detox center in Madison, Wisconsin, 68 times, McGovern writes in *Terry: My Daughter's Life-and-Death Struggle With Alcoholism*. Even a treatment program at the esteemed National Institutes of Health couldn't save her. Just after she was released, Terry told her father that she needed to pick up a prescription at the local drugstore; three hours later, a bartender called to say she had collapsed after having too many drinks. On December 13, 1994, Terry, who had tried repeatedly to heal herself, was found in an alley behind a Madison print shop. The 45-year-old mother of two girls had frozen to death in a bank of snow. Terry's death left her grieving father haunted by questions: "What could I have done differently? What if I had been a more concerned and actively involved parent when she was a little girl, or a fragile adolescent?" Most fundamental of all was this: "How did a beautiful, endearing, quick-witted, compassionate and perceptive little girl grow up to become an alcoholic powerless to control or save her life?"

⌁

MRS. FORD'S EARLY DAYS IN REHAB were not easy. For starters, she didn't like the idea of rooming with three other women at the naval hospital; she was a former first lady, after all. Didn't she deserve her own room? "I had a bit of the celebrity hang-up," she wrote in her memoir. At 60, she was also older than the other clients, she was reluctant to talk about her personal problems during group therapy, and she wasn't interested in exercising. Above all, Betty Ford initially refused to accept that she had a problem with alcohol. "I could *not* say I was an alcoholic," she recalled. "I didn't relate to any of the drunk stories I heard." Denial, frustration, anger, crying, mood swings—she experienced every bit of it.

Over the course of four weeks of treatment, however, Mrs. Ford began to bond with fellow patients and share stories over coffee breaks and card games. It was the denial of a fellow patient, who said her drinking hadn't caused her family any trouble, that jolted Betty Ford to finally admit that she had a drinking problem. "Suddenly I was on my feet, and I said, 'I'm Betty, and I'm an alcoholic, and I *know* my drinking has hurt my family,' " she recalled. "Because I thought, by God, if she isn't gutsy enough to say it, I will. It surprised me to hear myself and yet it was a relief." By the time she finished treatment, Mrs. Ford later recalled, "I was beginning to be happy again."

In 1982, four years after successfully completing rehab, Mrs. Ford co-founded the Betty Ford Center (now a part of the Hazelden Betty Ford Foundation) in Rancho Mirage, California, with a friend, former ambassador Leonard Firestone. She was especially interested in making rehab more accessible and targeted to women, whose addiction problems often stem from trauma associated with men. From the start, men and women have been separated for most of their treatment at the center, which is rooted in the principles of AA—a powerlessness over alcohol and a spiritual approach to support and fellowship. Since the center opened, patient demographics have changed significantly, says Betsy

Farver-Smith, vice president of philanthropy. "It used to be that you were a garden-variety alcoholic and you drank excessively," she says. Today, patients span generations, and they are dependent on a combination of substances. Older patients, often cognitively impaired, arrive at the center addicted to multiple prescription medications; younger ones, many of them teenagers, raid their parents' medicine cabinets to get high.

Over the last three decades of her life, Mrs. Ford visited the center regularly, greeting new patients with her experience and her honesty. "I will never forget the moment I heard 'I'm Betty, and I'm an alcoholic,'" says Farver-Smith, who was treated for alcohol dependence at the center in the mid-1990s. "That was life-changing for me." When patients threatened to leave, Mrs. Ford shared her story. "Nine times out of ten, she convinced them to stay in treatment," says Farver-Smith. Mary Tyler Moore attested to this in her 1995 memoir, *After All*. The "permanently perky, perennially composed" actress, as *People* magazine once described her, checked into the Betty Ford Center in 1984 to treat her alcohol dependence. Like Mrs. Ford, Moore bristled at some of the rules and expectations early on, which included mundane tasks like keeping a clean kitchen in the dorm. One night, Moore packed her bags and snuck out to a waiting taxi that whisked her off to the local Marriott. The next morning, the phone woke her. It was Betty Ford. "That phone call saved my life," Moore wrote. "I returned on my knees, pleading for reentry."

Since 1982, more than 90,000 people have been treated at the Betty Ford Center, including a long list of musicians, sports figures, politicians, television stars, and Hollywood actors—Elizabeth Taylor, Johnny Cash, Mickey Mantle, Drew Barrymore. Mrs. Ford's status as a former first lady made it clear that nobody was too famous or privileged to become an addict or to escape the hard work of recovery, and today her facility is one of the most recognized treatment centers in the country. Mrs. Ford also served as a catalyst and motivator, prompting patients to think, "If she can do it, so can I." Above all, Betty Ford was personally committed to everyone's recovery. At holiday barbecues at the center, she and Jerry threw on aprons and stood in the Southern California sun flipping burgers. "The lines went on forever," says Farver-Smith, "because Mrs. Ford wanted to talk to each and every person."

On July 8, 2011, Betty Ford died of natural causes at the age of 93. Her funeral took place at Grace Episcopal, the same church she and Gerald Ford had been married in 63 years earlier. Betty Ford was known to credit her husband with giving her the voice to speak out. Getting married to him, she once said, was "the best decision I made." But it took Betty Ford, the midwestern dancer with grit and candor, to use that voice to tackle the stigma of substance use disorders and transform the lives of countless Americans. It's hard to disagree with Gerald Ford, who once told a gathering at the Betty Ford Center that "when the final tally is taken, her contributions to our country will be bigger than mine."

Charles Darwin

JUNE 1858 WAS AN ESPECIALLY trying month for Charles Darwin, both personally and professionally. The great scientist, then 49 years old and a devoted father, had suffered through the agonizing illness and death of his beloved ten-year-old daughter, Annie, in 1851, most likely from tuberculosis. Another child, Mary, had died in infancy, and now both 14-year-old Henrietta and baby Charles, the youngest child of Darwin and his wife, Emma, were sick with infectious illnesses. "Etty" ultimately recovered, but Charlie, then about 18 months old, succumbed to scarlet fever. "Our poor Baby died on 28th at night," Darwin wrote in a letter to his cousin William Fox. "What a miserable fortnight we have had."

Andy Warhol Was a Hoarder

Trouble often comes in cascading torrents, and this was certainly true for Darwin. During that same month of June, Darwin received an envelope by mail that would not only catapult his professional life into a state of unexpected turmoil but change the course of scientific history. The correspondence came from Ternate, an island in the Dutch East Indies some 8,000 miles away from Downe, the small village southeast of London where Darwin and his family lived. Darwin knew and admired the writer, a fellow scientist and world traveler named Alfred Russel Wallace; his keen observations about native wildlife in a remote archipelago might have been welcome reading under other circumstances. But this correspondence contained far more than notes from a naturalist. Instead, in a concise essay, Wallace laid out an argument for evolution that was shockingly similar to the theory Darwin had been crafting—but not yet published—for almost two decades.

Wallace's paper hit Darwin with volcanic force. There was no mistaking the similarities in the two men's ideas about natural selection or the reality that Darwin, who had worked tirelessly to perfect his arguments, might be beaten to the punch on his life's work. "I never saw a more striking coincidence," Darwin wrote in a letter to his mentor, the esteemed scientist Charles Lyell, after reviewing Wallace's work. An exceptionally ethical man, Darwin felt compelled to act honorably and informed Lyell that he would forward Wallace's paper to a journal for publication, knowing full well what that would mean for his own painstaking research. "So all my originality," he wrote to Lyell, "whatever it may amount to, will be smashed."

These colliding events at home and at work would have been stressful for any human being. But the impact on Darwin was especially complicated, because he was a man of chronically bad health. For years, the scientist struggled with a long list of afflictions, including heart palpitations, stomachaches, and headaches, and throughout the course of his life his trials and his achievements were often paired with pain, immobilization, and isolation. We know this from his letters, his autobiography, his methodical health journal, and the observations of family and friends. "If the character of my father's working life is to be understood, the conditions of ill health under which he worked must be constantly borne in mind," the botanist Francis Darwin reflected after his father died. "For nearly 40 years he never knew one day of the health of ordinary men, and thus his life was one long struggle against the weariness and strain of sickness."

And yet doctors could find nothing intrinsically wrong with him. So what made Darwin so sick? Since his death in 1882, biographers, historians, physicians, and mental health experts have weighed in with dozens of hypotheses, most of which fall distinctly into one of two categories: an organic or "physical" disease, or a disorder of the mind. Is it possible that Charles Darwin was battling an infectious tropical bug, picked up on his famous travels aboard the *Beagle*? Was it irritable bowel syndrome or cyclical vomiting syndrome? Or were Darwin's lifelong symptoms psychosomatic—physical manifestations of ongoing mental stress?

The list of proposed diagnoses is so divergent you may as well be comparing a monarch butterfly to a great ape. But one key aspect stands out: Darwin was a worrier. He fretted about his children, about his work, about his deadlines, about his reputation, and, almost always, about what ailed him. Darwin, it could be argued, suffered from anxiety, one of the most common conditions on the planet. The revered scientist, the man who boldly proposed that "man is descended from a hairy quadruped furnished with a tail and pointed ears," was altogether very human. Sometimes, like the rest of us, he was one big bundle of nerves.

CHARLES ROBERT DARWIN WAS A perspicacious naturalist from his earliest days on earth. Born in Shrewsbury, England, on February 12, 1809, he was the fifth of six children of Robert Waring Darwin and Susannah Wedgwood. Robert, a monumental man of six foot two and more than 300 pounds, was a prominent and well-respected physician, as well as a successful financier; Susannah was the daughter of Josiah Wedgwood, an ambitious businessman who founded the Wedgwood pottery company and sold his elegant dinnerware to the highest ranks of British society, including the queen. His family's wealth afforded Darwin a privileged upbringing, giving him abundant freedom to travel and pursue his passion for science. Financial security meant he could dedicate his life to deep thinking and analysis, ultimately challenging centuries-old assumptions about how plants, animals, and humans came to be.

Smitten with the outdoors, young Charles was fond of taking long strolls on the grounds of The Mount, the Darwins' redbrick estate in Shrewsbury. Once, he became so lost in thought while walking to school that he fell off a high-set footpath, tumbling seven or eight feet to the ground. "Bobby," as he was called early on by his family, also enjoyed fishing on the riverbank and wandering in his father's vast garden, where he helped record details about the flowering of plants. Above all, young Charles loved collecting. His stockpile included household items, like coins and letter-sealing wax, but he was especially keen on the earth's natural wonders: shells, birds' eggs, plants, minerals, rocks, and insects. In an autobiography written during the latter years of his life, Darwin reflected on his enthusiasm for nature and how it distinguished him from his four sisters and his beloved older brother, Erasmus, who became a lifelong companion. "The passion for collecting, which leads a man to be a systematic naturalist, a virtuoso or a miser, was very strong in me," Darwin wrote, "and was clearly innate, as none of my sisters or brothers ever had this taste."

Darwin's father has been described as an overbearing man in both personality and size (legend has it that he ordered his footman to test the floorboards in a new patient's home to be sure they were strong enough to sustain his girth). In his autobiography, Darwin described his father in glowing terms: His kindness was "unbounded," he was "generally in high spirits," and "he was widely and deeply loved." But his reminiscences were also peppered with references to a demanding side of Dr. Darwin, a man who was easily upset. "Many persons," Darwin wrote, "were much afraid of him." Darwin's mother, by contrast, remained little more than a fleeting memory. Prone to intestinal upset and headaches, Susannah Darwin began experiencing severe stomach pains in July 1817, when Charles was just eight years old. She died just a few days later, possibly from an abdominal infection.

Studies have shown that the loss of a parent in early childhood can significantly increase the risk of both depression and anxiety later in life. Little is known about the full impact of his mother's death, because Darwin had so little to say about her in his later writings. "I can remember hardly anything about her except her death-bed, her black velvet gown, and her curiously constructed work-table," Darwin wrote in his autobiography. In a journal he noted that "except one or two walks with her I have no distinct remembrance of any conversations, & those only of very trivial nature." Indeed, Darwin's earliest memory had nothing to do with his mother at all. Instead, he remembered sitting on his sister's knee as she cut an orange for him and then being startled when a cow ran by the window. Still, although he never expressed great feelings of loss from his mother's death, he was profoundly affected by the *way* she died—quickly and inexplicably from pain in her stomach—according to Janet Browne, author of a highly acclaimed two-volume biography of Darwin. Darwin worried incessantly that he or his children had inherited a weak constitution from his mother's side of the family, and he knew from her experience that sickness could quickly turn deadly. "With all the increased sensibilities of an adult, and then the passionate absorption of a husband and father," Browne writes, "he came to dread the minutest sign of internal disorder for the destruction it might herald."

Robert Darwin never remarried. In the wake of their mother's death, Charles's older sisters stepped in to help raise him, and, soon after, Dr. Darwin sent his young son to a local boarding school in town. Charles was not intellectually stimulated there—he later described the school as a lackluster place that taught learning by rote—nor was he a standout student. He often escaped and ran home to spend time with his family. Darwin later depicted himself as a "very simple little fellow," who was considered by his teachers and his father to be "a very ordinary boy, rather below the common standard in intellect"—a modest appraisal that hardly matched the scientific genius he would become. Darwin found ways to enlighten himself, spending hours huddled under a window reading Shakespeare. But his chief passion early on was shooting birds. "I do not believe that anyone could have shown more zeal" for the sport, Darwin later reflected. "I became a very good shot." At some point during his education, Darwin remembered in his autobiography, his father took note and warned Charles that his hobbies did not bode well for his future: "You care for nothing but shooting, dogs and rat-catching, and you will be a disgrace to yourself and all your family."

To set him on a straight course, Dr. Darwin sent 16-year-old Charles to Edinburgh in 1825 to join his older brother, Erasmus, at medical school. It was something of a family tradition; both Dr. Darwin and his own father had studied to become physicians. The Darwin brothers enjoyed each other's company, attending lectures together and wandering to nearby fishing villages. But Charles couldn't bear the smells and spectacle of dissection or the eerie quality of the cadavers, some of which had been robbed out of graves and sold illegally to the school for profit. He was haunted, too, by the pain inflicted on patients during surgery (general anesthesia had yet to be discovered) and by the sight of blood, a phobia he claimed to have shared with his father. Although he dutifully showed up to observe two operations, he fled in horror before either one was completed and never went back. "To the end of his life he feared the sight of [blood], becoming almost hysterical if one of his own children accidentally grazed his or her skin, and quite unable to locate or apply a 'plaister' in his panic," according to Janet Browne. "Though the children laughed at him, it was a very real revulsion." Darwin, who lasted only two sessions at Edinburgh, never completed his medical studies.

With medicine no longer an option, Dr. Darwin proposed an alternative career for his son: clergyman. The path would start with an undergraduate university degree at Cambridge, followed by the steps required to receive ordination from the Church of England. It should come as no surprise that Darwin found his course of study at Cambridge less than inspired; he hated algebra, "did nothing" in the classics except attend a few required classes, and summed up his time there as "sadly wasted." Two experiences, however, had a lasting impact. First, Darwin became infatuated with collecting beetles, which helped lay the groundwork for his later work as a naturalist. (He was so enthusiastic that one day he popped a beetle into his mouth so that he wouldn't lose it; the insect, less thrilled about this arrangement than Darwin, expelled a noxious fluid, burning the scientist's tongue.) The second critical development was Darwin's friendship with John Stevens Henslow, a brilliant young professor of botany. The two became intellectual confidants, taking long walks together and discussing scientific developments of the day. Their friendship, Darwin later reflected, was "a circumstance which influenced my whole career more than any other."

It was Henslow, after all, who sent Darwin a letter in August 1831 asking him if he'd like to embark on a scientific journey on a ship called the *Beagle*. The vessel's captain, Robert FitzRoy, had been commissioned by the British Admiralty to take the *Beagle* on a second voyage (the first had taken place between 1825 and 1830) to continue a survey of the South American waterways. FitzRoy, who was aboard the first time, was looking for a scientific associate to keep him company and to engage in exploration. At first, Darwin's father, who would have to finance his son's expenses, vehemently objected. Worried, among other things, that Charles would never commit to a profession, he called the plan a "useless undertaking" and a "wild scheme." But Darwin had an ally in his uncle, Josiah Wedgwood, and he successfully sought Uncle Jos's help in changing his father's mind. "The undertaking would be useless as regards his profession," Wedgwood wrote to Darwin's father, "but looking upon him as a man of enlarged curiosity, it affords him such an opportunity of seeing men and things as happens to few."

On December 27, 1831, 22-year-old Charles Darwin set sail on a journey that would alter the trajectory of his life and transform the history of science. The trip would also serve as a signpost for

Darwin's health. Just before departing, Darwin exhibited signs of intense anxiety, and several months after returning, he began suffering from the symptoms that would debilitate him for decades, including what may have been panic attacks.

⌒

THERE IS OVERWHELMING EVIDENCE that Darwin was sick, often severely so, for much of the latter half of his life. He referred to his ill health repeatedly in his correspondence and painstakingly recorded his symptoms in a health diary whose entries included specific complaints ("boil under arm," "slight fit of flatulence") as well as overall ratings ("goodish" and "poorish" to "well very" and "well barely.") Darwin's extensive list of woes featured fatigue, dizziness, eczema, boils, muscle weakness, cold fingers and toes, black spots, and even hysterical crying. But his overwhelming complaint was abdominal distress, with ongoing bouts of nausea, vomiting, and flatulence. Over the years, Darwin's symptoms have spurred researchers to propose an alphabet soup of diagnoses: agoraphobia, anxiety, appendicitis, arsenic poisoning, barnacle preservative allergy, brucellosis (bacterial infection), Chagas' disease (infection resulting from a tropical bug bite), Crohn's disease, cyclical vomiting syndrome, depression, gastritis, gout, hepatitis, hypochondria, irritable bowel syndrome, lactose intolerance, malaria, Ménière's disease (inner ear disorder), mitochondrial disease (genetic disorder inherited from maternal lineage), neurasthenia (nervous disorder), obsessive-compulsive disorder, panic disorder, paroxysmal tachycardia (rapid heartbeat), peptic ulcer, pigeon allergy, pyroluria (blood disorder), and social anxiety. The only thing anyone can say with any certainty about Darwin and illness is that he died, at the age of 73, of heart disease.

Andy Warhol Was a Hoarder

What makes Darwin's case so intriguing is that it exemplifies the powerful interplay between body and mind—the reality that fatigue and vomiting can signify an intestinal infection in one case and emotional upheaval in another. Or both at the very same time. Even without a confirmed diagnosis, though, it is clear that Darwin struggled with a sensitive disposition. This became readily apparent as the scientist waited to board the *Beagle*. The 90-foot vessel had been scheduled to set sail from England's port town of Plymouth in October of 1831, but was delayed by bureaucratic impediments and heavy gales until the end of December. The intervening months were "the most miserable which I ever spent," Darwin later wrote, as he struggled with ailments. His symptoms during this time included chest pains, palpitations, abdominal discomfort, and fear of dying, according to Dr. Ralph Colp, Jr., a Columbia psychiatrist who spent decades poring over Darwin's letters, journals, and manuscripts. Darwin felt "giddy & uncomfortable" in the head and he was eager to escape the predeparture bustle of preparations. "I look forward even to sea sickness with something like satisfaction," he wrote in a letter to Henslow as the ship prepared to depart, "anything must be better than this state of anxiety."

People with anxiety often worry excessively about what *might* happen and anticipate the worst—"everyone's going to laugh at my speech," "my headache must be a brain tumor." As much as Darwin was eager to take the journey, he was nervous about what he might encounter along the way, according to Colp: the close quarters on the ship, the coarse behavior of the crew, the possibility that he might become ill or even drown. He also felt uneasy about being away for such an extended period: "I was out of spirits at the thought of leaving all my family and friends for so long a time, and the weather seemed to me inexpressibly gloomy," he later reflected.

And he began to exhibit a fear about his symptoms—hypochondria is rooted in anxiety—as well as an obsession about his health that would reappear throughout his life. "I was also troubled with palpitations and pain about the heart," Darwin wrote, "and like many a young ignorant man, especially one with a smattering of medical knowledge, was convinced that I had heart disease."

The journey, which spanned 40,000 miles from England to South America, Australia, and Africa, had plenty of challenges, both practical and social. In letters home, Darwin documented the rough seas and navigational mishaps. He struggled with occasional bouts of fever, intestinal distress, a swollen knee, occasional boils and headaches, and, more than anything, severe seasickness. Darwin spent much of his time at sea nibbling on raisins (his father's prescription), lying in his hammock, and retching. Although he and FitzRoy fared well together overall and engaged in deep and spirited discussions, Darwin remembered the captain (who would commit suicide years later) as exceedingly temperamental, suspicious, and morose. Darwin missed evening chats with his friends and fretted about what would become of his endeavors after the trip. "It is disheartening work to labour with zeal & not even know whether I am going the right road," he wrote to his cousin in October 1833.

The young adventurer was mostly in good physical form, however, while exploring on land, which composed the bulk of the journey. He rode hundreds of miles on horseback, sometimes through hail and snow; he slept outside; he climbed into the Andean foothills; he hunted animals for Christmas dinner; he ate roasted armadillo; he survived an earthquake and a near-capsizing of the boat by a glacier; he even "saved his crewmates by rescuing a rowboat from a tidal wave" in Tierra del Fuego, according to his biographer Janet Browne. Along the way, Darwin collected some

10,000 specimens—plants, fossils, rocks, animals—and shipped them home for analysis. In the end, Darwin "proved the fittest and, in many respects, the toughest man on board," the British physician Sir George Pickering noted in his book, *Creative Malady*. No mention was made of the illness that would later dominate his life, Pickering writes: "He was too active and too busy acquiring new experiences."

The *Beagle* journey, scheduled to last two years, stretched to five. When Darwin returned to England in October 1836, he was a changed man. His father, upon seeing him for the first time after the voyage, turned to Darwin's sisters and said, "Why, the shape of his head is quite altered"—a comment Darwin took as symbolic confirmation that his mind had developed through the course of his *Beagle* pursuits. No longer foraging for a career, Darwin was now a world-traveled naturalist who had assembled evidence— even if he didn't realize it at the time—for his theory of evolution.

Darwin's health would also undergo a dramatic metamorphosis. Stress of any kind is a common trigger for anxiety, and by the fall of 1837, when he was 28 years old and living in London, Darwin had taken on a weighty workload. His many activities included serving on the governing council of London's Geological Society, finishing a detailed account of the *Beagle* voyage, and scribbling out his earliest musings about evolution in a series of notebooks about the "transmutation of species." He also began to struggle with poor health. "I have not been very well of late with an uncomfortable palpitation of the heart," he wrote in a letter to Henslow that year, "and my doctors urge me *strongly* to knock off all work & go and live in the country, for a few weeks."

Worriers fear the unknown and tend to have difficulty making decisions. Around this time, Darwin was also wrestling with a major question in his personal life: whether or not to marry.

A thoughtful and exacting man, he scribbled out the pros and cons under "Marry" and "Not Marry" columns on scraps of paper. The upsides, Darwin noted, included companionship and "the charms of music and female chit-chat." The advantages to remaining single: no forced visits to relatives, relief from the "anxiety and responsibility" of children, and freedom to do as he liked. "Eheu!! I never should know French—or see the Continent—or go to America, or go up in a Balloon," he lamented about marriage, while at the same time bucking himself up to move forward. "Never mind my boy—Cheer up—One cannot live this solitary life, with groggy old age, friendless and cold and childless staring one in one's face, already beginning to wrinkle." By the time Darwin finally decided to propose to his cousin Emma Wedgwood, he was taxed by his reservations, not to mention the pressure of his work. His proposal was less than a boisterous occasion. "Darwin was exhausted by the nervous strain," wrote Janet Browne, "with a bad headache."

The couple would go on to enjoy a solid and loving 43-year marriage, and Emma became Darwin's dedicated caregiver throughout his many bouts of ill health. But his wife could not heal Darwin—far from it. During their early years of marriage, the scientist recorded a slew of debilitating symptoms, including chills, trembling, weakness, severe flatulence, vomiting, and headaches. His poor health fluctuated with his work and with Emma's first two pregnancies. Darwin's aversion to pain and bleeding may have made him especially sensitive to the discomfort his wife was going through, according to Colp. The period before delivery, Darwin wrote in a letter to his cousin William Fox, "knocked me up, almost as much as it did Emma herself." Darwin also worried excessively about the well-being of his children, fearing not only that they had inherited a weak constitution but that they might be affected by the effects of inbreeding, which increases the risk of birth defects and illness. "My dread is hereditary ill-health," Darwin wrote to Fox in 1852, when his ninth child was almost a year old. "Even death is better for them."

Ultimately, it was Darwin's work—primarily his writing of *On the Origin of Species*—that occupied most of his time and his worry. In 1844, Darwin completed a 189-page draft of his theory, with instructions for Emma to publish it if he died. But 14 years later, when Alfred Russel Wallace's correspondence arrived at his doorstep, Darwin still had not finalized his work. The cause for "Darwin's delay," as it has been dubbed, has been scrutinized and debated for years. He was of course busy with his marriage, his children (seven out of ten would survive into adulthood), and other major writing projects, including a five-volume collection documenting the plant and animal specimens he had collected during the *Beagle* voyage, and four reports on the diversity of barnacles. He also needed time to analyze everything, from the breeding habits of pigeons to the variation among strawberries and pears. And he wanted to be right. Well aware of half-baked speculations about evolution that had already been published, including an account by his grandfather Erasmus, Darwin's account needed to be as tight as an Anchor Bend knot.

There is little doubt that Darwin struggled with feelings of anxiety about publishing his theory, especially early on. Known to be a modest and affable man who hated both controversy and the public spotlight, he knew that his proposition that the earth's creatures were not uniquely designed by a higher power, but had instead evolved and adapted over time, would outrage the most pious members of society, upending centuries of religious belief about divine creation. Darwin had lost much of his own religious faith after the death of his daughter, Annie, in 1851, but his wife was a devout Christian; publishing could upset not only the greater masses but his most loyal supporter at home. His theory, he wrote to a friend, amounted to "confessing a murder."

It was competition that would finally push Darwin to publish his work. Charles Lyell, who had received Darwin's letter with Alfred Russel Wallace's correspondence, presented both scientists' theories jointly at a scientific meeting in July 1858—one month after Wallace's initial communication had arrived. It was a respectable solution that received surprisingly little notice and gave Darwin time to move forward honorably. Over the next year, he worked tirelessly to finalize his 500-page account. He also felt sick. As far back as 1838, Darwin had drawn a connection between his brain and his gut, writing that "I find the noddle & the stomach are antagonistic powers, and that it is a great deal more easy to think too much in a day, than to think too little." Now, as he raced to the finish line in 1859, Darwin again attributed his physical distress to the strain of completing his "abstract," as he called it, and he longed for it all to be over. "I have been extra bad of late, with the old severe vomiting rather often & much distressing swimming of the head," he wrote to Fox. "My abstract is the cause, I believe of the main part of the ills to which my flesh is heir to."

~⌒

THERE IS A CRITICAL DIFFERENCE BETWEEN fear and anxiety. Fear is like a guest who shows up without warning and leaves quickly; anxiety unpacks its suitcase, settles into your brain, and overstays its welcome. The difference comes down to real and imagined threats. Fear is a necessary part of our evolutionary makeup—a hardwired reaction to danger that compels us to run from a stampede of elephants or a tsunami and gives us the energy to do so. Our stress hormones spike, our hearts pump faster, our blood pressure increases. Anxiety, which causes some of the same physiological symptoms, is all about perceived hazards, not ones that are actually staring us in the face.

Scientists have pinpointed the circuitry for fear in a cluster of neurons called the amygdala, located deep inside the brain. Studies have revealed that a damaged or missing amygdala changes the way an animal responds to peril. Rats with an impaired amygdala will hang out with a sedated cat—an animal they'd normally flee from—and even nibble its ear. Healthy monkeys placed in close proximity to a snake, real or fake, will withdraw, avoid eye contact, and take their time reaching for tempting food situated near the reptile, be it M&M's, Froot Loops, or cocktail peanuts (we *are* related!). Monkeys whose amygdalas have been surgically removed, by contrast, act uninhibited; they go after the treats quickly, despite the possible risk, and even show curiosity about an animal they would otherwise evade.

Human studies are equally intriguing. Several years ago, researchers tried to evoke fear in a patient whose amygdala was destroyed by a rare congenital disorder. They took the patient, known as SM, to a spooky Halloween tour at the Waverly Hills Sanatorium, formerly a tuberculosis infirmary in Louisville, Kentucky, which was said to be haunted by dead patients and medical staff. As other adult members of the group screamed with fright, SM smiled and laughed at the monsters that jumped out to scare her. She even startled one of them by poking him in the head. Later, she reported feeling great excitement—as if she were riding a roller coaster—but zero fear.

The scientists showed SM movie clips from horror films, including *The Shining* and *The Silence of the Lambs*; she found them entertaining, not terrifying. And even though she said she hated snakes and spiders, SM showed no apprehension when taken to an exotic pet store, where she displayed an unusual compulsion to touch the animals, reporting that it was "so cool" to hold a slithering snake and feel its darting tongue. Her curiosity was so great, says Justin Feinstein, the study's lead author and a clinical neuropsychologist at the Laureate Institute for Brain Research in Tulsa, Oklahoma, that a store employee had to stop her from touching a tarantula so that she didn't get bitten.

It is well established that the amygdala acts as a warning system for external threats. Scanning the horizon like a searchlight, it sends chemical signals to other parts of the brain when danger is spotted. But as scientists unravel the science of fear, they are discovering that the amygdala's role is far more complex than originally imagined. It isn't, it turns out, the be-all and end-all of fear. This became clear recently when Feinstein and his colleagues put SM up to a different kind of challenge. Given her prior reactions, the scientists expected SM to respond without apprehension when they put a mask over her nose and asked her to inhale oxygen laced with carbon dioxide, a standard laboratory fear test. To the researchers' surprise, SM gasped for air, ripped off her mask, and had a full-blown panic attack. Her reaction turned out to be far more intense than most of the control subjects with fully functioning amygdalas; they had trouble breathing, but less than a quarter of them reacted with panic.

Feinstein's interpretation of these findings is that when a threat emerges *inside* the body—you breathe in bad air or feel pain in your heart—the primitive brain stem, not the amygdala, takes over. Not only that, when the amygdala is working as it should be, it may actually serve to damp down anxiety rather than ramp it up. This seems to be corroborated in other studies, which have found that people who suffer from panic attacks have a significant amount of atrophy in their amygdalas. If a damaged amygdala fails to inhibit panic, Feinstein explains, the brain might overreact to things that aren't really that dangerous—a bridge or a crowd of people—and trigger a series of panic attacks that ultimately leads to a condition known as agoraphobia, an avoidance of places and circumstances where panic might occur.

Just as allergies manifest in different ways—hives, rashes, watery eyes, sneezing—anxiety disorders can appear in multiple guises, often in the same individual. The *DSM* lists 11 types of anxiety disorders, including panic disorder and agoraphobia as well as selective mutism (anxiety so severe a child cannot speak in school or other social settings) and the more common generalized anxiety disorder (pervasive and chronic worry about a variety of everyday issues). Today, Darwin's aversion to blood would likely fall into the category of a specific phobia; other common phobias include a fear of spiders, heights, and flying. Darwin was also apprehensive about public speaking, a classic feature of what is now classified as social anxiety disorder and characterized by extreme worry about being scrutinized and humiliated. In a letter to his son Willy, Darwin wrote that when he was required to read papers as secretary of the Geological Society, "I was so nervous at first, I somehow could see nothing all around me, but the paper, & I felt as if my body was gone, & only my head left." At another time, he noted that speaking for just a few minutes at a scientific society meeting "brought on 24 hours [of] vomiting."

In a report published in the *Journal of the American Medical Association* in 1997, two medical doctors concluded that Darwin suffered from panic disorder, an anxiety disorder marked by recurrent panic attacks. These attacks are characterized by a sudden onset of fear accompanied by severe physical symptoms that can erupt unexpectedly. Darwin experienced a range of features associated with panic disorder, the researchers wrote, including palpitations, shortness of breath (which he described as "air fatigues"), crying, insomnia, abdominal distress, and feelings of imminent death. In the midst of a panic attack, it is not uncommon for people to worry that they are having a heart attack and are likely to die. The doctors also described Darwin's own accounts from his health journals—waking during the night feeling fearful and experiencing "swimming of the head," trembling hands, and "attacks of sickness"—as experiences consistent with the condition. Darwin's illness "followed a waxing and waning course typical of the disorder," the authors wrote. "His attacks caused him great distress and interfered with his work and social life."

The doctors theorized that Darwin also suffered from agoraphobia, a Greek and Latin term that translates as "fear of open spaces." The two conditions are often linked (until recently they fell under one diagnosis in the *DSM*), because people who have repeated panic attacks tend to avoid the places and situations that made them fearful in the first place—a bridge, a crowded theater, an elevator, or being alone. In Darwin's case, he actively shied away from public appearances, scientific meetings, and social interaction, because participating in these activities had a deleterious effect on his health. Soon after their marriage in 1839, Charles and Emma moved from London to Downe, where Darwin put stringent limitations on the time he spent out of his home. "During the first part of our residence we went a little into society, and received a few friends here; but my health almost always suffered from the excitement, violent shivering and vomiting attacks being thus brought on," he later reflected in his autobiography. Darwin did communicate actively with family, friends, and scientists by exchanging some 15,000 letters, but his preference was to stay physically close to home with his wife by his side. "I dread going anywhere, on account of my stomach so easily failing under any excitement," he wrote to his cousin in 1852. His life was comfortable, he told Fox, but "it is the life of a hermit." Even a major conference held to debate *On the Origin of Species* was too much for him. He wrote a note saying he couldn't attend because of stomach pain.

A series of landmark studies suggest that key features of anxiety, which runs in families, are detectable in the earliest days of life. In 1989, Harvard psychologist Jerome Kagan launched a long-term study in which he observed how a group of four-month-old babies responded to unfamiliar people and toys. Some of the babies remained calm and relatively unfazed, but about 20 percent had strong reactions—they cried, they pumped their arms and legs, they arched their backs. Kagan and his colleagues followed those babies for two decades and discovered that the highly reactive infants were more likely to be shy, cautious, and anxious children and adults.

Baby Darwin might have made an interesting research subject. In his youth, he exhibited physical symptoms—trembling, chills, shivering, and intestinal upset—in response to both pleasant and unpleasant events, according to Colp, the Columbia psychiatrist. He left a dog show early after seeing one of the animals react to its owner's reprimand, telling a friend, "I can't stand this any longer; how those poor dogs must have been licked." After shooting his first bird, Darwin later recalled, his hands were trembling so much with excitement that he could barely reload his gun. Listening to music prompted such intense enjoyment "so that my backbone would sometimes shiver," he wrote in his autobiography. Like the highly reactive babies in the Harvard study, Darwin responded to stimuli in a very physical way and may have been primed for anxiety from an early age.

He would have been in excellent company today. Anxiety disorders are the most ubiquitous of mental health conditions, affecting some 40 million Americans. We live at a time when it's easy to become nerve-racked by the minute choices that freedom affords us (not just should I buy organic milk, but what *brand* should I buy?), by the economy, by terrorism, by the mobile devices that interfere with our sleep. Inner peace is clearly hard to come by, as confirmed by how many people are desperately trying to find it. Guess what ranks as the top psychiatric medication prescribed in the country? The anti-anxiety drug alprazolam, which goes by the brand name Xanax. In 2012 alone, 49 million prescriptions were written.

We may think, in the 21st century, that we are more nervous than ever—that *our* "age of anxiety," as W. H. Auden dubbed it in his 1947 Pulitzer-winning poem, is the most skittish of all. The reality, of course, is that human beings have been worriers for millennia. As Scott Stossel, editor of *Atlantic* magazine and author of the book *My Age of Anxiety*, puts it: "As soon as the human brain became capable of apprehending the future, it became capable of being apprehensive about the future." Indeed, by the time Darwin died, anxiety had become a kind of cultural affliction. At the turn of the 20th century, the diagnosis du jour among accomplished and upper-crust Americans was "neurasthenia" or "nerve weakness." Symptoms, which included depression, insomnia, migraines, fatigue, anxiety, and even premature baldness, were deemed to be caused by the stresses of the industrial revolution and an overtaxed brain.

A host of well-known figures were said to suffer from neurasthenia, including the James siblings (Henry and Alice, both writers, and William, the influential philosopher) as well as President Theodore Roosevelt. Often, they were treated with "rest cures" and sent off to bed. In 1901, a Columbia University psychiatrist proposed that Darwin himself had neurasthenia—and a chronic and severe case of it, the doctor wrote, caused by the scientist's difficult journey on the *Beagle* and a "life of hard intellectual work." If only Darwin had given up all work for a year or two after his return and "had lived a life of rest and diversion, free from the daily toil of writing books, correcting proofs, and correspondence," the doctor lamented, "I believe a cure would have been brought about and his subsequent life more filled with joy and alleviation than it was."

If only it were that simple. Throughout the course of his illness, Darwin consulted numerous doctors—even Queen Victoria's own physician—and submitted himself to a wide array of treatments, including ice packs placed on his spine, mercury pills, antacids, bismuth (the active ingredient in Pepto-Bismol), lemons, codeine, and electrical stimulation of his abdomen. His favorite therapy, at least initially, was the Victorian "water cure," which required spending several months at a spa, where Darwin sweated next to hot lamps, had his body rubbed with cold towels, soaked his feet in cold baths, and had wet compresses pressed on his stomach. The treatment also required getting up early, eating moderately, avoiding sugar, drinking water, and walking. Back home, he kept up as best he could, taking frigid showers, even in the winter, and cutting back on his wife's sweet puddings. Nothing worked for long.

Scott Stossel can relate. A "twitchy bundle of phobias, fears, and neuroses" from around the age of two, Stossel has struggled with severe anxiety all his life, including panic attacks and a slew of specific phobias—heights (acrophobia), fainting (asthenophobia), flying (aerophobia), vomiting (emetophobia), and even cheese (turophobia, because the smell reminds him of throwing up). Although he has sought and tried a host of treatments, including medication, hypnosis, and even whiskey, "nothing has been a panacea," he says. Stossel finds comfort in Darwin's story, knowing that he is "hardly alone in having both a mind and a belly so easily perturbed by anxiety." Plenty of others are right there with him. Barbra Streisand was performing in Central Park in 1967 when she forgot the lyrics to the song she was singing, prompting a performance anxiety so intense that it kept her off the public stage (other than small clubs and charity events) for almost 30 years. Football player Ricky Williams, who was awarded a Heisman Trophy in 1998, suffered from such a bad case of social anxiety that he resorted to giving interviews with his helmet on.

Stossel believes, though, that some of the traits associated with his anxiety, including his conscientiousness and fear of screwing things up, may have helped make him the successful person he is today. A well-known scientific principle known as the Yerkes-Dodson law supports his theory in its assertion that if you're not worked up at all, you won't ace a test or hit a home run. Nor will you succeed if you're so overly stressed that you become paralyzed with fear. The key to optimal performance: a moderate dose of anxiety that will keep you energized, focused, and motivated.

Darwin was, of course, very sick. Even if anxiety did help fuel his momentous achievements, his physical symptoms were often overwhelming. "I'm staggered that he was able to persist through his extreme debilitation," says Stossel. Today, treatment for anxiety includes psychotherapy, medication, and lifestyle adjustments, including plenty of exercise and more sleep. The goal, says Dr. Craig Barr Taylor, director of the Anxiety Disorders Clinic at Stanford Medical Center in Palo Alto, California, is to calm down the worry to a level that allows an engaged and satisfying existence. "A lot of what we do in clinical treatment is not really to get rid of anxiety," he says, "it's to help you find a way to deal with it so you can lead a full life."

Andy Warhol Was a Hoarder

IT WOULD BE FOOLHARDY TO ASSERT that Darwin's problem was 100 percent anxiety, plain and simple. It's entirely possible that he suffered from other illnesses as well, including Chagas' disease, irritable bowel syndrome, or cyclical vomiting, any of which could have been exacerbated by stress. Still, anxiety seemed to infuse his very being, entwining itself with whatever else may have been coursing through his brain and his body.

In the end, *On the Origin of Species* did not set off quite as great an uproar as Darwin may have imagined, in part because he dedicated a chapter to "Difficulties on Theory," which anticipated and addressed the concerns of critics. But there was plenty of public debate, which Darwin managed to avoid as an alliance of supporters stepped forward to defend his work. His health problems persisted after publication of his celebrated dissertation, but during the last decade of his life—as he turned his attention to far less contentious topics—his symptoms subsided, and he finally found relief. His last book, one of his most popular, was about earthworms.

In the early months of 1882, Darwin experienced chest pains. Emma, his constant protector, attended to him and kept him company. On April 19, he died at age 73 of what doctors called "angina pectoris syncope," or heart disease, after reportedly telling Emma that he was not afraid to die. By the end of his life, this kind, modest and brilliant scientist had become an intellectual celebrity. He expected to be buried in the churchyard in his hometown, next to two of his children. But in one of history's great ironies, the man who overturned religious doctrine with barnacles and pigeons and apes found his final resting place in a velvet-draped coffin at the illustrious Westminster Abbey.

For Darwin, nothing was ever simple.

George Gershwin

GEORGE GERSHWIN FAMOUSLY WONDERED if his music would outlive him. He needn't have worried. From the start, the composer's songs lit up the sky like fireworks on the Fourth of July—bright, exhilarating, refreshingly new. Composing at breakneck speed, he mixed the sounds of Negro spirituals, Hebrew chants, Russian folk songs, and the cacophony of an emerging new world. Dazzling tunes like "I Got Rhythm," "Someone to Watch Over Me," and "Let's Call the Whole Thing Off" seemed to flow in an unending stream. Once, when asked how his work was going, Gershwin responded, "Too fast!" His mind surged with ideas.

The clamor of life around Gershwin infused his soul, starting in childhood with the hubbub of roller skates on city asphalt, honking traffic, and spirited street singers. As a composer, he found melodic inspiration in everyday noise. The blast of French taxicab horns catalyzed the frenetic street sounds in *An American in Paris*. The clickety-clack of a train's wheels, the whoosh of its steam engine, and the toot-toot of its whistle ignited the pulsating rhythms of *Rhapsody in Blue,* the masterpiece he completed in just three weeks.

Gershwin, the man, was just like his music: electric with energy. He walked swiftly and talked quickly, punctuating his words with "staccato beats of his left hand," a reporter once wrote. At the piano, Gershwin's technique was masterful, his playing luminous and bustling. "He would draw a lovely melody out of the keyboard like a golden thread. Then he would play with it and juggle it, twist it and toss it around mischievously, weave it into unexpected intricate patterns, tie it in knots and untie it and hurl it into a cascade of ever-changing rhythms and counterpoints," wrote the theater director Rouben Mamoulian. "George at the piano was like a gay sorcerer celebrating his Sabbath."

Gershwin's early life predicted none of this. By all accounts, he was a restless, inattentive, fist-fighting boy who thought music was for sissies. His father predicted that he'd grow up to be a bum. Instead, Gershwin became one of the most prolific composers in history. He composed hundreds of songs, dozens of solo piano pieces, major orchestral works, scores for Broadway musicals and feature films, and even an opera. After Gershwin died of a brain tumor at the age of 38 in 1937, memorial concerts were mobbed to overflowing—from Lewisohn Stadium in Manhattan, packed with a record-breaking 20,000 fans, to the Hollywood Bowl, where automobile traffic was so snarled that luminaries like Fred Astaire had to set out for the amphitheater on foot.

Gershwin captivated the nation and intoxicated its soul. But how? What propelled the brisk tempo of his body and mind? And how did he morph from a feisty street kid to one of the greatest composers of all time?

⌐⌐

GEORGE GERSHWIN WAS BORN on September 26, 1898, at home in Brooklyn—one of 28 residences in New York City that he and his family would inhabit over the course of his meandering childhood. His parents, Morris and Rose Gershwin, were Jewish immigrants from St. Petersburg, Russia. Like so many of their fellow countrymen, they had come to America seeking economic opportunity and relief from religious persecution. Morris Gershwin was a jobhopper, trying his hand at a slew of trades, from shoemaker and bookie to restaurant owner and even Turkish bath proprietor. He was an amiable guy, "a real shnook," according to Gershwin's younger sister, Frankie. Gershwin was especially close to his mother, whom he described as loving and also "nervous, ambitious and purposeful." Although not the doting type, Rose Gershwin insisted that her children become fully educated so that if all else failed, Gershwin later said, "we could always become schoolteachers."

Unlike his shy and quiet older brother, Ira, George Gershwin surged with untamed energy. "George, as he himself will remind you, was the rough-and-ready, the muscular type and not one of your sad, contemplative children," wrote Isaac Goldberg in his seminal 1931 biography of the composer. "He was a merry nature, always on the go." The Lower East Side, one of the neighborhoods where the Gershwins lived, teemed with European immigrants. Like many adventurous young children, Gershwin roamed the city streets uninhibited, surrounded by the chaos of peddlers haggling over prices for pickles and eggs. A natural athlete, he played stickball and soon became his neighborhood's roller-skating champion.

The Gershwins had reason to worry about young George, the second of their four children (which included another brother, Arthur, along with Ira and Frankie). As Ira, the studious one, read classics by Horatio Alger, Arthur Conan Doyle, and Harriet Beecher Stowe inside the family home, George got into brawls in the streets. He stole from pushcarts, set a few fires, got kicked in the nose by a horse, and had at least one run-in with police after he urinated behind a wagon, according to his biographer Howard Pollack. Once, he reportedly suffered a concussion after trying to run away from an Irish gang. His aunt described George as a "wild boy." Goldberg's assessment was even blunter: "He was, frankly, a bad child . . . With a little less luck he might have become a gangster."

He didn't fare a whole lot better in the classroom. Mischievous and impatient, Gershwin considered school a nuisance and often got into trouble with his teachers and school administrators. He had trouble sitting still and paying attention, and neglected to do his homework. Some of the time, he just didn't bother to go to class at all. When Gershwin's teachers sent notes home, Ira would come to the rescue, noted another biographer, Joan Peyser, assuring the authorities that his little brother would do better next time. The Gershwin brothers' collaboration started early.

Young George, it would seem, was more rambunctious and unruly than other kids inhabiting the whirling streets of New York at the turn of the 20th century. Dr. Richard Kogan, a Juilliard-trained pianist and a psychiatrist at Weill Cornell Medical College in New York, has a theory about what might have driven Gershwin's behavior. Kogan has analyzed the lives of myriad composers, including Mozart, Beethoven, and Tchaikovsky, to better understand how their minds influenced their music. He presents his accounts in riveting performances, where he plays biographer, shrink, and musician all in one, weaving anecdotes and history with dazzling piano playing.

In his analysis of Gershwin, Kogan found classic traits of childhood impulsivity and hyperactivity. One spring evening, Kogan presented his hypothesis at a performance at the Caramoor Center for Music and the Arts in Katonah, New York. After providing an overview of Gershwin's early life, Kogan wagered that the composer might have met the criteria for one of the most prevalent modern-day diagnoses in childhood. If Gershwin were growing up today, Kogan told the audience, "it's easy to envision him being sent by his school guidance counselor to a child psychiatrist who probably would have diagnosed the young George Gershwin with attention deficit hyperactivity disorder, and might have started him on a psychostimulant medication like Adderall or Ritalin."

Gershwin on Ritalin? Preposterous. Or is it? Gershwin's fevered energy propelled him throughout his life. "Whenever Stravinsky was asked about Gershwin, he always said the same thing: 'That man is just one bundle of nervous energy,' " Kogan said. "You can hear it in his music." To make his point, Kogan took to the keys and played a fast and spirited passage from *Rhapsody in Blue*. "Could that have been written by somebody who was *not* hyperactive?" he asked. "Any of you know this Gershwin song?" Kogan went on. He started with a slow and silky rendition of "Someone to Watch Over Me," Gershwin's hit from the musical *Oh, Kay!* Then he stopped and turned to the crowd. "This is how Gershwin played that song," Kogan said, setting a pace so brisk it sounded more like Scott Joplin's "Maple Leaf Rag." Gershwin once wrote, "We are living in an age of staccato, not legato." Kogan put his own spin on it: "I think Gershwin lived in a central nervous system of staccato, not legato."

Anybody whose child has been assessed for attention deficit hyperactivity disorder (ADHD) will find Gershwin's early behaviors familiar. The condition is defined by three overriding features: inattention, hyperactivity, and impulsivity, which play out in a variety of ways. Eighteen symptoms are described on the ADHD diagnostic checklist, including fidgeting and squirming, an inability to focus and pay attention, interrupting others, talking excessively, and restlessness. People with ADHD often feel as if they're "on the go" or "driven by a motor." To warrant an ADHD diagnosis, children must exhibit at least six of these symptoms, and their behaviors must interfere with how they function at school or in social settings.

Kogan says his proposition about Gershwin is pure speculation, but it rings true to Dr. Edward Hallowell, a psychiatrist and ADHD expert who has been treating children and adults with the condition for more than 30 years. Hallowell, who has ADHD himself, frames the intense energy of the condition in a positive light for his young patients, using analogies to explain what's going on in their heads. "I say to kids, 'Look, you're really lucky. You've got a Ferrari for a brain,' " says Hallowell. " 'The problem is you have bicycle brakes.' " The challenge is sorting out how to control all of that power and energy. Using Niagara Falls as another example, Hallowell explains that the force of the waterfall is phenomenal—but it needs to be strategically harnessed to make it productive. "Until you build a hydroelectric plant, it's just a lot of noise and mist," he says. "But once you build the hydroelectric plant, you light up the state of New York."

With all that noise and mist, it's not surprising that children with ADHD can find it hard to concentrate. The irony is that they often turn to risky and disruptive actions—not because they are inherently drawn to mayhem or danger, but as a way to calm themselves. The external commotion relieves them from their own internal chaos. "People with ADHD are always looking for ways to find focus, and one way to find focus is through stimulation," says Hallowell. There are maladaptive forms of stimulation (setting fires or pilfering) and adaptive forms (painting murals or starting a business). The goal must be to find positive inspiration that works.

For Gershwin, it was music: his stimulation, his calm, his focus—his hydroelectric plant. Interestingly, music was not particularly important to either of his parents. Morris enjoyed opera, had a knack for imitating the sound of a trumpet, and whistled a pretty good tune, but that was about the extent of it. Rose Gershwin hoped her son would go into business or law.

Gershwin's two most important introductions to music took place outside of the family home. The first occurred when he passed a penny arcade at the age of six and heard the strains of an automatic piano playing Anton Rubinstein's Melody in F. "The peculiar jumps in the music held me rooted," he later recalled. "To this very day, I can't hear the tune without picturing myself outside that arcade on One Hundred and Twenty-fifth Street, standing there barefoot and in overalls, drinking it all in avidly."

The second turning point took place several years later, when Gershwin was about ten. At P.S. 2 elementary school in the Lower East Side, he heard Maxie Rosenzweig, a fellow student, play Dvořák's Humoresque on the violin. The notes wafted out of the school auditorium, riveting Gershwin, who was entertaining himself outside. "It was, to me, a flashing revelation of beauty," he later recalled. Despite a heavy rainstorm, the story goes, Gershwin tracked down Rosenzweig's address and arrived at his house, dripping wet, to announce himself as an admirer. "From the first moment we became the closest of friends," Gershwin recalled. When they weren't wrestling, they talked, eternally, about music.

Within a couple of years, around 1910, the Gershwins acquired a secondhand upright piano of their own, which was hoisted through a window into the family home. It was meant, initially, for Ira, who had started taking piano lessons. But it was George who leapt onto the stool, lifted the cover off the keyboard, and began to play. The family was stunned. It turned out that George, then about 12, had been teaching himself how to play on a piano player at a friend's house. He had also been tinkering on the keyboards at a local piano store where he ran errands, according to biographer Pollack. Hooked, Gershwin asked his parents for lessons. Music became his salvation. "Studying the piano made a good boy out of a bad one," he said. "It took the piano to tone me down."

It is a common misperception that people with ADHD are incapable of focusing. What they need, says Hallowell, is to find a passion big enough to rein them in. When bored, the ADHD mind will wander, "like a toddler on a picnic," says Hallowell. "It's forever crawling around the woods looking for snakes and lizards. It goes wherever curiosity leads it, without any regard for danger or authority." But when these same people are captivated by what they love, they become hyperfocused and can concentrate better than even the most quiet of contemplators.

This was certainly true for Gershwin. His formal musical education began with 50-cent lessons from local neighborhood teachers, then progressed to a Hungarian band leader, who upped the price to $1.50. But it was Charles Hambitzer, a talented pianist and teacher who introduced Gershwin to Liszt, Chopin, and Debussy, who turned out to be what Gershwin called the "greatest musical influence in my life." As he studied with Hambitzer as a young teenager, Gershwin began attending concerts, where he heard eminent pianists of the time and familiarized himself with a sweep of composers, which almost certainly would have included Mozart, Brahms, and Beethoven. The "bad boy" of the streets found himself consumed by notes and melodies. He listened intensively, "not only with my ears but with my nerves, my mind, my heart," Gershwin wrote. "I had listened so earnestly that I became saturated with the music."

Gershwin's musical ear was evident from early on. At home after the concerts, he re-created the melodies in his head and played them on his piano. "I was becoming acquainted with that which later I would try to interpret—the soul of the American people," he later wrote. At 15, Gershwin dropped out of school to become a "plugger" for Jerome H. Remick, one of many music publishing companies clustered together on New York's west side and known collectively as Tin Pan Alley. It was 1914, a time when piano patrons flocked to hear pluggers like Gershwin play new sheet music before they purchased it. Gershwin plugged at Remick's shop and in cafés around town, where he accompanied singers and observed what inspired listeners and what did not. "Syrupy melodies" and worn-out harmonies were starting to feel old, like "tasteless filler for equally meaningless tunes," wrote biographer Isaac Goldberg. They were looking, happily, for precisely what Gershwin could offer. "The café patrons, he saw, wanted snap and 'pep,'" Goldberg wrote. "And pep was part of George's nature. He had been made for the new day."

Soon, Gershwin was performing around town as a concert accompanist and experimenting with his own compositions. He published his first song, "When You Want 'Em, You Can't Get 'Em," when he was just 17. An early collaboration with songwriter Irving Caesar produced "Swanee" in 1919, which Al Jolson incorporated into the Broadway musical *Sinbad*. "Swanee" became an instantaneous hit and sold one million copies of sheet music, making it the top seller of Gershwin's entire career. The lyrics "How I love you, my dear old Swanee" could not have been more appropriate. The song brought the composer stardom and fortune at the age of 21.

George's brother Ira, meanwhile, had bounced around from one job to the next, including a stint as a cashier for a traveling carnival. Along the way, he started writing song lyrics, and he and George began collaborating. The two teamed up to produce their first Broadway musical, *Lady Be Good*, in 1924. "The Gershwin brothers," as they came to be known, stayed close in every possible way, even living together—along with their parents, brother, and sister—in an apartment on the Upper West Side for several years in the early 1920s. George Gershwin's ability to focus amid the family din awed the playwright S. N. Behrman, who visited the composer there. "It was a perpetual wonder that Gershwin could do his work in the living room of this particular flat, the simultaneous stamping ground of the other members of the family and the numberless relatives and visitors who would lounge through, lean on the piano, chat, tell stories, and do their setting up exercises," Behrman wrote in a *New Yorker* magazine profile published in 1929. "I have seen Gershwin working on the score of the Concerto in F in a room in which there must have been six other people talking among themselves, having tea, and playing checkers."

George, handsome and lively, had an abundance of girlfriends, a ten-year love affair with the composer Kay Swift, and a yearning to be married. But he never settled down. Ira did, but his partnership with George never wavered. He and his wife, Leonore, spent their lives entwined with George—either living with him in one of the rambunctious Gershwin family homes or residing in separate apartments on the same block. As Leonore once commented: "I never saw a greater love than the love George and Ira had for each other."

The Gershwin brothers collaborated on lyrics and music throughout their lives, producing more than two dozen scores for the stage—including *Strike Up the Band* and *Girl Crazy*—and for Hollywood films. But they operated on very different metronomes: one slow, one fast. Ira labored over his words; George knocked his tunes out swiftly, working in a fury, sometimes all night long. Sleepless bursts of creativity can look like mania, a key feature of bipolar disorder, which is sometimes confused with ADHD and at other times overlaps with it. But hyperactivity can also kindle the mind at all hours. Many adults with ADHD characterize themselves as night owls whose lively minds surge with ideas after the sun goes down.

Gershwin's creative powers defied the clock, inspiring him with a velocity that captivated the music world. His Concerto in F, for piano and orchestra, was written at the same time that he was working on two musicals. He composed *An American in Paris*, which debuted at Carnegie Hall in December 1928, in just a few months. If you see "a tall, slender young man with thick, dark hair and large brown eyes toying with a bowl of porridge at a marble-top lunch on upper Broadway anywhere from 2 a.m. to 6 a.m.," a *New Yorker* "Talk of the Town" piece advised, "you may be watching the recuperation of a popular hero from the creation of a foxtrot or a piano prelude."

Gershwin's lightning-quick composition of *Rhapsody in Blue* is legendary. One day in 1924, the 25-year-old composer discovered that he was committed to producing a jazz piece for *An Experiment in Modern Music*, to take place at Aeolian Hall in midtown Manhattan. Although he'd felt the stirrings of a new composition, it was nowhere near completion, and the concert was only a month away. A train ride to Boston ignited his mind with its "steely rhythms, its rattle-ty-bang," Gershwin reflected. "I frequently hear music in the very heart of noise. And there I suddenly heard—and even saw on paper—the complete construction of the rhapsody, from beginning to end."

As with stimulating activities, noise can be soothing to people with ADHD, because it engages a part of the brain that might otherwise be distracted, says Hallowell. For Gershwin, ordinary sounds became music to his extraordinary ear. Bursting with drive and focus, he completed his magnum opus in just three weeks. He was determined, he later recalled, to do away with the misperception that jazz had to be written in the strict time of dance rhythms. Instead, he composed with "unwonted rapidity." Gershwin called

Rhapsody in Blue a "musical kaleidoscope of America—of our vast melting pot, of our incomparable national pep, our blues, our metropolitan madness." It was performed on schedule, as promised, bringing down the house with explosive applause and three curtain calls.

Gershwin's energy, his hyperactivity, infused everything—the zigzagging melodies he orchestrated, the way he thought, the way he moved. He was always on the go, always in a hurry. He tap-danced while waiting for elevators, cracked peanuts during rehearsals for *Porgy and Bess*, and chewed compulsively on pipes and cigars, according to Pollack. Sitting was rarely a sedentary pursuit. The actress Kitty Carlisle remembered Gershwin poking her in the ribs during a prizefight in the Bronx. "I came out with my whole side black and blue," she recalled. Gershwin filled notebooks with melodic ideas that gushed through his mind. His curiosity was boundless, even when the subject had nothing to do with music. A pretty plant would set him off on a quest for information about what kind of soil it liked and how often to water it, recalled Kay Swift. "Anything he wanted to learn, he hit with a terrific sock," Swift said. "He just tore into it."

A legendary partygoer, Gershwin entertained friends and acquaintances late into the night with his exuberant and propulsive artistry. Mostly, he played his own compositions, delighting his listeners with his virtuosity and magnetism. His audience became caught up in "the heady surf that inundates a room the moment he strikes a chord," Behrman wrote in the *New Yorker*. "It is a feat not only of technique, but of sheer virtuosity of personality."

Gershwin wrote that American music must "express the feverish tempo of American life." His compositions did that better than anyone else's—and along the way, he may have rescued himself. Kogan, the psychiatrist and pianist, believes strongly in the curative power of music. The act of creating, playing, and listening to melodies has provided inner harmony for many musicians, Kogan says, including Beethoven (who suffered from depression), Tchaikovsky (depression), and Schumann (bipolar disorder)—perhaps forestalling the worst of their mental illness. Gershwin's fortuitous encounter with Maxie Rosenzweig, who became an acclaimed violinist, prompted a young street kid to channel his innate exuberance into the keys of the piano, forever changing his destiny. "The Gershwin story," says Kogan, "is one of the best stories I know of music's capacity to truly transform the life of a youngster."

⌐

ATTENTION DEFICIT HYPERACTIVITY DISORDER has been documented in the medical literature for more than a century, but one of the earliest and liveliest descriptions appears in a children's poem called "The Story of Fidgety Philip." Written by a German physician for his young son in the mid-1800s, the verse describes a "naughty, restless" little boy who can't sit still at the dinner table, despite his parents' stern instructions. "He wriggles, And giggles, And then, I declare, Swings backwards and forwards, And tilts up his chair, Just like any rocking horse—'Philip! I am getting cross!' " Fidgety Phil soon became an allegory for ADHD and was even analyzed by contemporary medical researchers to refute the notion that the disorder is an "invention" of modern times.

ADHD was initially documented as a clinical condition in the medical literature in 1902, when a British pediatrician named George Still described a cluster of children, most of them boys, who showed "a quite abnormal incapacity for sustained attention" and an immediate need for gratification, no matter the consequences. They were not, however, intellectually impaired, but instead were "as bright and intelligent as any child could be." Over the next several decades, researchers documented similar symptoms in other children, amassing enough evidence for an official diagnosis in 1968, when the condition first appeared in the *DSM* as "hyperkinetic reaction of childhood." It was redefined as attention deficit hyperactivity disorder in 1987.

Researchers have found that ADHD, like other mental health conditions, runs in families, and they are searching for genes that may make some people more susceptible. Evidence suggests that preemies are at greater risk, as are babies born to mothers who smoked or consumed alcohol during pregnancy. Lead exposure, which is toxic to the growing brain and is linked to decreased IQ, has been associated with ADHD symptoms as well.

Does an ADHD brain *look* different? Scientists have discovered that the development of brain regions that control thinking, planning, and attention are delayed in kids with ADHD; one area does not develop fully until about age 10, compared to age 7 in unaffected kids. ADHD brains also show less mature connections between an area responsible for internal thoughts, including daydreaming, and an area that allows us to focus on tasks and get things done. The end result: distraction infringing on focus.

Despite these intriguing findings, there are few mental health conditions as heavily critiqued and controversial as ADHD, especially when it comes to kids. Today, one in ten children between the ages of 4 and 17 will receive a diagnosis of ADHD, and that number continues to rise. Critics charge that the condition, which is diagnosed in almost three times as many boys as girls, pathologizes normal childhood exuberance. Fidgeting with a pencil? Running around when you're not supposed to? Unable to pay attention? Everyone can relate, especially in our fast-paced, Internet-driven, instant-messaging world. With sensory overload all around us, who has time to concentrate? Long before ADHD became a go-to diagnosis, critics charge, kids were allowed to be kids. They weren't hauled off to the school psychologist.

The biggest concern is that children are being overmedicated. The condition is most often treated with stimulant drugs, which increase the level of dopamine, a brain chemical that is linked to sleep, mood, attention, and learning. Three and a half million American children now take ADHD medications, up from about 600,000 in 1990. Although the drugs can help some kids focus and excel socially and academically, they don't always work and can have serious side effects, including sleep problems, headaches, and irritability. The most extreme critics assert that ADHD isn't even real but has instead been manufactured by a profit-hungry pharmaceutical industry.

Mental health experts who treat children with ADHD struggle with these perceptions. Hallowell acknowledges that it can be difficult to tease out a true case, given the distracted lives our children lead. "But that doesn't mean ADHD doesn't exist," he says. "It just means you have to be careful when you make the diagnosis." This requires taking a meticulous history from parents and teachers and being judicious about prescribing drugs before trying alternative therapies, including behavioral and social skills training, exercise, and meditation.

Although not widely perceived as a debilitating condition, ADHD can in some cases cause severe distress. Children who are the most distractible cannot focus on schoolwork, and are often accused of being lazy, and badgered to shape up. Girls, especially, are often overlooked because their symptoms can make them look spacey or dreamy. Without help, these kids fall behind academically and lose self-esteem. Impulsive and hyperactive students disrupt classrooms and annoy their peers, making it difficult to form friendships. Viewed as troublemakers, they get punished and sent to the principal. Over time, the failures stack up. Children with ADHD are at risk for developing other mental health conditions, including depression, anxiety, and, later, substance use disorders. "It can be utterly crippling," says Hallowell.

ADHD can vary over a life span. In some cases, symptoms persist; in others, children appear to outgrow the condition by adulthood. Gershwin's early impulsivity receded, but his hyperactivity seems to have endured, says Kogan. Adults with ADHD sometimes discover that the problems they battle—forgetfulness, disorganization, restlessness—also come with favorable attributes: creativity, charisma, quick-wittedness, and abundant enthusiasm. People with ADHD are often risk-takers who think out of the box and burst with ideas. They're athletes, performers, teachers, journalists, Nobel Prize winners, and entrepreneurs. Michael Phelps applied his ADHD jumpiness to swimming and won 18 Olympic gold medals. David Neeleman, a college dropout, credits his ADHD brain with giving him the innovative vision to create JetBlue Airways. Thomas Edison, who had characteristics of ADHD, was pulled out of school for being inattentive. He gave the world light.

Hallowell is leading the charge for a positive conception of the condition. Rather than characterize ADHD solely as a disorder, he views it as the ultimate "American trait," rooted in the restlessness, originality, and vision of our earliest settlers. Gershwin embodied this vision. His rhythms were fresh and his melodies groundbreaking, meshing classical harmony with blues. Filled with color and humor, Gershwin's music tickled, provoked, and stretched the imagination and ear of its listener. "He broke the rules and created a whole new genre," says Hallowell. In 1925, when he was just 27 years old, the *New Yorker* pronounced Gershwin "new blood, beyond question." Four years later, in 1929, the financier Otto Kahn, a friend of Gershwin's, likened the composer to another trailblazer of his time: "George Gershwin is a leader of young America in music, in the same sense in which Lindbergh is the leader of young America in aviation," he wrote.

For Gershwin, it *was* all about America—its people, its voices, its cadences, its patchwork of personalities. He captured every morsel of it by embracing the dynamism of the streets while reaching high into the sky. "American music means to me something very specific, something very tangible. It is something indigenous, something autochthonous, something deeply rooted in our soil," Gershwin wrote in 1929. "In our music we must be able to catch a glimpse of our skyscrapers to feel that overwhelming burst of energy which is bottled in our life, to hear that chaos of noises which suffuses the air of our modern American city."

⌒

BY THE END OF HIS SHORT LIFE, Gershwin had become one of music's most ambitious and admired composers. It was not always easy. Despite seeming effortless, making music was sometimes a nerve-racking affair. "There are times when a phrase of music will cost me many hours of internal sweating," Gershwin wrote in 1930, when he was 31. "Rhythms romp through my brain, but they're not easy to capture and keep." Friends later recalled that beneath Gershwin's luminous joy, a brooding quality lurked, and he suffered from bouts of depression. "George was lonely inside himself," his sister said.

When he was 35, Gershwin sought out the counsel of a well-known psychoanalyst. For years, he had suffered from "composer's stomach"—indigestion and other intestinal problems—which he linked to the 1922 debut of his opera, *Blue Monday Blues*. And he was struggling with his indecision over whether or not to marry his great love, Kay Swift. He also hoped to delve deeper into his soul. "I want to know myself so I can know others," Gershwin said.

In the final year of his life, Gershwin was living in Los Angeles, where he and Ira had moved to write the score for *Shall We Dance*, the movie musical starring Ginger Rogers and Fred Astaire. Ira liked the sunny and slow pace of California; George wanted to go back to the dynamism of New York. He never got the chance. It was in Hollywood that Gershwin began to develop headaches, which became increasingly severe. In early 1937, Gershwin suffered a blackout during an appearance with the Los Angeles Philharmonic. He complained of smelling burning rubber and experienced repeated dizzy spells. A medical checkup in June found nothing unusual, and the normally vital composer, deemed nervous and overworked, was given a diagnosis of probable "hysteria." Over the next two weeks, his symptoms worsened, and he fell into a coma on July 9. Only then did neurosurgeons discover his brain tumor. Gershwin did not survive a five-hour emergency surgery and died on the morning of July 11, 1937.

Just a few months earlier, Gershwin had told his sister that he had not "scratched the surface" of what he wanted to do. The intrepid composer had taken his audiences from French cafés and taxicabs (in the lyrical and jubilant *An American in Paris*) to the tenements of Catfish Row (in his soulful opera *Porgy and Bess*). Until the end, his mind galloped forward with the next great idea—another opera, a string quartet, a symphony, a ballet.

Although he died tragically young, Gershwin's imprint on music was monumental. Indeed, it outlived him. "The world will always remember George Gershwin," Rouben Mamoulian wrote after Gershwin's death. "His music will remind them. As long as people dance and sing and play, as long as concert halls and radio remain on this earth—George Gershwin remains on this earth."

Fyodor Dostoevsky

THROUGHOUT HISTORY, many of the most powerful and incisive depictions of mental illness appear in great works of literature. Consider Shakespeare, revered by many as one of the world's greatest psychologists. The 16th-century playwright's dramas are rich with dramatic portrayals of madness. Macbeth suffers from delusions, hallucinations, and paranoia. Hamlet articulates key characteristics of depression, including emptiness and worthlessness. King Lear has been diagnosed with everything from senile dementia to bipolar disorder with psychotic features.

Enter Fyodor Dostoevsky, the great 19th-century essayist and novelist whose numerous works include *The Idiot*, *Crime and Punishment*, and *The Brothers Karamazov*. His masterpieces, drenched in the foibles of humanity, catapulted Dostoevsky into the highest ranks of Russian literature and left an enduring mark on Western writing, influencing authors as diverse as Friedrich Nietzsche, Ernest Hemingway, and Virginia Woolf. With his razor-sharp insight into the moods and minds of his countrymen, Dostoevsky crafted characters that throb with every human emotion from despair, rage, and shame to exuberance and exultation. Freud, the psychoanalysis pioneer, called *The Brothers Karamazov*, with its dramatic portrayal of three men and their father's murder, "the most magnificent novel ever written."

Dostoevsky's ability to penetrate human psychology would turn out to be his salvation during one of many financial crises in his life. In 1865, the author, 43 years old and besieged by a mountain of debt, agreed to a preposterous proposition from a publisher: to write a new novel in little more than a year. Desperate to meet his deadline, he turned to a plot that he could describe with flawless precision: addictive gambling.

For ten years of his life, Dostoevsky was a compulsive gambler, gouging both his wallet and his relationships. Drawing on this experience, the writer set his short novel *The Gambler* in the fictional resort town of Roulettenburg; his protagonist, Alexey Ivanovich, becomes tangled up in the delusional mind games that drive gambling addicts. Like Dostoevsky, Alexey Ivanovich is unable to walk away when he is ahead. Instead, he convinces himself that he knows how to beat the system, bets again, loses, and sinks deeper into the red.

Can too much roulette playing constitute a mental disorder? Yes, according to the latest version of the *DSM*. Researchers have found that compulsive gambling strikes at areas of the brain that are similar to those activated by addictive drugs. Marking a major shift in how psychiatrists view the condition, gambling disorder is the first "behavioral addiction" to emerge as a distinct diagnosis similar to substance use disorders.

You can't drink it, smoke it, snort it, or inject it, but money can seriously mess with your mind. Dostoevsky—the writer, the political activist, the addicted gambler—knew this better than anyone.

⌇

FYODOR MIKHAILOVICH DOSTOEVSKY WAS BORN, aptly enough, at the Mariinsky Hospital for the Poor in Moscow on November 11, 1821. His forebears once belonged to the great Lithuanian nobility, but the family had fallen on hard times long before Fyodor arrived on the scene. Both his grandfather and great-grandfather were priests, ranking low on the social hierarchy. His father, Mikhail Andreevich Dostoevsky, was a physician—a profession that brought him honor but not a great deal of money. Dr. Dostoevsky's dedicated service had nudged him up in society's ranks, and though the family would never achieve the upper-crust status of their long-gone relatives, he remained determined to keep up appearances, spending the little cash he had to hire servants and purchase a modest summer estate in the countryside. Most of the year, however, the family lived in a cramped apartment near a cemetery for criminals and the hospital, where disease and poverty collided every day. Not exactly breeding ground for Russian nobility.

Dr. Dostoevsky, a stern, disciplined man with rough features and a flaring temper, suffered from epilepsy as well as terrible headaches and bouts of melancholy triggered by bad weather. He was "naggingly unhappy" and suspicious of the people around him, according to his esteemed biographer Joseph Frank. Dostoevsky's mother, Maria Feodorovna, by contrast, was warm, loving, and upbeat—a woman of "natural gaiety," as she once described herself. Dostoevsky and his older brother, Mikhail, who became the writer's confidant and literary partner, spent much needed respites with their mother at their treasured country home. From his mother, Dostoevsky learned about compassion and the Bible; his father bequeathed to him a propensity for epilepsy, anxiety, and a fitful temper.

When he was just 15 years old, two monumental events transpired in Dostoevsky's life. First, his beloved mother died of tuberculosis, a disease she had battled for several years. Then Dostoevsky's father sent him off to the Academy of Military Engineers in St. Petersburg. The goal was to prepare his son for a financially secure career—but it did not align with Dostoevsky's interests. Evening reading sessions in the family home had introduced young Fyodor to the great works of Russian writers and poets, as well as the stories of English novelist Ann Radcliffe, which made him "agape with ecstasy and terror," as he would later recall. He wanted to be a writer, not an engineer.

It was around this time that Dostoevsky's dysfunctional relationship with money began. Despite financial assistance from wealthy relatives, Dr. Dostoevsky struggled to cover the assorted expenses of his son's education. His son, however, never hesitated to send home letters requesting more rubles. "How bitter it is to have to ask my flesh and blood a favor which so heavily oppresses," he wrote, with the tone of exaggerated humility in which he addressed his father. "Were I but free and independent, I should never have asked you for so much as a kopeck." Dostoevsky reported that he needed the money to buy an extra pair of boots, a locker for his books, and his own personal stash of tea—but none of these items were vital to his survival. He simply wanted to fit in with his wealthier peers. His father never said no, but in what would turn out to be the last letter he wrote to Fyodor before he died, Dr. Dostoevsky reported that drought and heat had decimated the estate's farm harvest, and he made it clear how little he had to spare. "After this, can you continue to grumble at your father for not sending you money?" he wrote.

During his student years, Dostoevsky escaped the drudgeries of engineering by discussing great works of literature—Homer, Shakespeare, Schiller—with a like-minded friend and poet named Ivan Shidlovsky. This was the world he was determined to inhabit. In 1841, after finishing his preliminary studies at the academy, 19-year-old Dostoevsky earned a commission, which provided a salary on top of a stipend he was receiving from his family's estate after his father's death. Now free to live away from school grounds, Dostoevsky indulged in the cultural delights of St. Petersburg, attending operas, concerts, plays, and ballets at the Alexandrinsky Theatre. "All of these amusements, of course, required a liberal supply of funds, and Dostoevsky was chronically short of cash," writes biographer Frank. Scrambling to cover the costs, Dostoevsky got into the bad habit of asking for an advance on his earnings, and took out loans at very high interest rates. His money troubles were well under way.

From his earliest adult years, the young intellectual lived beyond his means, at one point renting an enormous apartment that contained just a couch, a desk and a few chairs. Igor Riesenkampf, a young doctor who lived with him for a time, discovered that Dostoevsky was subsisting largely on bread and milk, which he obtained on credit from the neighborhood grocer. One day, Riesenkampf found his roommate pacing happily in his room with 100 rubles in hand; soon after, Dostoevsky asked Riesenkampf for a five-ruble loan. "It turned out that most of the sum was spent paying for previous debts," Riesenkampf reported. "The remaining money was all but lost yesterday at billiards, and the last small portion was simply stolen by his partner in the game."

Andy Warhol Was a Hoarder

After graduating from the military academy in 1843, Dostoevsky was assigned to a drafting position with the St. Petersburg Engineering Command, but it wouldn't last long. By then, the aspiring writer was spending his free time translating works of literature and writing his own fiction. Fed up with engineering and determined to get published, Dostoevsky quit his position after just one year, renouncing his salary for literary freedom. "I resigned because I just had to resign," he wrote to his brother, Mikhail in the fall of 1844. "I swear I couldn't stand the service any longer. Life is bleak if one's best time is wasted." Clearly, this was an imprudent financial decision, but in a characteristic display of financial wangling, Dostoevsky devised a solution, demanding a cash payment from his father's estate in return for giving up all rights to later funds. His brother-in-law, who managed the estate, thought it an unwise plan. Enraged, Dostoevsky asked Mikhail to intervene. "I haven't got one kopek to buy clothes," he wrote. "In the name of God, ask them to send me that money!"

Dostoevsky's transformation from engineering student to celebrated novelist evolved with staggering speed. By 1845, he had completed his first novel, *Poor Folk*, an epistolary tale told through the letters of an impoverished man and the young girl he pines for. A fellow engineering friend turned literary compatriot was so impressed by the work that he submitted it to a publisher he knew, who then shared it with Vissarion Belinsky, a preeminent literary critic. Just a few years earlier, Belinsky had made Gogol's 1842 novel, *Dead Souls*, the talk of the town with its stark portrayal of Russian society and character. Struck by Dostoevsky's revelation of the "secrets of life and characters in Russia as no one before him even dreamed of," Belinsky couldn't tear himself away. The story was simple, the critic noted, "but what drama, what types!" Word got out. Even before *Poor Folk* was published in January 1846, Dostoevsky, just 24 years old, had risen to literary acclaim.

Money, however, continued to be a problem. "Don't imagine that everything is roses," he wrote to his brother after his novel debuted. "I don't have a kopek to my name, as before." Although Dostoevsky was paid for his work and published numerous other short stories over the next several years—"The Landlady," "The Jealous Husband," "White Nights"—it was never enough to keep up with his daily expenses and the money he owed. As a result, he got into the habit of requesting advances on work that he had yet to complete, putting him in chronic debt to his publishers. His letters to family and friends include constant pleas for cash, sometimes peppered with apologies, other times blunt. "I need money," he writes to Mikhail at one point. "I have to live, brother."

In the late 1840s, Dostoevsky encountered professional turbulence as well. The early accolades for *Poor Folk* went to his head; his overwhelming egotism irked St. Petersburg's inner literary circle, which mocked and alienated him. He was also swept up in feuds with publishers about where his works would appear. But nothing could beat the events of 1849, when the writer, who by then belonged to a progressive literary group that opposed the tsarist autocracy, was arrested for alleged political crimes. He endured a terrifying mock execution—tied to the stake, rifles aimed—only to be spared by a last-minute pardon from the tsar and exiled to Siberia, where he was sentenced to four years of hard labor in a prison camp and five additional years in the Siberian regiment. At the camp, Dostoevsky slept on bare boards, ate boiled cabbage, endured hard labor in freezing temperatures, and began to experience his first severe bouts of epilepsy, which would plague him for the rest of his life. His harrowing experience gave him extraordinary access to the human psyche and provided fodder for his 1862 novel, *The House of the Dead*. It also heightened his underlying anxiety. At one point, Dostoevsky described himself as "devoured by gloom."

Gambling when feeling distressed is a key criterion for a gambling disorder diagnosis—and this was clearly a motivating factor for Dostoevsky's nonstop gambling spree in the 1860s. During his military service in Siberia, Dostoevsky had met and married Maria Dmitrievna Isaeva, a widow with a child. But by the time he returned to St. Petersburg in 1859, their relationship was falling apart. Dostoevsky's epilepsy, anxiety, and powerful irritability could not have been easy for his wife, and she was not a source of comfort for him. Known to be capricious and jealous, she was also sick with tuberculosis. By 1862, the 40-year-old writer was seeking solace elsewhere, and made the fateful decision to visit a casino in Germany. Right away, he got lucky at the roulette table, landing himself a hefty sum of 11,000 francs.

Big wins early on can lead amateur gamblers to mistakenly believe that they know how to beat the system, inspiring follow-up trips to the tables. One year later, Dostoevsky returned to Germany to try his hand again. At this point, he was still technically married to Maria, but the two lived apart, and Dostoevsky had struck up an affair with Polina Suslova, an aspiring writer 20 years his junior. In the spring of 1863, the two planned an illicit rendezvous in Paris. Suslova had arrived earlier and was waiting for Dostoevsky when he decided to make a four-day detour to the picturesque German gambling town of Wiesbaden. Once again, he did well, winning 10,400 francs. This trip, Frank notes, marked "the true beginning of the gambling mania that invariably swept over Dostoevsky whenever he came to Europe during the 1860s."

Roulette, the game that consumed Dostoevsky, is based on pure chance. Players bet money on red or black numbers, the croupier spins the wheel, the ball falls where it may. But in what is considered a classic early stage of gambling addiction, Dostoevsky deluded himself into thinking that he had figured out a foolproof betting system, which he described in a letter to his wife's sister after his visit to Wiesbaden. "Please do not think that in my joy over not having lost, I am showing off by saying that I possess the secret of how to win instead of losing," he wrote. "I really do know the secret—it is terribly silly and simple, merely a matter of keeping oneself under constant control and never getting excited, no matter how the game shifts. That's all there is to it—you just can't lose that way and are sure to win." In the same letter, Dostoevsky notes that he had initially locked his 10,400-franc win in his suitcase, but then succumbed to temptation, played again, and lost half of it.

With their intoxicating mix of money, bright lights, camaraderie, competition, risk, and thrill, casinos provide gamblers with a dramatic escape from the demands and traumas of everyday existence. Over the course of one year in 1864, Dostoevsky's life read like the Book of Job. The writer was sick with epilepsy and other illnesses, including a bladder infection. In February, his brother Mikhail's youngest daughter succumbed to scarlet fever; in April, the tuberculosis his wife had been battling finally took her life; in July, Mikhail died suddenly from a liver ailment. All of this devastated Dostoevsky and had a crippling effect on his already weak finances. He was now responsible for helping to support his stepson, Pasha, the surviving child of his late wife, Maria, as well as Mikhail's widow and her four children. In addition, his brother had taken on enormous debts to help him co-finance a literary magazine, *Epoch*, that was now floundering. With Mikhail's death, Dostoevsky made yet another unwise financial decision. Rather than shut down the journal, he tried to keep it alive—taking on not only an enormous professional responsibility but the prodigious financial burden his brother had left behind. It turned out to be a futile and costly error; in early 1865, less than a year after Mikhail's death, *Epoch* published its final issue.

This is the mess that Dostoevsky found himself in when he was presented with the seemingly impossible task of writing a novel in little more than a year. By then, he was well established as a writer, having published about a dozen short stories and a handful of novels, including his highly influential *Notes From Underground*, considered to be a precursor to the existential novel. Dostoevsky was also busy finishing up his first major narrative, *Crime and Punishment*, which initially appeared in monthly installments in a literary journal; this effort, according to biographer Frank, secured him a place in the elite literary ranks of novelists Ivan Turgenev and Leo Tolstoy. The shady publisher who proposed the deal to Dostoevsky offered 3,000 rubles up front for the new novel, plus the right to publish his entire set of past works. The stakes were dire: If Dostoevsky failed to meet his deadline, any future writing would be published for free over the course of nine years—without a ruble going to the author himself.

Dostoevsky struggled without success to produce under pressure, and by early October 1866, just weeks before his November 1 cutoff, he had no words on paper. In a panic, Dostoevsky disclosed his predicament to a friend, who arranged to have a stenographer take dictation to speed up the writing process. The young stenographer who showed up, Anna Grigoryevna Snitkina, had read the author's works and eagerly took on the job. Dostoevsky talked, Anna typed, and *The Gambler* made it to the publisher just two hours before deadline. The short novel, considered to be highly autobiographical, has it all: a window into Russian society, a tale of tortured romance (a character named Polina mirrors Dostoevsky's own tumultuous affair with Polina Suslova, who ultimately declined to marry him). It is also a quintessential account of the delusional thought processes that drive people with gambling disorder.

Through Alexey Ivanovich, his protagonist, Dostoevsky documents many of the features of gambling addiction that he struggled with himself—and that gamblers from Las Vegas to Monte Carlo battle today. Alexey Ivanovich was "possessed by an intense craving for risk," as Dostoevsky explained in the novel. "Perhaps passing through so many sensations, my soul was not satisfied but only irritated by them, and craved still more sensation—and stronger and stronger ones—till utterly exhausted." Even now, 150 years after its publication, gambling experts and literary critics alike continue to marvel at the novel's insightful depictions of the gambler's mind. Dr. Richard Rosenthal, a psychiatrist and co-director of the UCLA Gambling Studies Program, considers *The Gambler* a psychological masterpiece and "the best case of a compulsive gambler in or out of the professional literature."

Much of the thrill for gamblers, then and now, comes from the unpredictability of the game—those moments between laying down a bet and finding out whether you will win or lose. Some gamblers feel they must achieve a mastery over the challenge, no matter the costs. "They're flirting with the idea of disaster, and seeing how close they come to the line," says Rosenthal. Gamblers are also vulnerable to self-deception, a theme that runs through both the novel and Dostoevsky's own gambling experience. Although Dostoevsky had startling insight into the thought patterns of compulsive gamblers, he continued to buy in to the delusions that snare them. Even though every turn of the wheel is an independent event, with a roughly equal chance of red or black turning up, Dostoevsky and Alexey Ivanovich both put their faith in the illogical notion that previous results can predict the next spin. If red has won ten times in a row on the roulette wheel, for example, the gambler wagers that black is sure to win next. This is known as the "gambler's fallacy" or the "Monte Carlo fallacy," named after an infamous incident in 1913 when black won 26 times in a row and gamblers lost millions of francs betting on red.

Why did he do it? Financially, Dostoevsky needed the money. But his mind got caught up in the game. Compulsive gamblers often head for casinos when they are feeling anxious, depressed, helpless, or guilty. Guilt, especially, has emerged as a prominent theme in Dostoevsky's life, and experts have long theorized about where it came from and how profoundly it contributed to his addiction. Even Freud weighed in, arguing in a 1928 essay that Dostoevsky's excessive gambling was a form of self-inflicted punishment. But for what? Possibly his father's death. Just a week or two after writing to his son about the hardships at home, Dr. Dostoevsky was found dead by the roadside. Doctors reported that he'd suffered a stroke; the family believed that his own serfs murdered him. Whatever happened, experts have speculated that Dostoevsky felt deep remorse. Not only had he resisted the career his father set out for him, he had taken advantage of him by asking for money when there was little to spare.

Rosenthal, the UCLA gambling expert, believes that the author's guilt more likely stemmed from circumstances surrounding his birth. While his mother was pregnant with him, she developed a respiratory infection, which may have left her vulnerable to the tuberculosis that ultimately killed her. Viewed through this lens, Dostoevsky's very existence would have led to his mother's downfall and her death. Rosenthal points out that Dostoevsky's gambling began around the time that his first wife, Maria, became terminally ill with tuberculosis—a development that mirrored his mother's own suffering and early death. This gambling pattern could be viewed as a "defense against enormous feelings of loss and, especially, of guilt," says Rosenthal. Whatever the underlying triggers, the psychological payoff from gambling is an escape from the pain of negative feelings and the harsh realities of life. Immersed in noise, alcohol, anticipatory excitement, and the spin of the wheel, it's almost impossible to focus on anything else.

Writing *The Gambler* had an unexpected payoff: Forty-five-year-old Dostoevsky fell in love with his 20-year-old stenographer. Between dictations, the two talked about Russian literature, and Dostoevsky confided in Anna about his past, including the terrifying experience after his arrest when he thought he was going to be executed. Anna listened sympathetically, and over the course of just a few weeks in October 1866, the two developed a deeply personal relationship. Dostoevsky, eager to remarry, proposed just one month after they met. "I would answer that I love you and will love you all my life," she replied.

The couple was married in February 1867. It soon became clear that their new life would be far more challenging than the whirlwind weeks of their early romance. Among other issues, Dostoevsky's stepson resented Anna's presence in his stepfather's life, and Dostoevsky suffered two severe back-to-back epileptic attacks. Dostoevsky was often irritable, and the two had little quality time together. To alleviate the stress and in part to seek "some respite from the constant harassment of his creditors," Frank notes, the couple planned a trip to Europe that spring. Anna, who believed the trip was vital to the future of their marriage, pawned her wedding dowry to finance the initial part of their travel. In the end, they stayed away much longer than expected. Their journey, which took them to numerous cities (Dresden, Milan, Geneva, Prague,

Florence), turned into four years; much of the time, they barely managed to stay afloat. Anna's mother supplied some money, and Dostoevsky also pawned clothing and other belongings. As usual, he turned to friends for loans and to his editors for advances on his writing. Throughout it all, he paid frequent visits to the casinos.

By then, Dostoevsky was exhibiting many of the symptoms that constitute a gambling disorder diagnosis today: a preoccupation with how to get back to the tables; "chasing" losses to get even; relying on others to provide money lost at the casinos; and unsuccessful attempts to control, cut back, or stop gambling altogether. He articulated these thought patterns, behaviors, and self-deceptions in letters he wrote to Anna, his "sweet angel," who was far more patient and understanding of his incessant gambling than anyone else. In one correspondence written the year they were married, he told his new wife that if one gambles "coolly, calmly and with calculation, *it is quite impossible to lose!*" Then he went on to describe his elation over winning, his "maddening urge" to win more, and, as always, his ultimate demise and self-deception. "[I] lost *everything, the whole lot*, down to the last kopek," he wrote, but "if I could give myself just four more days . . . I surely could win everything back."

Anna put up with Dostoevsky's gambling, because she worried that the alternatives might be worse. While she was queasy and pregnant with their first child, the couple had taken a trip to the resort town of Baden-Baden in Germany. Despite being short on cash, Dostoevsky quickly set off to gamble. Although he initially handed his winnings over to his wife for safekeeping, he returned again, empty-handed, and begged for more. Dostoevsky worked himself up into such a state after his losses—remorseful, apologetic, self-flagellating—that Anna decided it was better to let him hit the casino than risk a possible epileptic attack. She also believed that her husband's gambling helped clear his muddled head and fuel his writing. Despite his ongoing losses (he pawned the couple's wedding rings, his wife's earrings and brooch, his coat, and her shawl), Anna stood by his side. "One had to come to terms with it," she later wrote, "to look at his gambling passion as a disease for which there was no cure."

WHAT PROPELS PEOPLE TO wager everything on a game of chance? There's no simple answer. Maureen O'Connor, a popular two-term mayor of San Diego from 1986 to 1992, started playing video poker after the 1994 death of her husband, Robert Peterson, the Jack in the Box fast-food tycoon. Between 2000 and 2009, O'Connor won more than a billion dollars at casinos in Las Vegas, Atlantic City, and San Diego, according to tax records cited in court papers filed by federal prosecutors in Southern California in 2013. But she lost even more. The ex-mayor, who had grown up in a working-class family and taught at Catholic school early in her career, liquidated her savings and took out second and third mortgages to cover her debts and continue gambling, according to prosecutors, who charged that she had misappropriated $2.1 million from her husband's charitable foundation, leaving it bankrupt. O'Connor's lawyer argued that her actions fit a pattern called "grief gambling" and that her behavior coincided with a slow-growing brain tumor, diagnosed in 2011, which can affect judgment and impulse control. Whatever the cause, her behavior was "totally out of character," her chief of staff told the *New York Times*. In a teary CBS News interview, O'Connor apologized and admitted that she thought she could beat the machine. "It was like electronic heroin," she said, acknowledging that she could lose more than $100,000 in one day. "You know the more you did, the more you needed—and the more it wasn't satisfied." Prosecutors later dismissed the case against O'Connor after she agreed to receive treatment for her gambling addiction and to pay back the $2.1 million when she was financially able to do so.

Gladys Knight, the Grammy Award–winning rhythm and blues singer, revealed in a memoir that she got hooked on the card game baccarat starting in the late 1970s, after her second marriage unraveled. She worried about paying funds she owed to the IRS and affording her kids' college educations—but it wasn't just money that spurred her decade-long addiction. "I had so much weighing on me at home: so many expectations, so many people depending on me, wanting things from me," she wrote. "When I was performing, it was the same thing. I had to be on all the time. When I gambled, I was a kid again in my private play space." Knight, who gambled in casinos from Las Vegas to Europe, rationalized her behavior while she made money. But over time, it became clear that she was in too deep. "Gambling became a substitute for actually dealing with my life," she reflected. One night, after losing $45,000, Knight called Gamblers Anonymous, a 12-step program similar to Alcoholics Anonymous. "I felt like I was going to throw up out of shame and self-revulsion," she recounted. "I *was* sick. I was an *addict*."

Most people who gamble do not become addicts. They play poker, cards, slots, and roulette with friends as entertainment for limited periods of time. So-called social gamblers don't risk inordinate sums or suffer other long-term consequences. A second tier of gamblers, referred to as "problem gamblers," spend a significant amount of time gambling, lose more money than they intend and may be at risk for developing a more serious fixation. Most worrisome are those gamblers who are so consumed by their game of choice—poker, slots, blackjack, craps—that they neglect their families, endanger their careers, and empty their pockets and bank accounts. Like Dostoevsky, they meet the criteria for gambling disorder.

In the United States, as many as two to three million people qualify for a gambling disorder diagnosis, and the numbers could rise. Over the last several decades, gambling has been legalized in almost every state, with new casinos doing brisk business. The gaming industry, which takes in more than $60 billion in revenues every year, promotes gambling as both entertainment and as a source of state revenue. The practice has become increasingly popular with niche demographics. College students are lured in by TV poker shows and the desire to win fast cash; gambling apps provide instant gratification. More men than women gamble, but the gap is beginning to close. The prototypical male gambler places heavy bets, wants to be the center of attention, and gets a rush from playing, says Nancy Petry, a gambling disorder expert at the UConn Health School of Medicine in Farmington, Connecticut. Women, by contrast, tend to gravitate to slot machines and gambling when they're depressed, and typically start later in life. For seniors who are lonely, isolated, or bored, gambling becomes a social outlet and an escape from the challenges of aging.

Excessive gambling can have adverse consequences on the body. With no clocks or windows, casinos are designed to lure people in, keep them playing, and ensure that they lose track of time. Pulling slots or playing cards all night can lead to sleep deprivation, which can trigger detrimental outcomes, including shut-eye at the wheel. Alcohol flows freely at casinos, and most allow smoking. All of this can exacerbate depression and anxiety in gambling addicts, who are more prone to mood disorders to begin with. The results can be dire: About 17 percent of people in treatment for gambling disorder have attempted suicide, often after suffering a substantial loss.

The most compelling research today revolves around scientists' game-changing conclusion that gambling disorder looks a lot like alcohol and drug addiction. The conditions have corresponding patterns and behaviors—the cravings, the risk-seeking, the lack of judgment, the inability to stop. Brain-imaging studies have found that people with gambling disorder, like individuals with other addictions, suffer from impaired decision-making, which leads them to choose immediate gratification over long-term consequences. There are similar patterns in family history, too. Children of gambling addicts run a higher risk of developing gambling disorder themselves; if one identical twin is addicted, the other is more likely to be as well. Compulsive gamblers are also more likely to have a parent, child, or sibling with a substance use disorder—Dostoevsky's father was said to have been an alcoholic—and demonstrate a greater probability of having one themselves, suggesting an overlap in genes that contribute to both varieties of addiction. As with substance use disorders, gambling disorder may start in adolescence or young adulthood; the earlier the onset, the more severe the condition tends to become.

Scientists now believe that addiction is rooted in the brain's "reward system"—the same system that releases the feel-good hormone dopamine when we do something pleasurable, like eat ice cream or have sex. When drugs and alcohol first activate this brain circuitry, levels of dopamine surge, making the person feel good. With repeated use, however, the brain becomes overwhelmed, and the addictive substance or behavior no longer provides the same satisfying jolt. This may lead people with addictions of all types to develop a tolerance and seek out risk as they try to regain the gratifying response they achieved early on.

Growing research shows that gambling strikes at similar pathways in the brain. What does that mean for other behaviors gone awry? According to the *DSM*, compulsive Internet gaming, which has been linked to extreme self-neglect and social isolation, most notably in Asia, warrants further research. Internet gaming disorder could become a diagnosable condition soon. Some experts believe that binge eating, which is currently classified as an eating disorder, looks like a behavioral addiction as well. What about shopping or sex? Is your brain wired to *make* you buy another pair of shoes or indulge in repeated affairs? You can see the challenge here: If overindulging is deemed to be a brain disorder, one could argue that we are no longer responsible for the bad choices we make. We've all got at least one vice that gives us pleasure, be it too much chocolate or too many hours on Twitter.

Behavioral addiction is an area that has garnered enormous debate in mental health circles. Diagnosing what might be nothing more than a troubling habit raises alarm bells about what psychiatrists perceive as "normal" versus "abnormal" behavior—as well as when and where the line is crossed. Critics argue that psychiatrists are already overpathologizing human behavior. Others wonder if addiction should be reconceptualized altogether. In her memoir *Desire*, the writer Susan Cheever, who has struggled with sex addiction and alcoholism, suggests that perhaps addiction should be categorized by intensity (" 'He's a level-five addict' or 'She's a level-two addict' ") instead of substance, since many people who are addicted to one thing are or will become addicted to another. "It's as if the addict is addicted to a feeling rather than a specific substance that triggers the feeling," she writes.

However addiction is defined, the biggest challenge is getting help to people whose lives are in peril. Few people with gambling disorder actively seek treatment. Lured by the prospect of winning, they often lack perspective on how serious their condition has become. As a result, most mental health clinicians have little experience treating the condition, says UConn Health's Petry. Cognitive-behavioral therapy, one of the therapeutic approaches used to treat substance abuse disorders, can be helpful in teaching patients how to identify the thoughts and feelings that motivate their gambling. Once these triggers are pinpointed, individuals are guided to find alternative activities that deter them from setting foot in a casino or gambling parlor. Some join self-help groups, including Gamblers Anonymous, which attempts to nurture recovery through mutual understanding and support. Antianxiety medications or antidepressants may be prescribed as well to combat the highly associated mood disorders. And given the similarities to substance use disorders, researchers are also testing the efficacy of a drug called naltrexone, used to combat cravings in alcoholism and drug addiction, to see if it can reduce gamblers' urges to play.

Rosenthal believes that the majority of compulsive gamblers can be treated successfully without medication. He uses psychodynamic therapy, which explores past experiences to identify a patient's underlying motivations. Most critical, says Rosenthal, is that patients understand why they gamble in the first place and "what it is that they're avoiding or escaping from."

⌒⌒

ANYBODY WHO'S STRUGGLED WITH ADDICTION knows how grueling it can be to stop. Gamblers who quit on their own usually do so for two reasons, says Rosenthal: Something terrible happens or they fear that it will (job loss, spouse filing for divorce, children walking away) or they experience some kind of breakthrough, perhaps a personal epiphany or some kind of spiritual awakening. Dostoevsky seems to have been motivated by both. In April 1871, he wrote a letter to Anna, then pregnant with their third child, explaining that once again he had lost everything on a gambling escapade—even the money she had sent him for his return trip. As usual, he begged her to send more cash. But he assured her that he was finally quitting. "A great thing has happened to me: I have rid myself of the abominable delusion that has *tormented* me for almost ten years," he wrote.

Dostoevsky expressed great anxiety about how much more his wife could take; in a dream, he had seen her hair turn white, he wrote, and he feared what might come next. He was also alarmed by a nightmare in which his father had appeared in a "terrifying guise" that he worried portended some disastrous event. All of this terrible foreboding appears to have helped push him toward salvation. "It seems as if I have been completely morally regenerated (I say this to you and before God)," Dostoevsky told Anna. "I realize that you have every right to despise me and to think: 'He will gamble again.' By what, then, can I swear to you that *I shall not*, when I have already deceived you before? But, my angel, I know that you would die (!) if I lost again! I am not completely insane after all!" he wrote.

This time, Dostoevsky stuck to his word. He spent the latter years of his life continuing to write, even as his own health declined and tragedy struck his family. By the time he and Anna moved back to St. Petersburg in 1871, they had lost their first child, a girl named Sonya, who succumbed to pneumonia when she was just a few months old. A second daughter, Lyubov, survived and returned with them to Russia, where two boys followed: Fyodor, and the couple's youngest child, Alyosha, who had a severe epileptic attack and died at the age of three in 1878.

Dostoevsky's final and epic novel, *The Brothers Karamazov*, was published in 1879. Two years later, on February 9, 1881, the writer experienced a pulmonary hemorrhage and died at the age of 59. Aware of the family's financial troubles, the government offered to pay Dostoevsky's burial expenses, but Anna claimed to have turned it down, saying it was her moral obligation to cover the costs, according to biographer Frank. She did, however, accept a lifetime pension provided in return for her husband's contributions to Russian literature. At his burial, the couple's daughter Lyubov cried out a goodbye to her "dear, kind, good papa." He was gone—leaving behind for his children, his wife, and the rest of us a trove of some of the most significant and affecting literature the world has ever seen.

Albert Einstein

THE HALLS OF THE ESTEEMED Mütter Museum in Philadelphia are filled with biological curiosities. A plaster death cast of the famous conjoined twins Chang and Eng. A human skeleton more than seven feet tall. Gruesome ulcers. A jar of peeled skin. Even a tumor removed from Grover Cleveland's mouth. But nothing can trump the contents of a wooden container, not much bigger than a cigar box, which sits in a temperature-controlled display case. Stacked inside are 46 microscope slides containing what look like a series of Rorschach inkblots. The color of tea, they are beautiful and beckoning. It is hard to believe that these elegant works of art are actually thin slices of brain tissue that once resided in the head of one of the greatest geniuses of all time: Albert Einstein.

Andy Warhol Was a Hoarder

Before his death in 1955, Einstein requested that his body be cremated and his ashes scattered, in part because he did not want to become a shrine for tourists. But Thomas Harvey, the pathologist who conducted the autopsy of the scientist's body, could not help himself: He removed Einstein's brain. Harvey kept several pieces in a glass jar (at one point reportedly stored in a cider box under a beer cooler) and sliced the rest into sections, which were mounted on slides and sent to a handful of scientists around the country. Now, decades later, one of these sets of brain slides had made its way to the Mütter Museum. Peering in at the display, curator Anna Dhody recalled the first time the box landed in her hands. "I thought, 'I'm holding a piece of Einstein. Wow!' " Then she paused for a moment. "Wouldn't it be nice if just holding him made you smarter?"

Few other brains in history have so captivated ordinary mortals. And rightly so. How could one three-pound mass of neurons and glial cells produce such genius? Einstein unraveled cosmic puzzles in his 20s, published his general theory of relativity in his 30s, and won the Nobel Prize in physics in his 40s. He was a giant, even among the greatest braniacs in the universe. But human beings are multifaceted, and Einstein's brain, like the rest of ours, did more than power his intellect. It triggered his emotions, juggled his conflicting desires, and made him act and speak and walk in his own Einsteinian way.

The physicist's brilliance, it turns out, was paired with behavioral traits and personality quirks that are less well known and celebrated. As a child, Einstein talked late and was a social misfit who distanced himself from other kids. In adulthood, he was disorganized and had rocky relationships. Throughout his life, he focused intensely on topics that interested him, and was such a tenaciously persistent thinker that he often retreated from people entirely.

"I am a truly a 'lone traveler,' " Einstein reflected, "and have never belonged to my country, my home, my friends, or even my immediate family, with my whole heart. In the face of all this, I have never lost a sense of distance and the need for solitude."

Yes, the way Einstein made sense of time and space is mind-blowing. But the way he acted has led some scientists to posit a hypothesis: Was Einstein on the autism spectrum?

IN 1944, HANS ASPERGER, an Austrian pediatrician, documented similar patterns of behavior in a group of children, whose primary characteristics included a lack of empathy, difficulty forming friendships, one-sided conversations, preoccupations with a special interest, and clumsy movements. These children tended to focus narrowly on their subjects of choice, which they would discuss at length with anybody who had the patience to listen. Social challenges were especially prominent; the youngsters did not engage and play with other kids. In general, they tended to be outsiders.

Although some of the children had significant intellectual disabilities, others had notable cognitive attributes—namely, the capacity to see things in novel ways and the ability to pursue their interests with a unique persistence unmatched by their peers. Children in this group, Asperger noted, often seemed predestined for a particular profession from early in childhood and were capable of achieving great success professionally. Despite their social challenges, he wrote, "their narrowness and single-mindedness, as manifested in their special interests, can be immensely valuable and can lead to outstanding achievements in their chosen areas." Asperger, who dubbed the condition "autistic psychopathy," called the children "little professors."

The condition received scant attention until 1981, when British psychiatrist Lorna Wing published an account of Asperger's work and proposed a new, less daunting name: Asperger's syndrome. Wing acknowledged similarities between Asperger's and autism, which had been deemed a distinct mental health diagnosis one year earlier, including problems in social communication and language. But she also noted differences. Children with autism could not speak or had delayed or abnormal speech; youngsters with Asperger's could talk, but what they said was often inappropriate. A child with autism was obsessed with repetitive routines (arranging toys in a row, for example); a child with Asperger's might become engrossed in math problems. The term "Asperger's syndrome" would be useful, Wing proposed, to distinguish people who exhibited some autistic characteristics but were not as significantly impaired as those with classical autism.

Throughout the 1980s, researchers studied the condition in earnest and in 1994, Asperger's disorder, as the *DSM* called it, joined autism as an official and related diagnosis. Many parents found relief, knowing that their unconventional kids were not alone and would be eligible for educational and support services. Over the next two decades, thousands of American children, teenagers, and even adults were diagnosed with Asperger's, and social consciousness about the condition evolved dramatically. As awareness grew, so did the recognition that despite their behavioral challenges, people with Asperger's also had unique abilities and talents to offer the world. A whole advocacy movement was spawned. Buoyed by the notion that quirkiness and brilliance are often intertwined, Asperger's support groups embraced historical icons who they believe share their condition. Albert Einstein tops the list.

In the world of autism and Asperger's, however, nothing is ever straightforward. Even as Asperger's gained new standing, many clinicians found it difficult to distinguish the condition from what has been deemed "high-functioning" autism because of their overlapping characteristics, most notably communication difficulties, social challenges, and repetitive behaviors. As a result, the two conditions were merged in 2013 under a new umbrella diagnosis known as autism spectrum disorder. Variation among patients is vast. At the most profound and regressive end of the continuum, tiny babies filled with vigor and promise slip into a world of solitude and silence. In some cases, toddlers who had learned to say their first words are suddenly banging their heads against the wall and unable to communicate. Parents use words like "kidnapped" and "stolen" to describe the way the condition robs the minds and the very essence of their children. The other end includes people who fit the characteristics of Asperger's. They may show keen intellectual curiosity, but struggle to fit in at school and on the job.

The autism/Asperger's dilemma—a debate about whether or not the conditions should be united is ongoing despite the official change—highlights the broader issue of how confounding mental health diagnoses can be. It also underscores the reality that so many brain conditions overlap and yet can also harbor both subtle and striking differences. Terminology will always be tricky in the autism arena, and it will likely evolve even more over time. Although "Asperger's" no longer exists as a *current* diagnosis—at least not now, anyway—people previously diagnosed with the condition still identify with it, and it continues to be used informally by many patients and doctors as a way to distinguish its unique characteristics. Today, the accepted way to make sense of all this confusion is to use a shorthand reference that covers all levels of diagnosis, from severe to moderately affected: "on the autism spectrum."

The symptoms that Einstein exhibited most closely resemble the Asperger's end of the autism spectrum. Hans Asperger's own assessment of the condition speaks to the kind of person Einstein was. Despite the social challenges of the condition, Asperger said, a child who pursues his passion with vigor "may find his way into an unusual career, perhaps into highly specialized scientific work, maybe with an ability bordering on genius." The critical ingredient, Asperger noted, was an ability to close off the outside world and rethink a subject in a wholly original way. "Indeed, it seems that for success in science," he said, "a dash of autism is essential."

⌒

ALBERT EINSTEIN WAS BORN to Jewish parents, Hermann and Pauline Einstein, in Ulm, in the southwest corner of Germany, on March 14, 1879. Although the family assimilated as best they could into German culture, anti-Semitic sentiments were on the rise. Hermann and Pauline considered naming their son Abraham, after Hermann's father, but decided that the name sounded "too Jewish" and chose Albert instead, according to biographer Walter Isaacson. Young Albert entered the world at a time of creative explosiveness. Literary masterpieces—*Anna Karenina*, *The Adventures of Tom Sawyer*, *A Doll's House*—were making their debut. Pointillism, an alternative to the more lyrical and fluid impressionist school, was shaking up the art world. And the second industrial revolution, with its electricity and automobiles, was transforming the way people lived and worked.

The great physicist's family origins give little clue to the towering genius that would ultimately emerge. Einstein's father showed a talent for math early on and was interested in pursuing the subject, but there was not enough money to advance his studies. After a brief and unimpressive stint selling feather beds, Hermann launched a gas and electrical engineering company with his brother and, later, installed power stations. With his formidable walrus mustache, he looked the part of a tough Prussian but was known to be gentle and kind. From his father, Einstein seems to have inherited a knack for numbers; his mother, a gifted pianist, imbued him with a lifelong passion for music. Practical and funny, she had the stronger personality of the two and encouraged Albert and his younger sister, Maja, to be self-sufficient. Maja later wrote in a biographical account that by the time her big brother was four years old, he was crossing busy city streets alone.

Albert stood out from the day he was born. His mother was immediately alarmed by the large size and angular shape of the back of his head and, according to Maja, "feared she had given birth to a deformed child." His grandmother thought he was overweight. "Much too fat! Much too fat!" she cried, throwing her hands up. Early on, young Albert was remarkably quiet. Although there is marked variation in children's linguistic development, most babies babble by about six months and say a few words around their first birthday. There are discrepant accounts of when, precisely, Einstein began speaking in full sentences, but it seems clear that he was at least two and might have been closer to three, qualifying him for what today would be called a "late talker."

Once he did begin speaking, the young boy engaged in what Maja described as "a characteristic, if strange, habit" of repeating sentences to himself, a habit that would persist for years. Delayed speech and the repetition of words or phrases, known as echolalia, are common features of autism. Echolalia, once regarded as problematic, is now viewed as a natural part of linguistic and cognitive development. At the time, Einstein's verbal obstacles caused considerable consternation. "He had such difficulty with language that those around him feared he would never learn to speak," Maja recalled. Einstein himself later remarked on this, too: "It is true that my parents were worried because I began to speak relatively late, so much so they consulted a doctor." The family maid called him "der Depperte," the dopey one.

Einstein's early social behaviors also showed several characteristic autistic traits. Young children often resort to anger when they are frustrated or anxious, a pattern that is often exacerbated in children with autism, who struggle to soothe themselves. Early in life, Einstein was known to be surprisingly volatile. Maja recalled a spate of temper tantrums so violent that her brother's face would go pale and the tip of his nose turn white. Then the hurling would begin. When he was five, Albert lobbed a chair at his school tutor, who fled and never returned. Maja didn't escape his wrath, either. Once, he threw a bowling ball at her head; another time, he came after her with a child's pickax. She survived. "This should suffice to show that it takes a sound skull to be the sister of an intellectual," she wrote.

With Einstein's temper came a piercing curiosity. People on the autism spectrum are often captivated by objects to the exclusion of friends and family. Einstein had great powers of concentration, becoming readily absorbed in single tasks. He was a solitary youngster who preferred playing on his own to engaging with other children—even his own cousins, who visited often. Instead, he played with puzzles, created complex structures out of building blocks, and crafted houses of cards that reached 14 stories high. At school, he was the oddball, the kid who had no interest in sports or his peers. The neighborhood boys, who preferred to tussle in the streets, nicknamed him "the bore." Biographer Dennis Overbye writes that Einstein's "more typical playmates were the chickens or pigeons, or the small boat he sailed in a pail of water."

Young Albert was captivated by things, ideas, unknowns. When he was about four years old, his father showed him a compass.

Other children might have found the device entertaining for a little while, then tossed it into the toy heap. Not Einstein. It was a transformative event, a moment of "wonder," as he later recalled. He was endlessly fascinated by how the needle moved with mysterious precision, driven by some external force. In his report, Hans Asperger noted that the children he studied had "the ability to see things and events around them from a new point of view, which often shows surprising maturity." For Einstein, the small device had a profound impact, stretching his young mind and stirring him to ponder the mysteries of science. "I can still remember—or at least I believe I can remember—that this experience made a deep and lasting impression on me," he later wrote. "Something deeply hidden had to be behind things."

Einstein's expansive mind was not well suited to the rigid teachings of his early education in Germany. A determined and contemplative thinker, he took his time mulling over questions. This did not go over well with his teachers, who expected quick and automatic answers. Einstein refused to suppress his contempt for the focus on memorization and harsh discipline, which he later likened to "the methods of the Prussian Army." Instead, he reveled in the independent learning provided by a young medical student named Max Talmud. Although the Einsteins did not belong to a synagogue or observe kosher laws or religious rituals, they invited Talmud to join them for a family meal each week as part of a Jewish custom to feed a needy scholar.

Starting at the age of ten, Talmud engaged Einstein in erudite conversations and brought him books, including a geometry text and works by the philosopher Immanuel Kant. He also introduced Einstein to a 21-volume series about biology and physics, which included an exploration of the speed of light—a principal component of what would become Einstein's special theory of relativity. Talmud's visits provided the intellectual stimulation Einstein craved. He devoured the books and, before long, even surpassed his young tutor in math. "In all those years, I never saw him reading any light literature," Talmud recalled. "Nor did I ever see him in the company of his schoolmates or other boys his age."

Though clearly brilliant, Einstein's performance at school was tumultuous. Although his grades were mostly very good, he lagged behind in languages, which were "never his forte," according to Maja. His Greek teacher, Herr Degenhart, was unimpressed by his efforts and told Einstein that he would never get anywhere in life. One day, Degenhart made it clear that he would rather not have him in class. When Einstein shot back that he had done nothing wrong, the teacher responded: "Yes, that is true, but you sit there in the back row and smile and your mere presence here spoils the respect of the class for me." Whether forced to leave or not, this was just the excuse Einstein needed to flee the drudgery of the systematic teaching he so despised. At 15, he dropped out of his Munich high school. Two years later, after completing the necessary coursework at a secondary school in Switzerland, he enrolled in the Polytechnic in Zurich.

There, Einstein persisted in his lackadaisical approach to educational norms; he regularly cut classes and once threw the instructions for a physics lab assignment into the trash, determined to do the work his own way. Hans Asperger noted this same tendency in the children he studied. "What they find difficult are the mechanical aspects of learning," he wrote. "They follow their own ideas, which are mostly far removed from ordinary concerns, and do not like to be distracted from their thoughts." They also had a penchant for disrespecting authority. A math teacher called Einstein a "lazy dog."

Einstein's nonconformity and irreverence—characteristics that would define him throughout his life—battered his relationships with his teachers. At first enamored of one of his professors, Heinrich Weber, Einstein soon concluded that Weber's lectures were too narrowly focused on the past. "Given his brash attitude, Einstein didn't hide his feelings. And given his dignified sense of himself, Weber bristled at Einstein's ill-concealed disdain," writes Isaacson. "By the end of their four years together they were antagonists." It didn't help that Einstein addressed his teacher informally as "Herr Weber," instead of the more respectful "Herr Professor."

Because they have difficulty detecting nonverbal cues and perceiving the feelings of others, people on the autism spectrum often speak bluntly and forcefully and may come off as tactless. However Einstein's utterances are interpreted—as brutally honest, disrespectful, or representative of an autistic trait—they struck many as cocky and impertinent, a problem that torpedoed his academic career early on. When Einstein graduated from the Polytechnic in 1900 at the age of 21, he was the only one in his division who had not landed a job offer. In hindsight, this was a boon to his career; it was while working as a patent examiner, the only position he could get, that Einstein had the time to come up with his special theory of relativity and his revolutionary ideas about the speed of light and the size of atoms. At the time, however, not getting a teaching job was discouraging. Einstein believed anti-Semitism played a role. But there were other factors working against him. When applying for jobs, he brashly pointed out other scientists' mistakes and suffered one rejection letter after the next. It wasn't until 1909, nine years after graduation, that Einstein got his first teaching job as an assistant professor at the University of Zurich. One of his peers once said he "had no understanding how to relate to people."

This shortcoming played out in the way Einstein interacted at times with his first wife, Mileva Marić, and his children, with whom he could be both supportive and loving, but also surprisingly distant. Einstein and Mileva met when they were fellow students at the Polytechnic. Although his mother vehemently disapproved of the relationship—Mileva was judged for being Serbian, older by a few years, and walked with a limp—Einstein pursued his girlfriend with the passion of early romance. "I miss the two little arms and the glowing little girl full of tenderness and kisses," he wrote to her in August 1900. "I can't wait for the moment when I'll be able to hug you and press you and live with you again." Two years later, a daughter was born out of wedlock and mysteriously disappeared (she may have died from scarlet fever or been adopted by another family). In 1903, Einstein, then almost 24, and Mileva, 28, married and soon had two sons, Hans Albert and Eduard. But the scientist threw himself into his work, leaving Mileva burdened by the demands of child rearing and forced to give up any hopes of having her own career in physics. A friend of Einstein's described her as gloomy.

By 1914, when Einstein moved his family from Zurich to Berlin to take on a professorship at the University of Berlin, the physicist was having an affair with his first cousin, Elsa, who was divorced, with two daughters of her own—Ilse and Margot. His marriage was in disarray. Romantic relationships can be rocky terrain for people on the autism spectrum, but they can be as interested in finding love as anyone else. Many *do* want social connections and intimate partnerships, despite the misconception that they are not interested or emotionally incapable. The challenge is figuring out how to go about initiating a relationship when it can be difficult to read social cues.

Sustaining relationships can be taxing as well. Sensory issues—a sensitivity to touch and a discomfort with physical contact—are common among people on the autism spectrum and can, in some cases, make intimacy uncomfortable. "Mindblindness," the inability to perceive how others are feeling, can lead to misunderstandings. And a preoccupation with work or hobbies is often frustrating for partners who feel they are not getting the attention and affection they desire.

Einstein was far more comfortable sorting out the complexities of physics than wrangling the emotional tumult of relationships. The manner in which he treated Mileva during the height of their marital upset seems to display a kind of mind-blindness about how his actions could affect her. In a letter to Elsa, who would later become his second wife, Einstein described Mileva as "an unfriendly, humorless creature who does not get anything out of life." Then he confronted Mileva with cold-hearted disdain, issuing a list of requirements that she would have to submit to in order for them to stay together for the sake of their two young children. These included bringing him three meals a day in his room, cleaning his bedroom and study, and doing his laundry. He also demanded that she "renounce all personal relations" with him—no sitting at home with him, no intimacy—and that she "desist immediately from addressing me if I request it" and "leave my bedroom or office immediately without protest if I so request."

It was clearly an untenable ultimatum, and the marriage ended soon after. Mileva took the boys back to Zurich while Einstein stayed on in Berlin with Elsa. Einstein's letters to his children show both fatherly love and a notable disconnect. Although he expressed delight in their activities and reported deriving great joy from his boys, he also disappointed them by not showing up for promised visits. Hans, who later became an engineer, wrote to his father with mechanical ideas, at one point posing a calculation about the sideward pressure of wind and the strength of a sail. But he was, at the same time, upset that Einstein was so removed from himself, his mother, and his brother. "We know absolutely nothing about each other; you have no idea what we need and require; I know nothing about you," he wrote. Einstein echoed this sentiment in a letter to his younger son, known as Tete, who would later be diagnosed with schizophrenia, a condition Einstein blamed on his wife's side of the family. "The two of us were so rarely together that I hardly know you at all, even though I am your father," he wrote in 1920. "I'm sure you have only a vague idea of me too."

Einstein admitted to having a problem with relationships, at one point writing in a letter that he had "grossly failed" at staying faithful to one woman. During his marriage to Elsa, which he plunged into just months after his divorce from Mileva in 1919, Einstein had a number of affairs. There's no way to know how deeply intimate these relationships were—or if they were at all—but Einstein seems to have treated many of them with a kind of nonchalance. Seemingly oblivious to how his escapades would come off, he even wrote a letter to Elsa's daughter, Margot, at one point in which he reported that one woman was chasing him and another was "absolutely harmless and decent."

Still, Elsa not only stood by Einstein, but devoted her life to caring for him. Often, this meant overseeing the way he presented himself. Disorganization is a classic trait on the autism spectrum, and it manifests both in the way people process information and in their inattention to how they look. Despite his razor-sharp intellect, Einstein was somewhat scattered, both inside and out. He was said to be an absentminded and confusing lecturer. In an article published in the *Journal of the Royal Society of Medicine*, Ioan James, a British mathematician, noted Einstein's haphazard teaching style, which involved "giving specific examples followed by seemingly unrelated general principles." "Sometimes," James wrote, "he would lose his train of thought while writing on the blackboard. A few minutes later he would emerge as if from a trance and go on to something different."

It is clear from photographs, correspondence, and Einstein's own writings that his appearance, which was often disorderly, was the least of his priorities. Among the children he studied, Hans Asperger observed a tendency to disregard cleanliness and physical care. "Even as adults," Asperger wrote, "they may be seen to walk about unkempt and unwashed, including those who have taken up an academic career." Einstein once wrote in a letter to Elsa that "if I were to start taking care of my grooming, I would no longer be my own self."

The physicist was well known for his disheveled dress. His clothes were often tattered, his shoelaces untied, his hair unbrushed, his pants wrinkled. He went without socks, even in winter. "Don't make yourself ridiculous in your dress coat, which is good for train travel but not for anything else," Elsa wrote to Einstein shortly after they were married. "Change your socks regularly, otherwise they get too large holes. And give a shirt and a nightshirt to the laundry now; you took hardly enough along with you."

Elsa took it upon herself to at least *try* to make Einstein presentable. The American artist S. J. Woolf, who visited Einstein in Berlin to draw his portrait, vividly depicted this in a piece he wrote for the *New York Times* in 1929. Woolf reported that he was greeted at the door by Elsa, whom he described as "a sweet, motherly woman, whose attitude toward her distinguished husband is that of a doting parent toward a precocious child." Einstein, described as average height with a notably large head, mostly gray hair, and a quizzical expression on his face, soon appeared in bare feet and a black-and-white bathrobe. "Patting him on the back, his wife told him to get dressed, and as he left the room she said with a smile: 'He is terribly hard to manage,'" Woolf reported. "In a few minutes he returned. His brown suit needed pressing and on his feet he wore, over wool socks, a pair of open-work sandals. His coat collar was half turned up in the back, and when we started to go upstairs Mrs. Einstein fixed his collar and arranged his hair."

What mattered to Einstein was not the aesthetics of the body but the substance of the mind. Asperger described the tendency of one of his patients to sit in a corner buried in a book, "oblivious to the noise or movement around him." Einstein's passion for the quandaries of gravity, time, and space left him little taste for socializing and conversation, and he often withdrew into himself—so much so that he would sometimes "go into some sort of trance or seizure, as if he had just disappeared into his own world," writes biographer Overbye. Woolf observed this during his visit. "Talking, he appears to be thinking of other things; gazing, he does not appear to be seeing the object at which he looks," Woolf wrote in his article. "In fact, these peculiarities are so marked as to appear almost abnormal." As the artist prepared to draw the physicist's portrait, Einstein began jotting notes on scraps of paper he had taken out of his pocket as if he were the only one in the room. "As far as he was concerned, I was not there," Woolf wrote. "To talk to him would have been out of the question."

Although amiable and unaffected ("I speak to everyone in the same way, whether he is the garbage man or the president of the university," Einstein is said to have remarked), his behavior could come off as aloof, shy, and removed—as if he had a shell around him. His mind was his constant and most alluring companion and, away from people, he found solitary pursuits that gave him time to think. Einstein liked to play Mozart sonatas on his violin while tackling gnarly theoretical problems. He also retreated to sailing, first in a sloop he was given for his 50th birthday in Germany and later in a dinghy sailboat in the United States. Although unable to swim, the physicist was comfortable on the water, drifting along various lakes and waterways on the East Coast while thinking through equations. At times, he was so impervious to the clock and the demands of the day that he had to be retrieved by local boatmen. Once, as Isaacson recounts, friends sent the Coast Guard out to find him at 11 p.m.

Temple Grandin, who is on the autism spectrum and is a leader in the field, readily identifies with Einstein's intense absorption in his hypotheses and theories. "Like me, he was more attached to ideas and work. I don't know what a deep relationship is. His deep passion was for science. Science was his life," she writes in her book, *Thinking in Pictures: My Life With Autism*. She relates to the way Einstein perceived information, too. Many people with autism excel at visual thinking—and, as the title of her book suggests, Grandin stands firmly among them. She stores information and memories in a "video library" in her head, which she draws on to design her revolutionary livestock equipment. Grandin suggests that the disorganization Einstein displayed as teacher and lecturer may have been the result of a brain that, like hers, processed in pictures, not in words.

Although Einstein was a prolific writer—he left behind thousands of letters and personal papers—he admitted to having a "bad memory for words and texts." Instead, he imagined physical problems in a simple, almost visually childlike way. Even the theory of relativity had a graphic beginning. One day when he was 16 years old, Einstein wondered what it would be like to chase a light beam and ride alongside it. Years later, while working at his patent job in Bern, Switzerland, Einstein made a stunning discovery inspired by the city's famous clock tower. He imagined that if a streetcar sped away from the clock tower at the speed of light, time on the clock would appear to have stopped, but it would continue ticking normally in the streetcar. "A storm broke loose in my mind," he recalled, revealing a simple truth: Time moves faster or slower depending on the point of view and speed of the observer. This revelation, sparked by visualization, would soon lead to his celebrated theory. "The words or language, as they are written or spoken, do not seem to play any role in my mechanism of thought," he once wrote in a letter. On another occasion he said simply: "I very rarely think in words at all."

One of the criteria for a diagnosis of autism is that a person's symptoms impair his everyday activities. Einstein clearly excelled in his mind's work. In navigating everyday practical affairs and social conventions, he was helped along. In addition to Elsa, Einstein's secretary, Helen Dukas, became his dedicated protector. Dukas began working for the physicist in 1928 in Germany and moved with the Einsteins to the United States in the early 1930s after they fled the rise of Nazi Germany. She handled Einstein's correspondence, forcefully shielded him from unwanted visitors, and guided him back to his home on Mercer Street in Princeton after his circuitous walks. One day, the famous story goes, the physicist called Princeton's Institute for Advanced Study, where he worked, and asked for Einstein's home address. "Please don't tell anybody," he whispered, "but I *am* Dr. Einstein, I'm on my way home, and I've forgotten where my house is."

Dr. Carl Feinstein, director of the Stanford Autism Center at Lucille Packard Children's Hospital, believes Einstein had personality traits that would be considered symptoms of the autism spectrum today. He wonders if Einstein would have inspired the same kind of assistance and acceptance from other people had he not been so brilliant. A person with similar behaviors and an average intelligence might have struggled to garner admiration and support—not to mention hold down a job and lead a relatively stable life. In Einstein's case, people seemed to adapt to his foibles and look past them because of his radiant mind and the wisdom he imparted, says Feinstein. "He was peculiar with other people, he was categorically different in numerous ways," he says, "but he was also a breathtaking genius."

THE SCIENCE OF AUTISM HAS come a long way since Hans Asperger published his paper in the 1940s. At the time, doctors blamed cold, unloving mothers for their children's detached and socially awkward behavior. Today, the "refrigerator mother" theory, long discredited, has been replaced by sophisticated biological research as scientists attempt to pinpoint causes and determine why the condition can vary so much from one child to the next. Early brain development appears to be one key factor. Neuroscientists have discovered that healthy brains prune their communication channels, known as synapses, in the first years of life to allow specialized areas to mature. In children with autism, however, this trimming is somehow compromised, and synapses propagate out of control. Scientists know that autism is highly heritable; when one identical twin has the disorder, there's a 70 percent or even higher chance the other twin will be on the spectrum as well. Now they are isolating specific genes associated with autism (there are likely hundreds) and studying their interplay with environmental factors that may also play a role, including older parents, exposure to infections or medications in the womb, and prematurity.

Simon Baron-Cohen, director of the Autism Research Centre in Cambridge, England (and, as it happens, the cousin of comic actor Sacha Baron Cohen), believes that there may be another strikingly positive force at work: a talent for science. In the 1990s,

Baron-Cohen gained attention with a provocative theory about autism and the brain. The average male brain, he proposed, is driven to understand how things work ("systemizing," he calls it), while the female brain is hardwired to interpret what people are thinking and feeling ("empathizing"). Baron-Cohen posits that people with autism have an extreme male brain, a concept first raised by Hans Asperger, which makes them exceedingly captivated by how train schedules and vacuum cleaners operate, but far less skilled at understanding social cues and making friends. Even newborn infants reflect this gender difference, according to Baron-Cohen, who found that girl babies show a stronger interest in the human face, while boy babies would rather look at a mechanical mobile. This could be triggered in part by exposure to elevated levels of prenatal testosterone, Baron-Cohen suggests, which might help explain why autism occurs almost five times more often in males than it does in females.

Baron-Cohen's quest to understand the brain-autism connection has led him to explore the link between the kinds of children Hans Asperger studied and minds that seem destined for science. Scientists have a unique ability to make sense of complex systems— the mysteries of the human body, weather patterns, or, in Einstein's case, the physical forces of the universe. Is it possible that scientists are prone to autism? Baron-Cohen has turned up some interesting data from surveys he has conducted: technically minded people scored higher on a checklist of autistic traits compared to nonscientists; math students at the University of Cambridge were nine times more likely to report a formal autism diagnosis than their peers studying the humanities; and children with Asperger's did better on tests of mechanical reasoning compared to older children who were not on the spectrum. In one of his studies, Baron-Cohen set out to determine if autism was more common in places overrun with techies. He and his colleagues looked at rates of autism in the Dutch city of Eindhoven, where roughly 30 percent of jobs are in the information-technology sector. They discovered that children living in what Baron-Cohen refers to as the "Silicon Valley of the Netherlands" were two to four times more likely to be diagnosed with autism than children in two non-tech cities of similar size.

All of this has led Baron-Cohen to surmise that genes that contribute to autism might overlap with genes that make people exceptionally good at systemizing—and that these genes might be passed down from parent to child. He has found that fathers and even grandfathers of children with autism are more likely to work in the field of engineering. Remember Einstein's father, Hermann? He had a knack for math and might have pursued a technical career if he'd had the chance; Hermann's brother, Jakob, did complete his studies in the field and later became a respected engineer. There's no cause and effect here—we'll never know how Einstein's DNA compared to his father's or, for that matter, if either one had genes linked to autism—but it's interesting to ponder.

Baron-Cohen's research is far from conclusive; critics say his findings need to be replicated in other studies. Without more research, there is no proof that a scientist is more likely to be on the autism spectrum than a poet—or that an engineer in Einstein's family had anything to do with the physicist's tenacious focus or wrinkled khakis. Still, the potential association between scientific talent and the autism spectrum is a rich area of exploration, and several experts have weighed in on the possibility that some of history's preeminent scientists may have had the condition.

Oliver Sacks, the neurologist and unrivaled explicator of the human mind, believed that the evidence for Henry Cavendish, the great 18th-century chemist and physicist who discovered hydrogen, is strong. In a report for the medical journal *Neurology*,

Sacks asserted that Cavendish's behavioral characteristics line up with Asperger's syndrome, and the evidence in his case is "almost overwhelming." Exceptionally quiet, Cavendish rarely communicated with anyone and had little understanding of social interaction and human relationships. He held unorthodox ideas and was single-minded in his scientific pursuits, passionate about number crunching, and strikingly literal and direct. "Many of these are the very traits he used so brilliantly in his pioneering scientific research," Sacks wrote, "and we are perhaps fortunate that he also happened to have the means and opportunity to pursue his 'eccentric' interests despite his lack of worldliness."

In his public talks about the science-autism link, Baron-Cohen cites the Royal Society of Medicine paper written by Ioan James, which was published in 2003. In that report, James suggested that not only Cavendish but also Isaac Newton, Marie Curie and her daughter, Irène Joliot-Curie, the theoretical physicist Paul Dirac, and, yes, Einstein, all exhibited traits consistent with Asperger's. In one of Baron-Cohen's lectures, he flashes a picture of Einstein onto the screen and ticks off the scientist's language delay and dearth of childhood friends. As an adult, Baron-Cohen says, "He wanted to be away from people and to really focus, some people would say obsessionally, on the world of physics." Baron-Cohen stops short of a diagnosis. "We don't really know whether if we saw them today, alive, would they meet the criteria," he says of Einstein and the other scientists, "but certainly it's pointing at this connection between great scientific talent and autism or Asperger's."

Had Einstein been born in the 21st century, it is almost certain that he would have been assessed for autism spectrum disorder as a very young child. His parents, already concerned about his delayed development, would have been bombarded by headlines about a surge in diagnoses—one in 68 children is now identified as falling somewhere on the spectrum—so they and their doctors would have surely been on the lookout. Pediatricians are now trained to identify initial signs of the disorder in young children, even in babies just a few months old. Early treatment, which includes intensive sessions of speech and language therapy and hands-on social skills building, can help improve verbal and nonverbal communication dramatically. If Einstein's parents had taken him for a checkup today, his late talking, intense focus, and social detachment would have raised red flags, prompted an autism screening, and possibly warranted a diagnosis.

Would Einstein have qualified for an autism spectrum diagnosis as an adult? Impossible to say. Several of his characteristics appear to fall outside the general conception of the condition, including his numerous romantic liaisons and his humor, which can be a challenge for people with autism given their literal interpretation of information. Reminiscences by people who knew him refer to Einstein's fondness for a good joke and his booming, enveloping laugh. In his writing, Sacks argued that while Cavendish's case is convincing, he found it highly unlikely that Einstein—or Newton or the philosopher Ludwig Wittgenstein, for that matter—was "significantly autistic."

Still, the condition varies widely, and it may come down to degree—the "dash" that Hans Asperger referred to. Grandin, who is a renowned professor of animal sciences at Colorado State University, likens small doses of autism to the marked creativity documented among people with bipolar disorder. Full-blown bipolar, she writes in her book, makes people unable to function; a mild form of the disorder, however, allows them to produce their best work. Similarly, "mild autistic traits can provide the singlemindedness that gets things done," she writes. Einstein, in Grandin's view, fits into this category.

Andy Warhol Was a Hoarder

Grandin exemplifies the ability of some people with autism to integrate themselves into the world while still maintaining their unique characteristics. Although she didn't speak until she was three and a half, Grandin is now a best-selling author and public speaker, lecturing at conferences worldwide. She states emphatically that a person's capacity for human interaction can evolve. "You keep learning more and more social rules," she says. New imaging studies show that therapy can even change the activity in the brains of children with autism, making them look more like typically developing children. Uta Frith, a pioneering autism researcher who brought Hans Asperger's original report to light when she translated it from German to English, has written that some people with Asperger's can achieve "near-normal" behavior by learning social routines well enough that they "strike others as merely eccentric."

In a foreword to Grandin's book, Oliver Sacks described Grandin's classic autistic characteristics—social awkwardness and difficulty processing human emotions—but noted that she had learned "many sorts of humanness" over the years he had known her. "Not least among these is a capacity for humor and even subterfuge," he wrote, "which one would have thought impossible in someone who is autistic." Grandin displays this trait in a point she often makes in interviews and in her public appearances. "Who do you think made the first stone spear?" she asked a *Wall Street Journal* reporter. "That wasn't the yakkity yaks sitting around the campfire. It was some Asperger sitting in the back of a cave figuring out how to chip rocks into spearheads."

It is not surprising that support groups for people with autism and their families are eager to claim visionaries like Grandin and Einstein as their own. Indeed, what used to be known as Asperger's has become something of a diagnosis du jour. Many historical figures, in addition to scientists, have attracted the label, including Thomas Jefferson, Mozart, and Bill Gates. Others have proudly announced their own diagnoses, including Tim Page, the Pulitzer Prize–winning music critic, who was diagnosed with Asperger's in 2000 at the age of 45. "My pervasive childhood memory is an excruciating awareness of my own strangeness," he writes in his memoir, *Parallel Play*. The title comes from his feeling that "my life has been spent in a perpetual state of parallel play, alongside, but distinctly apart from, the rest of humanity."

A whole movement of pride has developed with "Aspies," as they call themselves, relishing their unique characteristics and celebrating their "neurodiversity" as natural variation in the human genome. So what if they're not great cocktail party conversationalists? They might be math geeks who grow up to run billion-dollar software companies. T-shirts that read "Asperger's: Another kind of normal" and "Can't fix what's not broken" constitute one small part of their effort to raise awareness. Some even want to put an end to genetic research, because they fear that hunting down genes in the search for a cure could mean the end of the special qualities they offer the world. Grandin worries about this, too. "I feel very strongly that if you got rid of all of the autistic genetics, you're not going to have any scientists. There'd be no computer people. You'd lose a lot of artists and musicians. There'd be a horrible price to pay," she said in an interview with NPR.

People are intricate puzzles—biologically, genetically, behaviorally—and a psychological label cannot begin to do justice to our rich complexities. Nor can it or should it define anyone, including Albert Einstein and his extraordinary mind. In the end, an exploration of Einstein and the autism spectrum should not determine an absolute diagnosis, but rather unveil the phenomenal heights to which human beings can soar, no matter how "normal" or "odd" they may seem.

⌒

IN OCTOBER 1933, AFTER THE NAZIS seized power in Germany, Albert and Elsa Einstein moved to the United States. At 54, the physicist launched what would be a 22-year career at Princeton, where he remained as brilliant and offbeat as ever, spending much of his time in sweatshirts and baggy pants with no socks. He didn't drive, instead walking the mile or so from his home to his office. A neighbor remembered Einstein inviting her and two other girls in for lunch in his study one day. Einstein's hair shot out in every direction, she recalled, and his office was a mess, with stacks of books and papers everywhere. The physicist heated four cans of beans on a Sterno stove, stuck a spoon into each, and handed them out. "That," she told biographer Denis Brian, "was our lunch."

A lifelong pacifist, Einstein supported antiwar movements and civil rights, and identified strongly with his Jewish heritage. In the fall of 1952, he was offered the presidency of Israel. He turned it down. "All my life I have dealt with objective matters, hence I lack both the natural aptitude and experience to deal properly with people and to exercise official functions," he responded. "For these reasons alone I should be unsuited to fulfill the duties of that high office, even if advancing age was not making increasing inroads on my strength." Almost three years later, on April 18, 1955, Einstein died of a ruptured aortic aneurysm at the age of 76.

Einstein's brain, however, lives on. For years, researchers have been studying pieces of it to see if and how it differs from those of the average person. Several reports have emerged. One found that Einstein had a greater density of neurons in his brain; another determined that Einstein's inferior parietal lobe, which has been linked to mathematical wizardry, was 15 percent wider. Scientists have also reported unusual ridges and grooves, as well as a pronounced knoblike structure in an area linked to musical talent. One analysis even found that while Einstein's brain was average size overall, certain regions responsible for focus and perseverance were greatly expanded.

One of the simplest observations, however, may be the most telling of all. Dr. Lucy Rorke-Adams, a longtime neuropathologist at the Children's Hospital of Philadelphia, spent more time with Einstein's brain than just about anyone. She inherited one of the boxes of Einstein's brain slides from a colleague in the 1970s, and it was she who donated her box to the Mütter Museum after guarding it closely in a file drawer next to her desk for more than 30 years. What struck Rorke-Adams more than anything was the pristine quality of Einstein's brain. "I was extremely impressed," she says. There was very little evidence of a brownish pigment that tends to accumulate over a lifetime and is usually prominent by the time a person reaches the age Einstein was when he died. "The neurons were absolutely exquisite," she says. "It basically looked like the brain of a young person." Einstein's brain seemed untouched by the advance of years.

Youth. It was the essence of how Einstein lived and how he thought, his soaring intellect powered by a childlike curiosity and wonder. "The pursuit of truth and beauty," he once said, "is a sphere of activity in which we are permitted to remain children all our lives."

Afterword

RESEARCHING THIS BOOK has given me the extraordinary experience of feeling like a child with 12 imaginary friends. And what a privilege it has been. I have gotten to know these complex, intriguing historical figures at both a personal and public level through the luminous bits of creative energy they left behind—letters, diaries, autobiographies, films, literary works, paintings, scientific treatises, musical compositions, architectural designs, presidential proclamations.

Much of what I discovered in these pages came to life through the wonders of the Internet. In a matter of minutes, I was able to call up correspondence written by Dostoevsky in the 1800s and Einstein in the 1900s. I found stunning photos of Lincoln's second Inauguration in 1865 and a medical report about Darwin's ills dating back to 1901. YouTube made it possible to relive Princess Diana's walk down the aisle at St. Paul's Cathedral, watch Marilyn Monroe sing "Happy Birthday" to JFK, and marvel as Mike Wallace interviewed Frank Lloyd Wright in a cloud of cigarette smoke on black-and-white television. One of my greatest pleasures was listening to live recordings of Gershwin playing *Rhapsody in Blue* while I tapped away on my keyboard.

Andy Warhol Was a Hoarder

When possible, I also visited places where these historical figures live on in tangible ways. In Pittsburgh, I studied Warhol's silk screens and "oxidation" paintings at the Andy Warhol Museum; in Alexandria, Virginia, I toured the Pope-Leighey House, one of Frank Lloyd Wright's Usonian homes; in Philadelphia, I stared with disbelief at slices of Einstein's brain—Einstein's brain!—at the Mütter Museum.

I do not presume to know everything about these 12 minds and the infinite thoughts, fears, and desires that swirled through them. Far from it. But I learned enough to appreciate, more deeply than ever, the disparity that often exists between our inner and outer selves—despite their inseparable connection.

Science is doing its best to unravel the mysteries that drive the interaction between inner and outer—why we feel and act the way we do, what happens when something goes wrong. This is a tough and valiant effort. Mental health research is often overlooked, underfunded, and stigmatized. The scientists I interviewed impressed me deeply with their commitments to better understanding the brain so that they can help people emerge from the depths of depression, stop injuring themselves, or quit their addictions to drugs and alcohol. As they continue to sort out the entanglement of genes, life experiences, and environmental risk factors that contribute to mental health conditions, some torment may be alleviated, and some lives bolstered and rejuvenated.

My research has also made clear that there are no absolutes when it comes to behaviors, diagnoses, and treatments. In some cases, shyness may just be shyness, not a symptom of an illness that needs to be treated. In other situations, a mental health diagnosis will be warranted so that therapy can make life more purposeful and satisfying. Medication may be enormously helpful for certain patients; others might do as well or even better with psychotherapy, support groups, lifestyle changes (more exercise, better sleep, relaxation techniques), or a combination. Probing the biology of the brain is critical—but so is a more holistic approach that explores a person's experiences, feelings, and motivations. There are valid concerns about overtreating human behavior, and equally important worries about undertreating serious disorders. Patient privacy is important, as is an openness that will help reduce stigma. Language and terminology are shifting, and fresh concepts are emerging. Distinct diagnoses are giving way to an understanding of the similarities that underlie many mental health conditions, which is in turn driving research in new directions.

All of these intricacies have made writing this book equal parts daunting, challenging, and fascinating. I view my exploration of these 12 historical figures and their minds as an entrée into this complex world, not a journey that has ended. I hope the hypotheses I've explored and the questions I've raised will lead to a better appreciation of the many tangled forces that make up our collective minds—and a greater empathy for the trials we all face.

It seems fitting to end this book with a reflection on Charles Darwin, whose 19th-century pilgrimage into nature resonates with a 21st-century expedition of the mind. In early 1832, while traveling aboard the *Beagle*, Darwin wrote in his journal about the "transports of pleasure" he encountered while exploring the landscapes and forests of Brazil. He described an abundance of nature's splendor—"the elegance of the grasses, the novelty of the parasitical plants, the beauty of the flowers" and the "paradoxical mixture of sound & silence." This intoxicating jumble, with its butterflies and fruits and soft air, brought him enormous joy.

It was a place of beauty and bewilderment. In describing his reaction to all that he was seeing, Darwin wrote that "the mind is a chaos of delight."

Simple words for the vast enigmas of the mind. A chaos of delight it is.

—Claudia Kalb
May 2015

Sources and Notes

Throughout the course of my research, I conducted dozens of interviews with mental health professionals, scientists, and academic researchers. A wide variety of source materials informed my biographical research, including diaries, letters, newspaper and magazine articles, autobiographies, and biographies. In my analysis of mental health conditions, I consulted medical and scientific journals and books, as well as content published by mental health associations, medical associations, and government health organizations. These included the American Academy of Pediatrics, American Psychiatric Association, American Psychological Association, Centers for Disease Control and Prevention, Harvard Health Publications, National Alliance on Mental Illness, and National Institute of Mental Health. For each chapter, I consulted the American Psychiatric Association's *Diagnostic and Statistical Manual of Mental Disorders*, fifth edition (*DSM-5*, 2013), as well as fact sheets on the APA's website.

In my notes below, I have highlighted materials mentioned within each chapter's text as well as additional sources that helped inform my understanding of the historical figures and the mental health conditions presented.

Introduction

Conversations with experts in the field provided me with invaluable insights into the state of mental health research as well as the value and challenge of evaluating historical figures and the mind. These individuals include Dr. Jeffrey Borenstein, Brain and Behavior Research Foundation; Dr. David Kupfer, University of Pittsburgh School of Medicine; Dr. Philip Mackowiak and Dr. David Mallott, University of Maryland School of Medicine; Dr. Michael Miller, Harvard Medical School; Dr. Osamu

Andy Warhol Was a Hoarder

Muramoto, Center for Ethics in Health Care, Oregon Health and Science University; Dr. David Rettew, University of Vermont College of Medicine; and Mark Smaller, president, American Psychoanalytic Association.

Numerous books informed my understanding of mental health and historical diagnosis. These include Philip Marshall Dale, *Medical Biographies: The Ailments of Thirty-Three Famous Persons* (Norman, OK: University of Oklahoma Press, 1952); Brian Dillon, *The Hypochondriacs: Nine Tormented Lives* (New York: Faber and Faber, 2010); Douglas Goldman et al., *Retrospective Diagnoses of Historical Personalities as Viewed by Leading Contemporary Psychiatrists* (Bloomfield, NJ: Schering Corporation, 1958); Kay Redfield Jamison, *Touched with Fire: Manic-Depressive Illness and the Artistic Temperament* (New York: Free Press, 1993); Jeffrey A. Kottler, *Divine Madness: Ten Stories of Creative Struggle* (San Francisco: Jossey-Bass, 2006); Philip Mackowiak, *Post-Mortem: Solving History's Great Medical Mysteries* (Philadelphia: American College of Physicians, 2007); Roy Porter, *Madness: A Brief History* (New York: Oxford University Press, 2002); David Rettew, *Child Temperament: New Thinking About the Boundary Between Traits and Illness* (New York: W. W. Norton, 2013).

Articles include: Nancy C. Andreasen et al., "Relapse Duration, Treatment Intensity, and Brain Tissue Loss in Schizophrenia: A Prospective Longitudinal MRI Study," *American Journal of Psychiatry* 170, No. 6 (June 1, 2013), 609–15; Milton Cameron, "Albert Einstein, Frank Lloyd Wright, Le Corbusier, and the Future of the American City," Institute for Advanced Study, *Institute Letter* (Spring 2014), 8–9; D. S. Carson et al., "Cerebrospinal Fluid and Plasma Oxytocin Concentrations Are Positively Correlated and Negatively Predict Anxiety in Children," *Molecular Psychiatry* (online ed.; November 4, 2014), doi: 10.1038/mp.2014.132; Cross-Disorder Group of the Psychiatric Genomics Consortium, "Identification of Risk Loci With Shared Effects on Five Major Psychiatric Disorders: A Genome-Wide Analysis," *Lancet* 381, No. 9875 (April 2013), 1371–79; Eric Kandel, "The New Science of Mind," *New York Times,* December 6, 2013; Callie L. McGrath et al., "Toward a Neuroimaging Treatment Selection Biomarker for Major Depressive Disorder," *JAMA Psychiatry* 70, No. 8 (August 2013), 821–29; Richard Milner, "Darwin's Shrink," *Natural History* 114, No. 9 (November 2005), 42–44.

A note about the increase in mental disorders in the *DSM* (from 80 in the first edition to 157 in the fifth edition): These numbers were provided by the American Psychiatric Association and refer to the total number of distinct disorders contained in the manual. They do not include subtypes of disorders, variation in severity within disorders (mild, moderate, or severe, for example), or "unspecified" disorders. I chose to cite the APA's tally of distinct diagnoses, but it should be noted that the number of possible diagnoses contained in the *DSM* is higher.

Sources and Notes

Marilyn Monroe
Books

Lois Banner, *Marilyn: The Passion and the Paradox* (New York: Bloomsbury, 2012); Arnold M. Ludwig, *How Do We Know Who We Are? A Biography of the Self* (New York: Oxford University Press, 1997); Arthur Miller, *Timebends: A Life* (New York: Grove Press, 1987); Marilyn Monroe, *Fragments: Poems, Intimate Notes, Letters* (New York: Farrar, Straus and Giroux, 2010); Marilyn Monroe, *My Story* (New York: Cooper Square Press, 2000); Sarah K. Reynolds and Marsha M. Linehan, "Dialectical Behavior Therapy," in *Encyclopedia of Psychotherapy* 1, eds. Michel Hersen and William H. Sledge (Academic Press, 2002), 621–28; Donald Spoto, *Marilyn Monroe: The Biography* (New York: HarperCollins, 1993); Gloria Steinem and George Barris, *Marilyn: Norma Jeane* (New York: East Toledo Productions, 1986); Anthony Summers, *Goddess: The Secret Lives of Marilyn Monroe* (New York: Macmillan, 1985); J. Randy Taraborrelli, *The Secret Life of Marilyn Monroe* (New York: Grand Central Publishing, 2009).

Newspapers, Magazines, and Medical Reports

Lois Banner, "The Meaning of Marilyn," *Women's Review of Books* 28, No. 3 (May/June 2010), 3–4; Robert S. Biskin and Joel Paris, "Diagnosing Borderline Personality Disorder," *Canadian Medical Association Journal* 184, No. 16 (November 6, 2012), 1789–94; Benedict Carey, "Expert on Mental Illness Reveals Her Own Fight," *New York Times*, June 23, 2011; Richard Ben Cramer, "The DiMaggio Nobody Knew," *Newsweek*, March 22, 1999; John Gunderson, "Borderline Personality Disorder," *New England Journal of Medicine* 364, No. 21 (May 26, 2011), 2037–42; John Gunderson et al., "Borderline Personality Disorder," *Focus* 11, No. 2 (Spring 2013); John Gunderson et al., "Family Study of Borderline Personality Disorder and Its Sectors of Psychopathology," *Archives of General Psychiatry* 68, No. 7 (July 2011), 753–62; Barbara Grizzuti Harrison, "Vengeful Fantasies," *New Republic*, February 28, 1991; James Harvey, "Marilyn Reconsidered," *Threepenny Review* 58 (Summer 1994), 35–37; Constance Holden, "Sex and the Suffering Brain," *Science* 308 (June 10, 2005), 1574–77; Sam Kashner, "The Things She Left Behind," *Vanity Fair*, October 2008; Susan King, "Marilyn Monroe's Last Film Work Resurrected for New Documentary," *Los Angeles Times*, May 28, 2001; Robert E. Litman, "Suicidology: A Look Backward and Ahead," *Suicide and Life-Threatening Behavior* 26, No. 1 (Spring 1996); Larry McMurtry, "Marilyn," *New York Review of Books*, March 10, 2011; Daphne Merkin, "Platinum Pain," *New Yorker*, February 8, 1999; Richard Meryman, "A Last Long Talk With a Lonely Girl," *Life*, August 17, 1962; Richard Meryman, "Marilyn Monroe Lets Her Hair Down About Being Famous: 'Fame Will Go By and—So Long, I've

Andy Warhol Was a Hoarder

Had You,' " *Life*, August 3, 1962; Andrada D. Neacsiu et al., "Impact of Dialectical Behavior Therapy Versus Community Treatment by Experts on Emotional Experience, Expression, and Acceptance in Borderline Personality Disorder," *Behaviour Research and Therapy* 53 (2014), 47–54; Joel Paris, "Borderline Personality Disorder," *Canadian Medical Association Journal* 172, No. 12 (June 7, 2005), 1579–83; Patrick Perry, "Personality Disorders: Coping With the Borderline," *Saturday Evening Post*, July/August 1997; Carl E. Rollyson, Jr., "Marilyn: Mailer's Novel Biography," *Biography* 1, No. 4 (Fall 1978), 49–67; William Todd Schultz, "How Do We Know Who We Are? A Biography of the Self," *Biography* 22, No. 3 (Summer 1999), 416–20; Lee Siegel, "Unsexing Marilyn," *New York Review of Books*, NYR Blog, January 5, 2012; Diana Trilling, "The Death of Marilyn Monroe," *Encounter*, August 1963; Diana Trilling, " 'Please Don't Make Me a Joke,' " *New York Times*, December 21, 1986; Christopher Turner, "Marilyn Monroe on the Couch," *Telegraph*, June 23, 2010.

Online

Georges Belmont, interview with Marilyn Monroe, video, *Marie Claire*, April 1960, https://vimeo.com/76791522; Jesse Greenspan, " 'Happy Birthday, Mr. President' Turns 50," History.com, www.history.com/news/happy-birthday-mr-president-turns-50; John Gunderson, "A BPD Brief: An Introduction to Borderline Personality Disorder: Diagnosis, Origins, Course, and Treatment," www.borderlinepersonalitydisorder.com/professionals/a-bpd-brief/.

Howard Hughes
Books

Donald L. Barlett and James B. Steele, *Howard Hughes: His Life and Madness* (New York: W. W. Norton, 1979); Peter Harry Brown and Pat H. Broeske, *Howard Hughes: The Untold Story* (New York: Dutton, 1996); Richard Hack, *Hughes: The Private Diaries, Memos and Letters* (Beverly Hills: New Millennium Press, 2001); Jeffrey Schwartz with Beverly Beyette, *Brain Lock: Free Yourself From Obsessive-Compulsive Behavior* (New York: ReganBooks, 1996).

Newspapers, Magazines, and Medical Reports

Riadh T. Abed and Karel W. de Pauw, "An Evolutionary Hypothesis for Obsessive Compulsive Disorder: A Psychological Immune System?" *Behavioural Neurology* 11 (1998/1999), 245–50; Lisa Belkin, "Can You Catch Obsessive-Compulsive Disorder?" *New York Times*, May 22, 2005; Nicholas Dodman, "Obsessive Compulsive

Disorder in Animals," *Veterinary Practice News* (November 2012); Raymond D. Fowler, "Howard Hughes: A Psychological Autopsy," *Psychology Today* (May 1986), 22–33; Jon E. Grant, "Obsessive-Compulsive Disorder," *New England Journal of Medicine* 371, No. 7 (August 14, 2104), 646–53; Jerome Groopman, "The Doubting Disease," *New Yorker*, April 10, 2000; Edward D. Huey et al., "A Psychological and Neuroanatomical Model of Obsessive-Compulsive Disorder," *Journal of Neuropsychiatry and Clinical Neuroscience*s 20, No. 4 (Fall 2008), 390–408; Michael Jenike, "Obsessive-Compulsive Disorder," *New England Journal of Medicine* 350, No. 3 (January 15, 2004), 259–65; Gilbert King, "The Rise and Fall of Nikola Tesla and His Tower," *Smithsonian*, February 4, 2013; Salla Koponen et al., "Axis I and II Psychiatric Disorders After Traumatic Brain Injury: A 30-Year Follow-Up Study," *American Journal of Psychiatry* 159, No. 8 (August 2002), 1315–21; David L. Pauls, "The Genetics of Obsessive-Compulsive Disorder: A Review," *Dialogues in Clinical Neuroscience* 12, No. 2 (June 2010), 149–63; Dan J. Stein, "Obsessive-Compulsive Disorder," *Lancet* 360 (August 2002), 397–405; Steve Volk, "Rewiring the Brain to Treat OCD," *Discover*, November 2013.

Online

Anxiety and Depression Association of America, www.adaa.org; College of Physicians of Philadelphia, "History of Polio," www.historyofvaccines.org/content/timelines/polio; Rebecca Murray, "Leonard DiCaprio Talks About 'The Aviator,' " movies.about .com/od/theaviator/a/aviatorld121004.htm; "Obsessive Compulsive Disorder—History, Imaging, and Treatment: An Expert Interview with Judith L. Rapoport, MD," April 30, 2007, www.medscape.com/viewarticle/554732.

Films

Martin Scorsese, *The Aviator* (2004); *Howard Hughes Revealed* (2007), National Geographic Channel.

Andy Warhol
Books

Victor Bockris, *Warhol: The Biography* (New York: Da Capo Press, 2003); David Bourdon, *Warhol* (New York: Harry N. Abrams, 1989); Bob Colacello, *Holy Terror: Andy Warhol Close Up* (New York: HarperCollins, 1990); Randy O. Frost and Gail Steketee, *Stuff: Compulsive Hoarding and the Meaning of Things* (New York: Houghton Mifflin Harcourt, 2010); Kenneth Goldsmith, ed., *I'll Be Your Mirror: The Selected*

Andy Warhol Was a Hoarder

Andy Warhol Interviews (New York: Carroll and Graf, 2004); Pat Hackett, ed., *The Andy Warhol Diaries* (New York: Warner Books, 1989); Wayne Koestenbaum, *Andy Warhol* (New York: Viking Penguin, 2001); Tony Scherman and David Dalton, *Pop: The Genius of Andy Warhol* (New York: HarperCollins, 2009); John W. Smith, ed., *Possession Obsession: Andy Warhol and Collecting* (Pittsburgh, PA: Andy Warhol Museum, 2002); Andy Warhol, *The Philosophy of Andy Warhol (From A to B and Back Again)* (New York: Harcourt Brace Jovanovich, 1978); Robin Zasio, *The Hoarder in You: How to Live a Happier, Healthier, Uncluttered Life* (New York: Rodale, 2011).

Newspapers, Magazines, and Medical Reports

Jennifer G. Andrews-McClymont et al., "Evaluating an Animal Model of Compulsive Hoarding in Humans," *Review of General Psychology* 17, No. 4 (2013), 399–419; Deborah Bright, "Shopping the Leftovers: Warhol's Collecting Strategies in *Raid the Icebox I*," *Art History* 24, No. 2 (April 2001), 278–91; William Bryk, "The Collyer Brothers, Past & Present," *New York Sun,* April 13, 2005; Harold Faber, "Body of Collyer Is Found Near Where Brother Died," *New York Times,* April 9, 1947; Randy O. Frost, "Hoarding: Making Disorder an Official Disorder," *Insight,* September 14, 2012; Melissa Grace, "Jackie Kin, Model Edith Beale Dies," *New York Daily News,* January 27, 2002; Julie Hannon, "Face Time," *Carnegie,* Spring 2008; James C. Harris, "Before and After and Superman: Andy Warhol," *JAMA Psychiatry* 71, No. 1 (January 2014); "Inside the Collyer Brownstone, the Story of Harlem's Hermits and Their Hoarding," *New York Daily News,* October 19, 2012; Ann Kolson, "Warhol's Collection 10,000 Items—From Cookie Jars to Precious Gems—Will Be Auctioned Starting Saturday in New York," *Philadelphia Inquirer,* April 20, 1988; Jesse Kornbluth, "The World of Warhol," *New York,* March 9, 1987; Bridget M. Kuehn, "Trouble Letting Go: Hoarders," *Journal of the American Medical Association* 308, No. 12 (September 26, 2012), 1198; Scott O. Lilienfeld and Hal Arkowitz, "Hoarding Can Be a Deadly Business," *Scientific American* 24, No. 4 (September 2013); Douglas Martin, "Edith Bouvier Beale, 84, 'Little Edie,' Dies," *New York Times,* January 25, 2002; David Mataix-Cols, "Hoarding Disorder," *New England Journal of Medicine* 370 (May 22, 2014), 2023–30; Cathleen McGuigan, "The Selling of Andy Warhol," *Newsweek,* April 18, 1988; Louis Menand, "Top of the Pops," *New Yorker,* January 11, 2010; Suzanne Muchnic, "Rummaging Through the Andy Warhol Estate," *Los Angeles Times,* February 21, 1988; Cristina Rouvalis, "Unpacking Andy," *Carnegie,* Spring 2012; Gail Sheehy, "A Return to Grey Gardens," *New York,* May 28, 2007; Richard F. Shepard, "Warhol Gravely Wounded in Studio," *New York Times,* June 4, 1968; John W. Smith, "Saving Time: Andy Warhol's Time Capsules," *Art Documentation: Journal of the Art Libraries Society of North America* 20, No. 1 (Spring 2001); John Taylor, "Andy's

Empire: Big Money and Big Questions," *New York*, February 22, 1988; John Taylor, "Andy's Empire II: Rosebud," *New York,* March 7, 1988; David F. Tolin et al., "Neural Mechanisms of Decision Making in Hoarding Disorder," *Archives of General Psychiatry* 69, No. 8 (August 2012), 832–41; Bonnie Tsui, "Why Do You Hoard?" *Pacific Standard,* April 29, 2013; Matt Wrbican, "Warhol's Hoard a Treasure Trove," *Sydney Morning Herald,* November 20, 2007.

Films
David Maysles, Albert Maysles, Ellen Hovde, Muffie Meyer, Susan Froemke, *Grey Gardens* (1975).

Princess Diana

Books

Tina Brown, *The Diana Chronicles* (New York: Doubleday, 2007); Joan Jacobs Brumberg, *Fasting Girls: The History of Anorexia Nervosa* (New York: Vintage Books, 2000); Jonathan Dimbleby, *Prince of Wales: A Biography* (New York: William Morrow, 1994); Andrew Morton, *Diana: Her True Story* (New York: Simon & Schuster, 1997); Andrew Morton, *Diana: In Pursuit of Love* (London: Michael O'Mara Books, 2004); Sally Bedell Smith, *Diana in Search of Herself: Portrait of a Troubled Princess* (New York: Times Books, 1999).

Newspapers, Magazines, and Medical Reports

Scott J. Crow et al., "Increased Mortality in Bulimia Nervosa and Other Eating Disorders," *American Journal of Psychiatry* 166, No. 12 (December 2009), 1342–46; Laura Currin et al., "Time Trends in Eating Disorder Incidence," *British Journal of Psychiatry* 186 (March 2005), 132–35; Nigel Dempster, "Diana, Princess of Wales," *People*, December 27, 1982; Clive James, "Requiem," *New Yorker*, September 15, 1997; Frank Kermode, "Shrinking the Princess," *New York Times*, August 22, 1999; John Lanchester, "The Naked and the Dead," *New Yorker*, June 25, 2007; Daniel Le Grange et al., "Academy for Eating Disorders Position Paper: The Role of the Family in Eating Disorders," *International Journal of Eating Disorders* 43, No. 1 (2010), 1–5; Rachel Marsh et al., "Deficient Activity in the Neural Systems That Mediate Self-Regulatory Control in Bulimia Nervosa," *Archives of General Psychiatry* 66, No. 1 (2009), 51–63; Rachel Marsh et al., "An fMRI Study of Self-Regulatory Control and Conflict Resolution in Adolescents with Bulimia Nervosa," *American Journal of Psychiatry* 168, No. 11 (November 2011); David Noonan, "Di Struggled With Mental Demons: New Biography Reveals Her Personality Disorder," *New York Daily News*, August 15, 1999; Richard

Smith, "Death of Diana, Princess of Wales: A Special Life Forged from Adversity," *British Medical Journal* 315 (September 6, 1997), 562; Charles Spencer, "Brother's Eulogy for Diana: 'The Very Essence of Compassion,'" *New York Times*, September 7, 1997.

Online

Tom Clark, "Queen Enjoys Record Support in Guardian/ICM Poll," *Guardian*, www.theguardian.com/uk/2012/may/24/queen-diamond-jubilee-record-support; "Interview With Earl Charles Spencer," transcript, CNN, *Larry King Weekend*, August 31, 2002, transcripts.cnn.com/TRANSCRIPTS/0208/31/lklw.00.html; "Interview With Princess Diana Biographer Andrew Morton," transcript, CNN, *Larry King Live*, March 10, 2004, transcripts.cnn.com/TRANSCRIPTS/0403/10/lkl.00.html; "The Princess and the Press," interview of Princess Diana by Martin Bashir, transcript, BBC, *Panorama,* November 1995, www.pbs.org/wgbh/pages/frontline/shows/royals/interviews/bbc.html; "Princess Diana: Growing Up to Be Princess," transcript, CNN, *People in the News,* aired September 1, 2001, www.cnn.com/TRANSCRIPTS/0109/01/pitn.00.html; K. D. Reynolds, "Diana, Princess of Wales (1961–1997)," *Oxford Dictionary of National Biography*, online edition, January 2014, dx.doi.org/10.1093/ref:odnb/68348; "The Royal Wedding of HRH The Prince of Wales and the Lady Diana Spencer," television program, BBC One, aired July 29, 1981, www.bbc.co.uk/programmes/p00frtkf; James Whitaker, "The People's Princess I Knew: Diana's Extraordinary Life Remembered by Our Legendary Royal Reporter James Whitaker," *Mirror*, August 30, 2012, www.mirror.co.uk/news/uk-news/princess-dianas-life-and-death-obituary-1282386.

Abraham Lincoln
Books

Michael Burlingame, *The Inner World of Abraham Lincoln* (Chicago: University of Illinois Press, 1997); David Herbert Donald, *Lincoln* (New York: Simon & Schuster, 1995); Daniel Mark Epstein, *The Lincolns: Portrait of a Marriage* (New York: Ballantine Books, 2008); Don E. Fehrenbacher and Virginia Fehrenbacher, eds., *Recollected Words of Abraham Lincoln* (Palo Alto, CA: Stanford University Press, 1996); Nassir Ghaemi, *A First-Rate Madness: Uncovering the Links Between Leadership and Mental Illness* (New York: Penguin Press, 2011); Nassir Ghaemi, *On Depression: Drugs, Diagnosis, and Despair in the Modern World* (Baltimore: Johns Hopkins University Press, 2013); Doris Kearns Goodwin, *Team of Rivals: The Political Genius of Abraham Lincoln* (New York: Simon & Schuster, 2005); Harold Holzer, ed., *Lincoln as I Knew Him: Gossip, Tributes and Revelations From His Best*

Sources and Notes

Friends and Worst Enemies (Chapel Hill, NC: Algonquin Books, 1999); Peter Kramer, *Against Depression* (New York: Viking, 2005); James M. McPherson, *Abraham Lincoln* (Oxford: Oxford University Press, 2009); Joshua Wolf Shenk, *Lincoln's Melancholy: How Depression Challenged a President and Fueled His Greatness* (New York: Houghton Mifflin, 2005); Andrew Solomon, *The Noonday Demon: An Atlas of Depression* (New York: Scribner, 2001); Anthony Storr, *Churchill's Black Dog, Kafka's Mice, and Other Phenomena of the Human Mind* (New York: Grove Press, 1988); William Styron, *Darkness Visible: A Memoir of Madness* (New York: Random House, 1990).

Newspapers, Magazines, and Medical Reports

David Brent et al., "The Incidence and Course of Depression in Bereaved Youth 21 Months After the Loss of a Parent to Suicide, Accident, or Sudden Natural Death," *American Journal of Psychiatry* 166, No. 7 (July 2009), 786–94; Caleb Crain, "Rail-Splitting: Two Opposite Approaches to Honest Abe," *New Yorker*, November 7, 2005; Richard A. Friedman, "A New Focus on Depression," *New York Times*, December 23, 2013; Adam Goodheart, "Lincoln: A Beard Is Born," *New York Times*, November 24, 2010; Allen C. Guelzo, "Blue Beard: A Revealing Look at Why Lincoln's Depression Didn't Cost Him Politically," *Washington Monthly*, December 2005; Norbert Hirschhorn et al., "Abraham Lincoln's Blue Pills: Did Our 16th President Suffer from Mercury Poisoning?" *Perspectives in Biology and Medicine* 44, No. 3 (Summer 2001), 315–32; Harold Holzer, "Five Myths About Abraham Lincoln," *Washington Post*, February 17, 2011; Huguette Martel, "If They Had Prozac in the Nineteenth Century," cartoon, *New Yorker*, November 8, 1993; Michael T. Moore and David M. Fresco, "Depressive Realism: A Meta-Analytic Review," *Clinical Psychology Review* 32 (May 2012), 496–509; Mark Olfson and Steven C. Marcus, "National Patterns in Antidepressant Medication Treatment," *Archives of General Psychiatry* 66, No. 8 (August 2009), 848–56; Erik Parens, "Do Think Twice: Kramer and Shenk on Depression," *Perspectives in Biology and Medicine* 50, No. 2 (Spring 2007), 295–307; Joshua Wolf Shenk, "Lincoln's Great Depression," *Atlantic*, October 2005; George M. Slavich et al., "Early Parental Loss and Depression History: Associations with Recent Life Stress in Major Depressive Disorder," *Journal of Psychiatric Research* 45 (September 2011), 1146–52; Andrew Solomon, "Anatomy of Melancholy," *New Yorker*, January 12, 1998; Andrew Solomon, "The Blue and the Gray," *New York*, October 17, 2005; Ida M. Tarbell, "Lincoln Greater, Says Ida M. Tarbell, Each Passing Year," *New York Times*, February 11, 1917; Brian Vastag, "Decade of Work Shows Depression Is Physical," *Journal of the American Medical Association* 287, No. 14 (April 10, 2002), 1787–88.

Online

"Address of Carl Sandburg Before the Joint Session of Congress, February 2, 1959, www.nps.gov/carl/learn/historyculture/upload/Address-of-Carl-Sandburg-before-the-Joint-Session-of-Congress.pdf; William H. Herndon and Jesse W. Weik, *Abraham Lincoln: The True Story of a Great Life*, vols. 1 and 2 (1888–1896; Project Gutenberg, 2012), www.gutenberg.org/ebooks/38483 and www.gutenberg.org/ebooks/38484; Elizabeth Keckley, *Behind the Scenes* (New York: G. W. Carleton, 1868; Project Gutenberg, 2008), www.gutenberg.org/ebooks/24968; Douglas F. Levinson and Walter E. Nichols, "Major Depression and Genetics," Stanford University School of Medicine, depressiongenetics.stanford.edu/mddandgenes.html; Ida M. Tarbell, ed., "Abraham Lincoln," *McClure's*, December 1895 (Project Gutenberg, 2004), www.gutenberg.org/files/11548/11548-h/11548-h.htm.

Christine Jorgensen

A note about names and pronouns: After careful consideration, I chose to identify Jorgensen as George and to use male pronouns in my descriptions of her childhood and early adulthood before her transition. This is in no way meant to be disrespectful; instead, my goal was to maintain a consistency with Jorgensen's own account in her autobiography, along with her doctors reports at the time, and to make the narrative and medical history clear for readers.

Books

Chaz Bono, *Transition: The Story of How I Became a Man* (New York: Dutton, 2011); Jennifer Finney Boylan, *She's Not There: A Life in Two Genders* (New York: Broadway Books, 2003); Paul de Kruif, *The Male Hormone* (New York: Harcourt Brace, 1945); Richard F. Docter, *Becoming a Woman: A Biography of Christine Jorgensen* (New York: Haworth Press, Taylor and Francis Group, 2008); Christine Jorgensen, *A Personal Autobiography* (New York: Bantam Books, 1967); Pagan Kennedy, *The First Man-Made Man: The Story of Two Sex Changes, One Love Affair, and a Twentieth-Century Medical Revolution* (New York: Bloomsbury, 2007); Joanne Meyerowitz, *How Sex Changed: A History of Transsexuality in the United States* (Cambridge, MA: Harvard University Press, 2002); Jan Morris, *Conundrum* (New York: New York Review of Books, 2002).

Newspapers, Magazines, and Medical Reports

Jacob Bernstein, "A Barney's Campaign Embraces a Gender Identity Issue," *New York Times,* January 29, 2014; Amy Bloom, "The Body Lies," *New Yorker*, July 18, 1994;

Sources and Notes

Jennifer Finney Boylan, " 'Maddy' Just Might Work After All," *New York Times*, April 24, 2009; William Byne et al., "Report of the APA Task Force on Treatment of Gender Identity Disorder," *American Journal of Psychiatry* 169, No. 8 (August 2012), 1–35; Peggy T. Cohen-Kettenis et al., "Puberty Suppression in a Gender-Dysphoric Adolescent: A 22-Year Follow-Up," *Archives of Sexual Behavior* 40, No. 4 (August 2011), 843–47; Peggy T. Cohen-Kettenis and Friedemann Pfäfflin, "The *DSM* Diagnostic Criteria for Gender Identity Disorder in Adolescents and Adults," *Archives of Sexual Behavior* 39, No. 2 (April 2010), 499–513; Annelou L. C. de Vries et al., "Puberty Suppression in Adolescents With Gender Identity Disorder: A Prospective Follow-Up Study," *Journal of Sexual Medicine* 8 (August 2011), 2276–83; Alice Dreger, "Gender Identity Disorder in Childhood: Inconclusive Advice to Parents," *Hastings Center Report* 39, No. 1 (January/February 2009), 26–29; Jack Drescher, "Controversies in Gender Diagnoses," *LGBT Health* 1, No. 1 (2013), 9–15; Jack Drescher et al., "Minding the Body: Situating Gender Identity Diagnoses in the ICD-11," *International Review of Psychiatry* 24, No. 6 (December 2012), 568–77; Jack Drescher and William Byne, "Gender Dysphoric/Gender Variant (GD/GV) Children and Adolescents: Summarizing What We Know and What We Have Yet to Learn," *Journal of Homosexuality* 59 (March 2012), 501–10; Christian Hamburger et al., "Transvestism: Hormonal, Psychiatric, and Surgical Treatment," *Journal of the American Medical Association* 152, No. 5 (May 30, 1953); Melissa Hines, "Prenatal Endocrine Influences on Sexual Orientation and on Sexually Differentiated Childhood Behavior," *Frontiers in Neuroendocrinology* 32, No. 2 (April 2011), 170–82; Michele Ingrassia, "In 1952, She Was a Scandal: When George Jorgensen Decided to Change His Name—and His Body—the Nation Wasn't Quite Ready," *Newsday*, May 5, 1989; Baudewijntje P. C. Kreukels and Peggy T. Cohen-Kettenis, "Puberty Suppression in Gender Identity Disorder: The Amsterdam Experience," *Nature Reviews Endocrinology* 7 (August 2011), 466–72; Paul McHugh, "Transgender Surgery Isn't the Solution," *Wall Street Journal*, June 12, 2014; Joanne Meyerowitz, "Transforming Sex: Christine Jorgensen in the Postwar U.S.," *OAH Magazine of History* 20, No. 2 (March 2006); Hilleke E. Hulshoff Pol et al., "Changing Your Sex Changes Your Brain: Influences of Testosterone and Estrogen on Adult Human Brain Structure," *European Journal of Endocrinology* 155 (November 1, 2006), S107–14; Roni Caryn Rabin, "Medicare to Now Cover Sex-Change Surgery," *New York Times*, May 30, 2014; Yolanda L. S. Smith et al., "Adolescents with Gender Identity Disorder Who Were Accepted or Rejected for Sex Reassignment Surgery: A Prospective Follow-Up Study," *Journal of the American Academy of Child and Adolescent Psychiatry* 40, No. 4 (April 2001), 472–81; Norman Spack, "Management of Transgenderism," *Journal of the American Medical Association* 309, No. 5 (February 6, 2013), 478–84; Katy Steinmetz, "The Transgender Tipping Point," *Time*, May 29, 2014; Margaret Talbot, "About a Boy: Transgender Surgery at Sixteen," *New Yorker*, March 18, 2013; Laura Wexler, "Identity Crisis," *Baltimore Style*, January/Feburary 2007; George Wiedeman, "Tranvestism," *Journal of the American Medical Association* 152, No. 12 (July 18, 1953), 1167; Cintra Wilson, "The Reluctant Transgender Role Model," *New York Times*, May 6, 2011.

Online

Jaime M. Grant et al., "Injustice at Every Turn: A Report of the National Transgender Discrimination Survey," National Center for Transgender Equality and National Gay and Lesbian Taskforce, 2011, www.endtransdiscrimination.org; Beth Greenfield, "Transgender Author Jennifer Finney Boylan Went from Dad to Mom: How It Changed Her Family," Yahoo! Shine, May 3, 2013, ca.shine.yahoo.com/blogs/mothers-day/transgender-author-jennifer-finney-boylan-went-from-dad-to-mom--how-it-changed-her-family-162811616.html.

Frank Lloyd Wright
Books

William Cronon, "Inconstant Unity: The Passion of Frank Lloyd Wright" in *Frank Lloyd Wright: Architect*, ed. Terence Riley (New York: Museum of Modern Art, 1994), 8–31; Roger Friedland and Harold Zellman, *The Fellowship: The Untold Story of Frank Lloyd Wright and the Taliesin Fellowship* (New York: HarperCollins, 2006); Brendan Gill, *Many Masks: A Life of Frank Lloyd Wright* (New York: G. P. Putnam's Sons, 1987); Anne C. Heller, *Ayn Rand and the World She Made* (New York: Anchor Books, 2010); Ada Louise Huxtable, *Frank Lloyd Wright: A Life* (New York: Penguin Books, 2008); Walter Isaacson, *Steve Jobs* (New York: Simon & Schuster, 2011); Jeffrey Kluger, *The Narcissist Next Door: Understanding the Monster in Your Family, in Your Office, in Your Bed—in Your World* (New York: Riverhead Books, 2014); Linda Martinez-Lewi, *Freeing Yourself from the Narcissist in Your Life* (New York: Jeremy P. Tarcher/Penguin, 2008); Bruce Brooks Pfeiffer, ed., *The Essential Frank Lloyd Wright: Critical Writings on Architecture* (Princeton, NJ: Princeton University Press, 2008); Meryle Secrest, *Frank Lloyd Wright: A Biography* (New York: Alfred A. Knopf, 1992); Edgar Tafel, *About Wright: An Album of Recollections by Those Who Knew Frank Lloyd Wright* (New York: John Wiley & Sons, 1993); Jean M. Twenge and W. Keith Campbell, *The Narcissism Epidemic: Living in the Age of Entitlement*

Sources and Notes

(New York: Free Press, 2009); Frank Lloyd Wright, *An Autobiography* (New York: Horizon Press, 1977); Frank Lloyd Wright, *A Testament* (New York: Horizon Press, 1957); John Lloyd Wright, *My Father, Frank Lloyd Wright* (Mineola, NY: Dover Publications, Inc., 1992); Olgivanna Lloyd Wright, *The Shining Brow: Frank Lloyd Wright* (New York: Horizon Press, 1960).

Newspapers, Magazines, and Medical Reports

Mamah Borthwick and Alice T. Friedman, "Frank Lloyd Wright and Feminism: Mamah Borthwick's Letters to Ellen Key," *Journal of the Society of Architectural Historians* 61 No. 2 (June 2002), 140–51; Eddie Brummelman et al., "Origins of Narcissism in Children," *Proceedings of the National Academy of Sciences of the United States of America* 112, No. 12 (March 24, 2015), 3659–62; Tamra E. Cater et al., "Narcissism and Recollections of Early Life Experiences," *Personality and Individual Differences* 51, No. 8 (December 1, 2011), 935–39; Grace Glueck, "In Guggenheim Restoration, Wright Laughs Last," *New York Times*, August 12, 1991; Erica Hepper et al., "Moving Narcissus: Can Narcissists Be Empathic?" *Personality and Social Psychology Bulletin* 40, No. 9 (September 2014), 1079–91; Bernard Kalb, "The Author: Frank Lloyd Wright," *Saturday Review*, November 14, 1953; Arthur Lubow, "The Triumph of Frank Lloyd Wright," *Smithsonian*, June 2009; Thomas Mallon, "Possessed: Did Ayn Rand's Cult Outstrip Her Canon?" *New Yorker*, November 9, 2009; Joshua D. Miller, Thomas A. Widiger, and W. Keith Campbell, "Narcissistic Personality Disorder and the *DSM-V*," *Journal of Abnormal Psychology* 119, No. 4 (2010), 640–49; Lewis Mumford, "The Sky Line: What Wright Hath Wrought," *New Yorker*, December 5, 1959, 105–29; Charles A. O'Reilly III et al., "Narcissistic CEOs and Executive Compensation," *Leadership Quarterly* 25, No. 2 (April 2014), 218–31; Jack Quinan, "Frank Lloyd Wright's Guggenheim Museum: A Historian's Report," *Journal of the Society of Architectural Historians* 52, No. 4 (December 1993), 466–82; Elsa Ronningstam and Igor Weinberg, "Narcissistic Personality Disorder: Progress in Recognition and Treatment," *Focus* 11, No. 2 (Spring 2013), 167–77; Eleanor Roosevelt, "Eleanor Roosevelt's Story: This I Remember," *Milwaukee Sentinel*, February 3, 1950; Lars Schulze et al., "Gray Matter Abnormalities in Patients with Narcissistic Personality Disorder," *Journal of Psychiatric Research* 47, No. 10 (October 2013), 1363–69; Jean M. Twenge et al., "Egos Inflating Over Time: A Cross-Temporal Meta-Analysis of the Narcissistic Personality Inventory," *Journal of Personality* 76, No. 4 (August 2008), 875–901; S. Mark Young and Drew Pinsky, "Narcissism and Celebrity," *Journal of Research in Personality* 40 (2006), 463–71; Charles Zanor, "A Fate That Narcissists Will Hate: Being Ignored," *New York Times*, November 29, 2010.

Online

"Frank Lloyd Wright to His Neighbors," letter, www.pbs.org/flw/buildings/taliesin/taliesin_wright03.html; "Keeping Faith With an Idea: A Time Line of the Guggenheim Museum, 1943–59," web.guggenheim.org/timeline/index.html; *The Mike Wallace Interview*, Frank Lloyd Wright, September 1 and 28, 1957, transcript, www.hrc.utexas.edu/multimedia/video/2008/wallace/wright_frank_lloyd_t.html; Katy Waldman, "Are You a Narcissist?" *Slate*, August 24, 2014, www.slate.com/articles/health_and_science/medical_examiner/2014/08/narcissistic_personality_disorder_is_narcissism_a_personality_trait_or_mental.html.

Betty Ford
Books

James Cannon, *Gerald R. Ford: An Honorable Life* (Ann Arbor: University of Michigan Press, 2013); Betty Ford, *Healing and Hope: Six Women From the Betty Ford Center Share Their Powerful Journeys of Addiction and Recovery* (New York: Putnam, 2003); Betty Ford with Chris Chase, *Betty: A Glad Awakening* (New York: Doubleday and Company, 1987); Betty Ford with Chris Chase, *The Times of My Life* (New York: Harper & Row, 1978); George McGovern, *Terry: My Daughter's Life-and-Death Struggle With Alcoholism* (New York: Villard Books, 1996); Mary Tyler Moore, *After All* (New York: G. P. Putnam's Sons, 1995; Sheila Rabb Weidenfeld, *First Lady's Lady: With the Fords at the White House* (New York: G. P. Putnam's Sons, 1979).

Newspapers, Magazines, and Medical Reports

Center on Addiction and Substance Abuse at Columbia University, "Addiction Medicine: Closing the Gap Between Science and Practice," June 2012; Anna Rose Childress et al., "Prelude to Passion: Limbic Activation by 'Unseen' Drug and Sexual Cues," *Public Library of Science (PLoS) ONE* 3, No. 1 (February 2008), e1506; Robin Marantz Henig, "Valium's Contribution to Our New Normal," *New York Times*, September 29, 2012; Louise Lague, "Addicted No Moore," *People*, October 1, 1984; Robert Lindsey, "Mrs. Ford, in Hospital Statement, Says: I Am Addicted to Alcohol," *New York Times*, April 22, 1978; Enid Nemy, "Betty Ford, Former First Lady, Dies at 93," *New York Times*, July 8, 2011; Leesa E. Tobin, "Betty Ford as First Lady: A Woman for Women," *Presidential Studies Quarterly* 20, No. 4 (Fall 1990), 761–67; Brian Vastag, "Addiction Poorly Understood by Clinicians," *Journal of the American Medical Association* 290, No. 10 (September 10, 2003), 1299–1303; Kimberly A. Young et al., "Nipping Cue Reactivity in the Bud: Baclofen Prevents Limbic

Activation Elicited by Subliminal Drug Cues," *Journal of Neuroscience* 34, No. 14 (April 2, 2014), 5038–43.

Online

"The Best of Interviews With Gerald Ford," transcript, CNN, *Larry King Live Weekend*, February 3, 2001, transcripts.cnn.com/TRANSCRIPTS/0102/03/lklw.00 .html; "Betty Ford: The Real Deal," television program, *PBS NewsHour*, aired July 11, 2011, video.pbs.org/video/2050830175; "Good Medicine, Bad Behavior: Drug Diversion in America," www.goodmedicinebadbehavior.org/explore/history_of_ prescription_drugs.html; IMS Health, "Top 25 Medicines by Dispensed Prescriptions (U.S.)," www.imshealth.com/deployedfiles/imshealth/Global/Content/Corporate/ Press%20Room/2012_U.S/Top_25_Medicines_Dispensed_Prescriptions_U.S.pdf; "Interview With Former First Lady Betty Ford," transcript, CNN, *Larry King Live*, January 3, 2004, transcripts.cnn.com/TRANSCRIPTS/0401/03/lkl.00.html; Interview of Robert DuPont by Richard Norton Smith, October 26, 2010, Gerald R. Ford Oral History Project, geraldrfordfoundation.org/centennial/oralhistory/robert -dupont; William Moyers, "My Name Is Betty," Creators.com, www.creators.com/ health/william-moyers/-my-name-is-betty.html; "The Remarkable Mrs. Ford: *60 Minutes* Revisits a Very Candid Interview With the Former First Lady," CBSNews .com, January 5, 2007, www.cbsnews.com/news/the-remarkable-mrs-ford.

Charles Darwin
Books

John Bowlby, *Charles Darwin: A New Life* (New York: W. W. Norton, 1991); Janet Browne, *Charles Darwin: The Power of Place* (New York, Alfred A. Knopf, 2002); Janet Browne, *Charles Darwin: Voyaging* (New York: Alfred A. Knopf, 1995); Janet Browne, *Darwin's Origin of Species: A Biography* (New York: Atlantic Monthly Press, 2006); Frederick Burkhardt, ed., *Charles Darwin: The 'Beagle' Letters* (New York: Cambridge University Press, 2008); Ralph Colp, Jr., *Darwin's Illness* (Gainesville, FL: University Press of Florida, 2008); Charles Darwin, *The Autobiography of Charles Darwin, 1809–1882*, edited by Nora Barlow (New York: W. W. Norton, 1958); Charles Darwin, *From So Simple a Beginning: The Four Great Books of Charles Darwin*, edited by Edward O. Wilson (New York: W. W. Norton, 2005); Charles Darwin, *On the Origin of Species*, edited by David Quammen (Toronto: Sterling Publishing, 2011); Adrian Desmond and James Moore, *Darwin: The Life of a Tormented Evolutionist* (New York: Warner Books, 1992); Tom Lutz, *American Nervousness, 1903:*

Andy Warhol Was a Hoarder

An Anecdotal History (Ithaca, NY: Cornell University Press, 1991); George Pickering, *Creative Malady: Illness in the Lives and Minds of Charles Darwin, Florence Nightingale, Mary Baker Eddy, Sigmund Freud, Marcel Proust, and Elizabeth Barrett Browning* (New York: Oxford University Press, 1974); Daniel Smith, *Monkey Mind: A Memoir of Anxiety* (New York: Simon & Schuster, 2012); Scott Stossel, *My Age of Anxiety: Fear, Hope, Dread, and the Search for Peace of Mind* (New York: Alfred A. Knopf, 2014).

Newspapers, Magazines, and Medical Reports

Thomas J. Barloon and Russell Noyes, Jr., "Charles Darwin and Panic Disorder," *Journal of the American Medical Association* 277, No. 2 (January 8, 1997), 138–41; Anthony K. Campbell and Stephanie B. Matthews, "Darwin's Illness Revealed," *Postgraduate Medical Journal* 81 (May 2005), 248–51; Sidney Cohen and Philip A. Mackowiak, "Diagnosing Darwin," *Pharos* (Spring 2013), 12–20; Ralph Colp, Jr., "More on Darwin's Illness," *History of Science* 38, No. 2 (2000), 219–36; Ralph Colp, Jr., "To Be an Invalid, Redux," *Journal of the History of Biology* 31, No. 2 (Summer 1998), 211–40; M. Davis and P. J. Whalen, "The Amygdala: Vigilance and Emotion," *Molecular Psychiatry* 6, No. 1 (January 2001), 13–34; Kathryn Amey Degnen and Nathan A. Fox, "Behavioral Inhibition and Anxiety Disorders: Multiple Levels of a Resilience Process," *Development and Psychopathology* 19 (February 2007), 729–46; Justin S. Feinstein et al., "Fear and Panic in Humans with Bilateral Amygdala Damage," *Nature Neuroscience* 16, No. 3 (March 2013), 270–72; Justin S. Feinstein et al., "The Human Amygdala and the Induction and Experience of Fear," *Current Biology* 21 (January 2011), 34–38; John Hayman, "Charles Darwin's Mitochondria," *Genetics* 194, No. 1 (May 1, 2013), 21–25; John A. Hayman, "Darwin's Illness Revisited," *British Medical Journal* 339, No. 7735 (December 14, 2009), 1413–15; Robin Marantz Henig, "Understanding the Anxious Mind," *New York Times Magazine*, October 4, 2009; Douglas Hubble, "Charles Darwin and Psychotherapy," *Lancet* 241, No. 6231 (January 1943), 129–33; W. W. Johnston, "The Ill Health of Charles Darwin: Its Nature and Its Relation to His Work," *American Anthropologist*, New Series 3, No. 1 (January/February 1901), 139–58; Ned H. Kalin et al., "The Primate Amygdala Mediates Acute Fear but Not the Behavioral and Physiological Components of Anxious Temperament," *Journal of Neuroscience* 21, No. 6 (March 15, 2001), 2067–74; Richard Milner, "Darwin's Shrink," *Natural History*, November 2005; Fernando Orrego and Carlos Quintana, "Darwin's Illness: A Final Diagnosis," *Notes and Records of the Royal Society* 61, No. 1 (January 22, 2007), 23–29; Robert J. Richards, "Why Darwin Delayed, or Interesting Problems and Models in the History of Science," *Journal of the History of Behavioral Sciences* 19 (1983), 45–53; Fergus Shanahan, "Darwinian Dyspepsia: An Extraordinary Scientist, an Ordinary Illness, Great Dignity," *American Journal of Gastroenterology* 107 (February 2012), 161–64; Keith Thomson, "Darwin's Enigmatic Health," *American Scientist* 97, No. 3 (May/June 2009), 198–200; A. W. Woodruff, "Darwin's Health in Relation to His Voyage to South America," *British Medical Journal* 1 (1965), 745–50.

Online

Darwin Correspondence Project, available online at www.darwinproject.ac.uk; Darwin Online, darwin-online.org.uk/; Emma Darwin, *A Century of Family Letters, 1792–1896* (New York: D. Appleton and Company, 1915; Archive.org, 2007), archive.org/details/emmadarwincentur02litc; Jerome Kagan, "New Insights into Temperament," Dana Foundation, January 1, 2004, www.dana.org/Cerebrum/2004/ New_Insights_into_Temperament.

George Gershwin
Books

Merle Armitage, ed., *George Gershwin* (New York: Da Capo Press, 1995); Isaac Goldberg, *George Gershwin: A Study in American Music* (New York: Frederick Ungar, 1958); Edward M. Hallowell and John J. Ratey, *Driven to Distraction: Recognizing and Coping With Attention Deficit Disorder From Childhood Through Adulthood* (New York: Anchor Books, 2011); Heinrich Hoffman, *Struwwelpeter: Merry Tales and Funny Pictures* (New York: Frederick Warne & Co.); William G. Hyland, *George Gershwin: A New Biography* (Westport, CT: Praeger Publishers, 2003); Edward Jablonski, *Gershwin: A Biography* (New York: Doubleday, 1987); Robert Kimball and Alfred Simon, *The Gershwins* (New York: Atheneum, 1973); Howard Pollack, *George Gershwin: His Life and Work* (Berkeley and Los Angeles: University of California Press, 2006); Katharine Weber, *The Memory of All That: George Gershwin, Kay Swift, and My Family's Legacy of Infidelities* (New York: Crown Publishers, 2011); Robert Wyatt and John Andrew Johnson, eds. *The George Gershwin Reader* (New York: Oxford University Press, 2004).

Newspapers, Magazines, and Medical Reports

S. N. Behrman, "Troubadour," *New Yorker*, May 25, 1929; "Blues," *New Yorker*, December 12, 1925; Heidi M. Feldman and Michael I. Reiff, "Attention Deficit-Hyperactivity Disorder in Children and Adolescents," *New England Journal of Medicine* 370, No. 9 (February 27, 2014), 838–46; Malcolm Gladwell, "Running From Ritalin,"

New Yorker, February 15, 1999; Klaus W. Lange et al., "The History of Attention Deficit Hyperactivity Disorder," *Attention Deficit and Hyperactivity Disorders* 2, No. 4 (December 2010), 241–455; Mark Leffert, "The Psychoanalysis and Death of George Gershwin: An American Tragedy," *Journal of the American Academy of Psychoanalysis and Dynamic Psychiatry* 39, No. 3 (2011), 421–52; Claudia Roth Pierpont, "Jazzbo: Why We Still Listen to Gershwin," *New Yorker*, January 10, 2005; David Schiff, "Composers on the Couch," *Atlantic Monthly*, January 1994; Alan Schwarz, "The Selling of Attention Deficit Disorder," *New York Times*, December 15, 2013; P. Shaw et al., "Attention-Deficit/Hyperactivity Disorder Is Characterized by a Delay in Cortical Maturation," *Proceedings of the National Academy of Sciences of the United States of America* 104, No. 49 (December 4, 2007), 19649–54; Robert A. Simon, "Gershwin Memorial—Turn Out the Stars?" *New Yorker*, August 21, 1937; Chandra S. Sripada et al., "Lag in Maturation of the Brain's Intrinsic Functional Architecture in Attention-Deficit/Hyperactivity Disorder," *PNAS* 111, No. 39 (September 30, 2014), 14259–64; George Still, "Some Abnormal Psychical Conditions in Children," *Lancet* 159, No. 4104 (April 26, 1902), 1163–68; "Talk of the Town," *New Yorker*, January 1, 1927; J. Thome and K. A. Jacobs, "Attention Deficit Hyperactivity Disorder (ADHD) in a 19th Century Children's Book," *European Psychiatry* 19, No. 5 (2004), 303–6.

Online

Attention-Deficit/Hyperactivity Disorder, Centers for Disease Control and Prevention, www.cdc.gov/ncbddd/adhd/data.html; Parizad Bilimoria, "3 Interesting Characters in ADHD History," E/I Balance, April 27, 2012, eibalance.com/2012/04/27/3-interesting-characters-in-adhd-history; "Brain Matures a Few Years Late in ADHD, but Follows Normal Pattern," press release, National Institute of Mental Health, November 12, 2007, www.nimh.nih.gov/news/science-news/2007/brain-matures-a-few-years-late-in-adhd-but-follows-normal-pattern.shtml; Anne Trafton, "Inside the Adult ADHD Brain," MIT News on Campus and Around the World, June 10, 2014, www.newsoffice.mit.edu/2014/inside-adult-adhd-brain-0610.

Fyodor Dostoevsky
Books

Susan Cheever, *Desire: Where Sex Meets Addiction* (New York: Simon & Schuster, 2008); Fyodor Dostoevsky, *The Gambler*, translated by Constance Garnett (New York: Modern Library, 2003); Joseph Frank, *Dostoevsky: The Mantle of the Prophet, 1871–1881* (Princeton, NJ: Princeton University Press, 2002); Joseph Frank, *Dostoevsky:*

Sources and Notes

The Miraculous Years, 1865–1871 (Princeton, NJ: Princeton University Press, 1995); Joseph Frank, *Dostoevsky: A Writer in His Time* (Princeton, NJ: Princeton University Press, 2010); Joseph Frank and David I. Goldstein, eds., *Selected Letters of Fyodor Dostoyevsky*, translated by Andrew R. MacAndrew (New Brunswick, NJ: Rutgers University Press, 1987); Richard Freeborn, *Dostoevsky* (London: Haus Publishing, 2003); Loenid Grossman, *Dostoevsky: A Biography*, translated by Mary Mackler (Indianapolis/New York: Bobbs-Merrill Company, 1975); Gladys Knight, *Between Each Line of Pain and Glory: My Life Story* (New York: Hyperion, 1997); Richard J. Rosenthal, "The Psychodynamics of Pathological Gambling: A Review of the Literature," *The Handbook of Pathological Gambling*, edited by T. Galski (Springfield, IL: Charles C. Thomas, 1987); David G. Schwartz, *Roll the Bones: The History of Gambling* (New York: Gotham Books, 2006); Peter Sekirin, *The Dostoevsky Archive: Firsthand Accounts of the Novelist from Contemporaries' Memoirs and Rare Periodicals* (Jefferson, NC: McFarland & Company, 1997); Howard Shaffer, *Change Your Gambling, Change Your Life* (San Francisco: Jossey-Bass, 2012); Sam Skolnik, *High Stakes: The Rising Cost of America's Gambling Addiction* (Boston: Beacon Press, 2011); Lorne Tepperman, Patrizia Albanese, Sasha Stark, and Nadine Zahlan, *The Dostoevsky Effect: Problem Gambling and the Origins of Addiction* (Ontario: Oxford University Press, 2013).

Newspapers, Magazines, and Medical Reports

Sheila B. Blume, "Pathological Gambling," *British Medical Journal* 311 (August 26, 1995), 522–23; Daniel Bortz, "Gambling Addiction Affects More Men and Women, Seduced by Growing Casino Accessibility," *U.S. News & World Report*, March 28, 2013; Henrietta Bowden-Jones and Luke Clark, "Pathological Gambling: A Neurobiological and Clinical Update," *British Journal of Psychiatry* 199, No. 2 (August 2011), 87–89; Julian W. Connolly, "A World in Flux: Pervasive Instability in Dostoevsky's *The Gambler*," *Dostoevsky's Studies*, New Series 12 (2008), 67–79; Timothy W. Fong, "The Biopsychosocial Consequences of Pathological Gambling," *Psychiatry* 2, No. 3 (March 2005), 22–30; Joseph Frascella et al., "Shared Brain Vulnerabilities Open the Way for Nonsubstance Addictions: Carving Addiction at a New Joint?" *Annals of the New York Academy of Sciences* 1187, No. 1 (February 2010), 294–315; Constance Holden, "Behavioral Addictions Debut in Proposed *DSM-V*," *Science* 327, No. 5968 (February 19, 2010), 935; Ferris Jabr, "How the Brain Gets Addicted to Gambling," *Scientific American*, October 15, 2103; Raanan Kagan et al., "Problem Gambling in the 21st Century Healthcare System," National Council on Problem Gambling, July 3, 2104; Howard Markel, "The D.S.M. Gets Addiction Right," *New York Times*, June 5, 2012; Jennifer Medina, "San Diego

Andy Warhol Was a Hoarder

Ex-Mayor Confronts $1 Billion Gambling Problem," *New York Times*, February 14, 2013; Denise Phillips, "Gambling: The Hidden Addiction," *Behavioral Health Management* 25, No. 5 (September/October 2005), 32–37; Marc N. Potenza et al., "Neuroscience of Behavioral and Pharmacological Treatments for Addictions," *Neuron* 69, No. 4 (February 24, 2011), 695–712; Christine Reilly and Nathan Smith, "The Evolving Definition of Pathological Gambling in the *DSM-V*," White Paper, National Center for Responsible Gaming; Richard J. Rosenthal, "The Gambler as Case History and Literary Twin: Dostoevsky's False Beauty and the Poetics of Perversity," *Psychoanalytic Review* 84, No. 4 (August 1, 1997), 593–616; Howard J. Shaffer et al., "Estimating the Prevalence of Disordered Gambling Behavior in the United States and Canada: A Meta-Analysis," Harvard Medical School Division on Addictions, December 15, 1997; David Surface, "High Risk Recreation—Problem Gambling in Older Adults," *Social Work Today* 9, No. 2 (March/April 2009), 18; Carol A. Tamminga and Eric J. Nestler, "Pathological Gambling: Focusing on the Addiction, Not the Activity," *American Journal of Psychiatry* 163, No. 2 (February 2006), 180–81; Caroline E. Temcheff et al., "Pathological and Disordered Gambling: A Comparison of *DSM-IV* and *DSM-V* Criteria," *International Gambling Studies* 11, No. 2 (August 2011), 213–20.

Online

American Gaming Association, "Groundbreaking New Research Reveals Impressive Magnitude of U.S. Casino Gaming Industry," October 7, 2014, www.american gaming.org/newsroom/press-releases/groundbreaking-new-research-reveals -impressive-magnitude-of-us-casino-gaming; American Gaming Association, "Problem Gambling Pioneer: Fyodor Dostoevsky," September 1, 2004, www.americangaming .org/newsroom/newsletters/responsible-gaming-quarterly/problem-gambling -pioneer-fyodor-dostoevsky; Cambridge Health Alliance, "The Ticket to Addiction: Fyodor Dostoevky," Addiction and the Humanities, Vol. 3, No. 1, www.basisonline .org/2007/01/addiction_the_h.html; "Disgraced Former San Diego Mayor Maureen O'Connor: Brain Tumor Contributed to Gambling Addiction," CBSNews.com, February 22, 2013, www.cbsnews.com/news/disgraced-former-san-diego-mayor -maureen-oconnor-brain-tumor-contributed-to-gambling-addiction; Sigmund Freud, "Dostoevsky and Parricide," 1928, www.slideshare.net/341987/dostoevsky-and -parricide; National Center for Responsible Gaming, "Gambling and the Brain: Why Neuroscience Research Is Vital to Gambling Research," Vol. 6 of *Increasing the Odds: A Series Dedicated to Understanding Gambling Disorders,* 2011, www.ncrg.org/sites/ default/files/uploads/docs/monographs/ncrgmonograph6final.pdf.

Sources and Notes

Albert Einstein
Books

Jennifer Berne, *On a Beam of Light: A Story of Albert Einstein* (New York: Chronicle Books, 2013); Denis Brian, *Einstein: A Life* (New York: John Wiley & Sons, 1996); Denis Brian, *The Unexpected Einstein: The Real Man Behind the Icon* (New York: John Wiley & Sons, 2005); Alice Calaprice, ed., *The Expanded Quotable Einstein* (Princeton, NJ: Princeton University Press, 2000); Helen Dukas and Banesh Hoffmann, eds., *Albert Einstein, The Human Side: Glimpses From His Archives* (Princeton, NJ: Princeton University Press, 2013); Albert Einstein, *Autobiographical Notes*, translated and edited by Paul Arthur Schilpp (La Salle, IL: Open Court, 1996); Albrecht Fölsing, *Albert Einstein: A Biography*, translated by Ewald Osers (New York: Viking, 1997); Uta Frith, ed., *Autism and Asperger Syndrome* (Cambridge, UK: Cambridge University Press, 1991); Temple Grandin, *Thinking in Pictures: My Life With Autism* (New York: Vintage Books, 2006); Temple Grandin and Richard Panek, *The Autistic Brain: Thinking Across the Spectrum* (New York: Houghton Mifflin Harcourt, 2013); Gerald Holton, *Einstein, History, and Other Passions: The Rebellion Against Science at the End of the Twentieth Century* (Cambridge, MA: Harvard University Press, 2000); Walter Isaacson, *Einstein: His Life and Universe* (New York: Simon & Schuster, 2007); Ioan James, *Asperger's Syndrome and High Achievement: Some Very Remarkable People* (London: Jessica Kingsley Publishers, 2005); Ioan James, *Remarkable Physicists: From Galileo to Yukawa* (Cambridge, UK: Cambridge University Press, 2004); Dennis Overbye, *Einstein in Love: A Scientific Romance* (New York: Viking, 2000); Tim Page, *Parallel Play: Growing Up with Undiagnosed Asperger's* (New York: Doubleday, 2009); Ze'ev Rosenkranz, *The Einstein Scrapbook* (Baltimore: Johns Hopkins University Press, 2002).

Newspapers, Magazines, and Medical Reports

Hans Asperger, "Problems of Infantile Autism," *Communication* 13 (1979), 45–52; Jeffrey P. Baker, "Autism at 70—Redrawing the Boundaries," *New England Journal of Medicine* 369, No. 12 (September 19, 2013), 1089–91; Simon Baron-Cohen, "Autism and the Technical Mind," *Scientific American*, November 2012, 72–75; Simon Baron-Cohen et al., "Why Are Autism Spectrum Conditions More Prevalent in Males?" *Public Library of Science (PLoS) Biology* 9, No. 6 (June 2011); Lizzie Buchen, "Scientists and Autism: When Geeks Meet," *Nature* 479 (November 3, 2011), 25–27; Jennifer Connellan et al., "Sex Differences in Human Neonatal Social Perception," *Infant Behavior and Development* 23, No. 1 (2000), 113–18; Geraldine Dawson et al., "Early Behavioral Intervention Is Associated With Normalized

Andy Warhol Was a Hoarder

Brain Activity in Young Children with Autism," *Journal of the American Academy of Child and Adolescent Psychiatry* 51, No. 11 (November 2012), 1150–59; Marian C. Diamond et al., "On the Brain of a Scientist," *Experimental Neurology* 88, No. 1 (April 1985), 198–204; Dean Falk, "New Information About Albert Einstein's Brain," *Frontiers in Evolutionary Neuroscience* 1 (May 2009); Dean Falk, Frederick E. Lepore, and Adrianne Noe, "The Cerebral Cortex of Albert Einstein: A Description and Preliminary Analysis of Unpublished Photographs," *Brain: A Journal of Neurology* 136 (2012), 1304–27; David C. Giles, " '*DSM-V* Is Taking Away Our Identity': The Reaction of the Online Community to the Proposed Changes in the Diagnosis of Asperger's Disorder," *Health* 18, No. 2 (March 2014), 179–95; Ioan James, "Singular Scientists," *Journal of the Royal Society of Medicine* 96, No. 1 (January 2003), 36–39; Hazel Muir, "Einstein and Newton Showed Signs of Autism," *New Scientist*, April 30, 2003; Oliver Sacks, "Autistic Geniuses? We're Too Ready to Pathologize," *Nature* 429 (May 20, 2004), 241; Oliver Sacks, "Henry Cavendish: An Early Case of Asperger's Syndrome?" *Neurology* 57, No. 7 (October 9, 2001), 1347; Bari Weiss, "Life Among the 'Yakkity-Yaks,' " *Wall Street Journal*, February 23, 2010; Lorna Wing, "Asperger's Syndrome: A Clinical Account," *Psychological Medicine* 11 (February 1981), 115–29; Lorna Wing, "Reflections on Opening Pandora's Box," *Journal of Autism and Developmental Disorders* 35, No. 2 (April 2005), 197–203; Sandra F. Witelson, Debra L. Kigar, and Thomas Harvey, "The Exceptional Brain of Albert Einstein," *Lancet* 353 (June 19, 1999), 2149–53; S. J. Woolf, "Einstein's Own Corner of Space," *New York Times*, August 18, 1929.

Online

Simon Baron-Cohen, "Autism, Sex and Science," TEDx Talk, April 13, 2013, www.ted xkingscollegelondon.com/simon-baron-cohen-autism-sex-and-science; Simon Baron-Cohen, "Scientific Talent and Autism: Is There a Connection?" www.youtube.com/watch?v=FUbn2G2Ra-8; "A Conversation With Temple Grandin," transcript/audio, National Public Radio, January 20, 2006, www.npr.org/templates/story/story.php?storyId=5165123; Albert Einstein, *The Collected Papers of Albert Einstein*, www.einstein papers.press.princeton.edu; Michio Kaku, "The Theory Behind the Equation," NOVA, October 11, 2005, www.pbs.org/wgbh/nova/physics/theory-behind-equation.html; Ian Steadman, "Watch Simon Baron-Cohen's Full Wired 2012 Talk About Autism," January 18, 2013, www.wired.co.uk/news/archive/2012-10/26/simon-baron-cohen.

Acknowledgments

I am indebted to an enormous circle of very smart and generous people who made this book possible. My deepest appreciation to Gail Ross, my agent at the Ross Yoon literary agency, and Hilary Black, my editor at National Geographic Books, for their support and guidance throughout this fascinating journey.

From the start, Hilary buoyed me with her enthusiasm, patience, wisdom, deft editing, and championing of this book. I lucked into a most wonderful partnership. Many thanks also to National Geographic associate editors Anne Smyth, who diligently worked on the early stages of the book, and Allyson Dickman, who helped get me to the finish line with her abundant cheer, masterly deadline schedules, and editorial prowess.

My research for this book relied on many great minds, past and present. I am extremely grateful to the mental health scientists and clinicians who stepped out of their busy lives to share their expertise and to guide my understanding of extraordinarily challenging terrain. Although I could not quote everyone I interviewed, all informed my knowledge and contributed to the whole immensely. A special tip of the hat to those who were uncomfortable discussing "patients" they did not know but were nonetheless willing to talk about these 12 conditions in the spirit of educating the public. If we recognize ourselves and the people we love in these pages—and I certainly did—you have served us well and, I hope, moved us one step closer to eradicating stigma and embracing empathy.

Reading about celebrated lives in history is one of my favorite pastimes; writing about them is supremely daunting. I could not have begun to craft the chapters in this book without the cadre of authoritative biographers whose works brought these 12 individuals to life. I am obliged to these writers for the biographical nuggets that I was able to share. On the subject of biographies: a shout-out to public libraries everywhere and especially to my local branch, Beatley Central Library in Alexandria, Virginia, where I spent many hours scouring the shelves and interacting with a wonderfully good-natured and helpful staff.

I am extraordinarily privileged to be the daughter of two loving and adventurous parents who are exceptional writers and thinkers. My mother Phyllis's graceful and reflective writing inspired my love for language early on, as did my father Bernard's insatiable curiosity, wit, and literary flair. My mother read early drafts, offered sage suggestions, and listened patiently and compassionately during moments of writerly angst. My father helped brainstorm, cheered me on, and, much to my delight, provided reporting. While I was researching Frank Lloyd Wright, he mentioned that he had interviewed the architect in the fall of 1953 at the Plaza Hotel in New York City. In a matter of minutes, I Googled his column, "The Author: Frank Lloyd Wright," and found the reporting gems I needed to wrap up the chapter. Bernard Kalb is the *Saturday Review* writer who makes an appearance. Nothing could be more humbling and gratifying than drawing on my father's esteemed journalistic work for my own.

Acknowledgments

Several individuals offered immense guidance, input, and support. My sister Marina enthusiastically and generously read chapter drafts, made each one better, and bolstered my confidence. I cannot possibly thank her enough. Ongoing conversations with Joanna Spiro, friend and dedicated mental health professional, provided both sustenance and wise counsel as she answered complicated questions and walked me through challenging material. Steve Fainaru, loyal comrade and exemplary journalist, helped me navigate my entrée into book writing and provided ongoing encouragement, as did mentor extraordinaire Larry Tye, whose books have inspired me and who cares as deeply about the good work of others as he does about his own.

A coterie of friends and colleagues, many of whom I had the tremendous privilege of working with at *Newsweek*, helped in immeasurable ways. Lucy Shackelford cheered me on from the beginning, took on the critical task of fact-checking with her exacting eye, and answered my many "one last question" e-mails with unbounded patience. Pat Wingert graciously stepped in at the end, read the full manuscript with great care, and made many welcome improvements. Other generous souls talked through profile candidates, suggested sources, made introductions, provided information or expertise on specific subject matter, read a chapter draft, or offered much appreciated support along the way. Enormous thanks to: Ruth Arkell, Sharon Begley, Hannah Bloch, Bob Cohn, Sophia Colamarino, Nancy Edson, Yonit Hoffman, Dottie Jeffries, Barbara Kantrowitz, Fred Kaplan, Catherine Karnow, Anna Kuchment, Kevin Peraino, Stanley Rabinowitz, Joan Raymond, Debra Rosenberg and David Lipscomb, Karen Springen, Jamie Stiehm, Steve Tuttle, Anne Underwood, and Katie Waxman.

My 17 years at *Newsweek* steeped me in the best of journalism—deep reporting, thoughtful analysis, and compelling writing—and provided a vast network of exceptional colleagues. My deepest gratitude to Ann McDaniel for her generous and steadfast guidance, counsel, and friendship throughout my journalistic journey. Much appreciation to Jeff Bartholet, Dan Klaidman, John McCormick, Jon Meacham, Lisa Miller, David Noonan, and Mark Starr, who supported my career in countless ways. On the health team, special thanks to Alexis Gelber and a salute to Geoff Cowley, gone much too soon and greatly missed. And to many others who have inspired me throughout the years, a collegial thank-you to all.

My family members provided welcome support and much needed distractions along the way. Abundant love and gratitude to my sisters and their families: Tanah, Hilmar, Max, Talia, and Camila; Marina, David, Elijah, and Wolf; Sarinah, Jaron, Leo, Susannah, and Bella. Big thanks to Hilmar for a superfun photo shoot and for sharing his great talent. For their ongoing and warm encouragement, many thanks to my aunt and uncle, Mady and Marvin Kalb, and to my cousins Deborah and Judith and their families. Debby's terrific blog about books and authors provided inspiration. Judy and her husband, Alex, talked Dostoevsky with me; Judy reviewed the chapter and, among many other helpful suggestions, explained the intricacies of Russian names. Much love to my cousins in New York, London, Mexico, and Argentina, and a special tribute to my grandparents and aunts and uncles who are deeply missed and with whom I would have loved to share this book.

Wonderful friends have provided companionship and fortification throughout my writing career. Heartfelt thanks to: Susan Berfield and Tim Brewer, Alex Bernstein and Sonia Daccarett, Katherine and Tim Dilworth, Jack Flyer and Winnie Hahn, Trina Foster, Beth Fouhy, Trent Gegax and Samara Minkin, Carmen MacDougall, Dan McGinn, Susan McKeever, Norah McVeigh and Peter Szabo,

Acknowledgments

Cindy Peterson, and Jessica Portner. I am blessed to have a large circle—beyond those named—and offer my gratitude to every one of you.

Above all, I want to extend my deepest love, thanks, and appreciation to my husband, Steve, and to Molly and Noah. Molly left home to launch her great adventures at college as I started this book; I am thrilled to see her flourishing with the wind at her back, both on and off the water. Noah provided glorious smiles and hugs; worked alongside me; wrote and illustrated several books of his own, including *A Tiger's Tale;* and made me enormously happy and proud as he, too, began a love affair with biography. (Thank you, children's literature!) From the start, Steve supported this project wholeheartedly. A fellow journalist, he lobbed questions, extracted meaning out of complexity, and provided many welcome laughs. When I needed time to work, he and Noah played, watched, and strategized baseball. Most important, Steve's unwavering encouragement made me believe that I could not only write this book but finish it. I am immensely grateful.

About the Author

CLAUDIA KALB is an award-winning journalist in the fields of medicine, health, and science. A former senior writer at *Newsweek,* she is now a freelance writer and editor. Her writing has also appeared in *Smithsonian* and *Scientific American.* She lives with her family in Alexandria, Virginia.